I0229273

LISZT'S DANTE SYMPHONY

Liszt Memorial *by Rich DiSilvio*

Liszt's

Dante Symphony

A Historical Thriller about
The Arts & Deceptive Arts

Rich DiSilvio

PUBLISHER'S NOTE:
This book is a work of historical fiction, and as such contains both factual and fictional characters, places, and incidents. An attempt to clarify some of the historical characters has been made at the end of this work, yet not every detail has been covered, as it would take a book to properly address and separate all the facts from creative fiction that occur throughout this integrated work. However, most information about the historical characters and events herein have been as factual as possible, with the obvious exception of those directly related to the fictional characters or storylines of the Altar Eagles and the *Dante Symphony* cipher.

Copyright © 2011 Rich DiSilvio
All Rights Reserved. No part of this book may be used or reproduced in any manner whatsoever without written permission, except in the case of brief quotations embodied in critical articles or reviews.
Published ℗ 2011 by DV Books, an imprint of Digital Vista, Inc.
Printed in the USA.

Cover art and interior book layout by © Rich DiSilvio. Illustrations of Dante's Inferno on Contents page by Gustave Doré. Photographs & images are from purchased collections or courtesy of Wikipedia's public domain images.
Photo of Hitler on back cover: Bundesarchiv, Bild 183-S33882 / CC-BY-SA

Author's Website: www.richdisilvio.com

PUBLISHER'S CATALOGING-IN-PUBLICATION DATA
(PREPARED BY THE DONOHUE GROUP, INC.)

NAMES: DISILVIO, RICH.
TITLE: LISZT'S DANTE SYMPHONY: A HISTORICAL THRILLER ABOUT THE ARTS & DECEPTIVE ARTS / RICH DISILVIO.
DESCRIPTION: NEW YORK, USA : DV BOOKS, AN IMPRINT OF DIGITAL VISTA, INC., 2011.
IDENTIFIERS: ISBN 978-0-9817625-3-1 (PAPERBACK) | ISBN 978-0-9817625-4-8 (HARDCOVER) | ISBN 978-0-9976807-1-3 (EBOOK)
SUBJECTS: LCSH: SPIES--EUROPE--FICTION. | CIPHERS--EUROPE--FICTION. | LISZT, FRANZ, 1811-1886. SYMPHONIE ZU DANTE'S DIVINA COMMEDIA--FICTION. | FRANCO-PRUSSIAN WAR, 1870-1871--FICTION. | WORLD WAR, 1939-1945--FICTION. | NAZIS--EUROPE--FICTION. | REVENGE--FICTION. | LCGFT: THRILLERS (FICTION) | HISTORICAL FICTION.
CLASSIFICATION: LCC PS3604.I85 L57 2011 (PRINT) | LCC PS3604.I85 (EBOOK) | DDC 813/.6--DC23

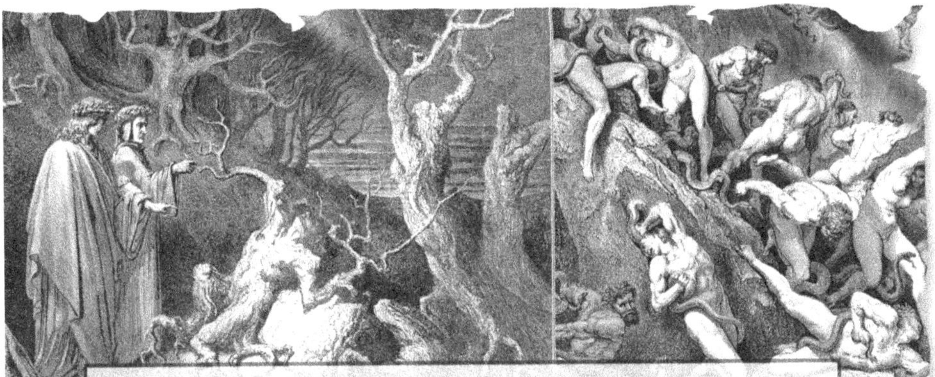

Contents

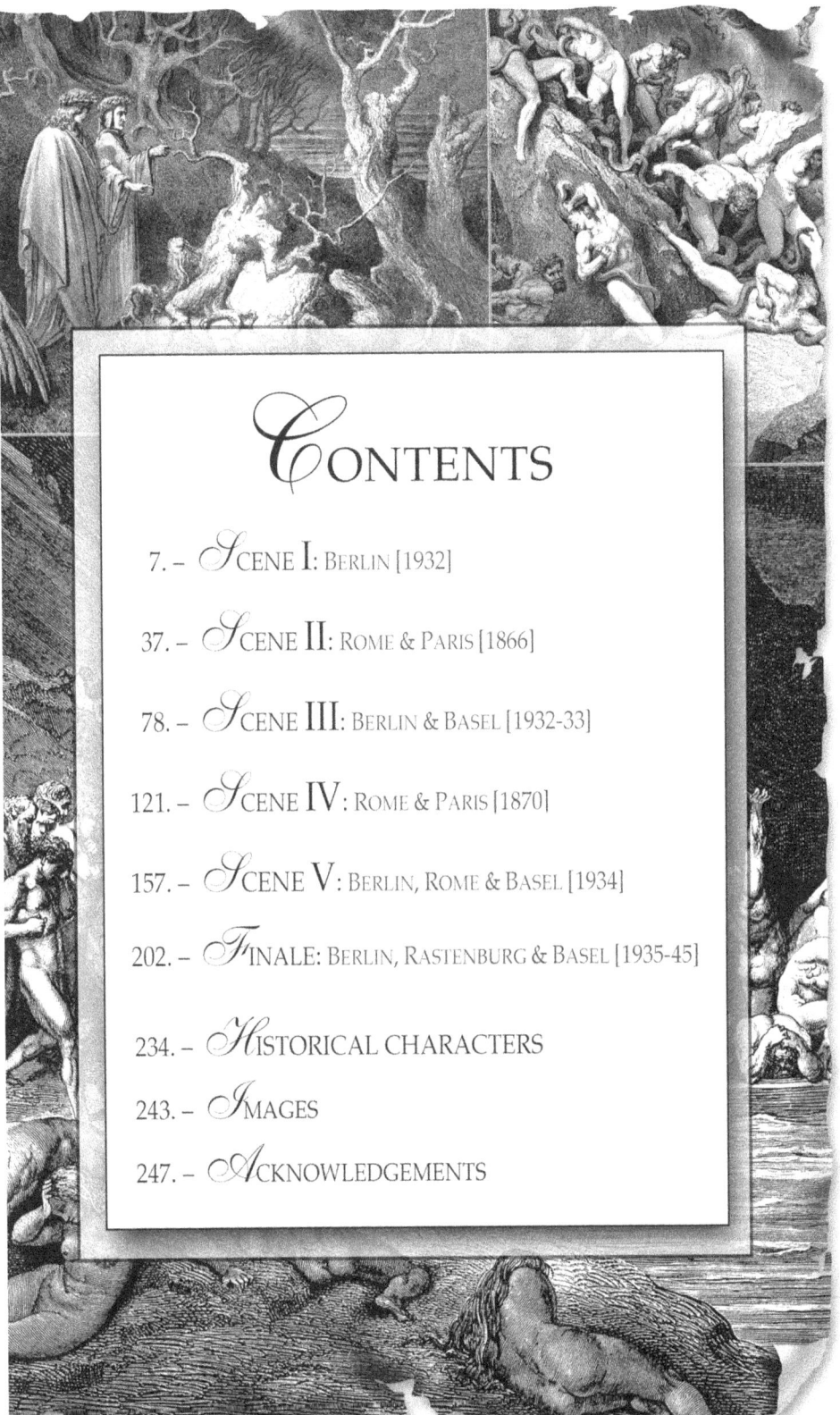

Scene I: Berlin [1932]

All Hell broke loose!

With a sweep of the baton, a cataclysmic wave of bone-chilling riffs soon vilified the stately chamber. Diabolical dissonances erupted as rolls of tympanic thunder clashed with the ominous tolling of a gong. Tubas and trombones belched and blasted brimstone and fire, while the searing clashes of cymbals pierced eardrums like shards of glass. In the pit, violins and violas squealed and sighed, as they sang of tortured souls forever doomed to freeze or fry. These are the pitiless souls who lived their lives unwisely. These are the sinful souls that met their ultimate fate. These are the forlorn souls that shall forever suffer in Satan's sadistic cyclone of Hell. The Lord has had his say and Satan would now and forever have his way.

The *Inferno* movement of Franz Liszt's *Dante Symphony* was now in full fury, evoking the horrors so eloquently committed to words by Dante Alighieri in his *Divine Comedy*.

Convulsing on the podium, Felix Weingartner—a disciple of Liszt's—looked possessed as he led the Berlin Philharmonic into the very bowels of Hell.

Sitting in the front row, with adrenaline pumping and clenched fists violently rocking to the rapacious rhythm, was Germany's rising death star, Adolf Hitler.

To Hitler's right sat his new Aryan beauty, Eva Braun. She had recently replaced his former lover, and half-niece, Geli Raubal. Ten months earlier the young and defiled Geli had committed suicide, suffering her own Hell. In three months, Eva, too, will attempt suicide by shooting herself because of her new lover, yet will miraculously survive that attempt—she will try again. Hitler was toxic; and as time would tell, anything he touched would wither and die or be set ablaze. Either way, all would be reduced to ashes.

Seated to Hitler's left was his long-time friend and muse, Winifred Wagner, widow of Siegfried Wagner and daughter-in-law of the famed German opera composer Richard Wagner. In fact, it was Winifred who supplied Hitler with the paper on which to write his bigoted book of bile, *Mein Kampf (My Struggle).* At the time, Hitler had been incarcerated in a Munich prison for a failed coup d'état known as the Beer Hall Putsch, and Winifred made sure Adolf kept busy, and diabolically active his scheming mind was.

But that was eight years ago. It was now July 18, 1932, and Winifred invited Hitler to Berlin to celebrate the seventh anniversary of the world premiere of his hateful and quasi-fallacious book. Hitler's struggle had led him to a position that anyone of sound mind found unfathomable, however, the downtrodden middle and lower classes now seemed to adore him. The shrewd Nazi leader zealously exalted his followers' superior bloodline, thus brainwashing his Aryan calves to become wolves—eager to spill innocent blood in their racial quest for hegemony, a blood lust that began a century earlier.

Winifred was delighted to have Hitler sitting at her side again, yet not particularly thrilled about his new bauble. It wasn't that Eva was a raving beauty. In fact, Winifred felt she surpassed her in the looks department. But Eva was fifteen years younger; and no woman can beat the clock, especially since Eva was vivacious and physically equipped to offer pleasures that the cultured Winifred could no longer match, or even cared to. Yet, despite her aging deficit, Winifred still managed to exude an air of confidence over her young rival, knowing that her famous father-in-law had seduced Hitler like few others could, and certainly far more than any other composer. Richard Wagner may have died six years before Hitler was even born, but his dramatic operas captured Adolf's imagination so powerfully that he even adopted Wagner's *Rienzi Overture* for his Nazi Party's anthem. And to Winifred's credit, she quite calculatingly knew that today's performance featured the *Rienzi Overture,* followed by two other Wagner overtures, consuming the first half of the program.

Winifred always made sure Adolf received ample doses of her father-in-laws *musikdroge,* yet she was somewhat hesitant about today's matinée concert. In fact, even before taking their seats, as she and Eva escorted the Nazi leader down the aisle, she balked, "Adolf, darling, please remember, if you wish to leave after the first half of the concert, I'm all for it."

Hitler gazed up from reading the playbill. "We shall see. Granted, we have rarely listened to the dribble of foreign composers in the past, but some of Liszt's works do seem commendable. And I just read here that Liszt dedicated this piece to your great father-in-law."

A smirk etched Winifred's face. "That's true, but you must know that the *Dante Symphony* met with catcalls when it premiered, and at subsequent performances. So why waste our time with Hungarian goulash when we have a feast of Germany's most brilliant delicacies being served up first?"

Amused, Hitler chuckled. "True, my dear Winifred. Very true! But, this piece actually piques my curiosity. Quite frankly, I'm curious to hear Liszt's interpretation of Dante's *Inferno.*"

With a touch of jealousy, Eva grasped Adolf's arm, as she located their seats. "Here we are!" Then looking at

Winifred, she added, "And I agree with Adolf. I think Liszt's symphony looks like it might be interesting. And besides, weren't the two composers friends?"

Winifred nodded haughtily. "Yes, Eva, of course they were friends. My father-in-law married Liszt's daughter Cosima, for Christ's sake! Everyone knows that, but—"

Hitler interjected, "No need to get cross, Winifred. Eva is right—you Wagners are bound by blood to the Liszt clan. So even though Liszt is not of superior Aryan stock, we might wish to hear the Gypsy out."

As the three took their seats, Winifred grimaced. "Adolf, we may be bound by blood, but I know how much you esteem German art. As we've discussed many times, it resides far above the trifling nonsense that often fills these chambers. Except for Beethoven, Bach or Bruckner, there really are very few composers worth listening to these days. And—"

Hitler nodded. "Naturally, but—"

Winifred continued undaunted, "you must know, Adolf, that there have been unsavory rumors about our dear Richard—namely that he plagiarized Liszt's advanced chromatic harmonies. And those vile rumors have not subsided; rather, they have gained more press and attention over the years. It's infuriating! Not to mention insulting to our great master, nay, to Germany's ultimate master. So, I simply suggest that we demonstrate to our fellow citizens that we abhor such nonsense by making our exit very pronounced and, in turn, newsworthy. As you know, Adolf, your actions do carry tremendous weight these days, and the German people *will* follow your wise example."

Hitler smiled affectionately. "Winifred, you always were an astute and most treasured voice of reason, but let's just do the musically prudent thing, and play it by ear."

To Winifred's utter dismay, Hitler had not only opted to stay for Liszt's symphony but, worst yet, he was now emotionally and physically reveling in the verve and venom spewing from the vast assortment of instruments. Winifred's consternation was written on her face as she thought: *My Lord. Could these be the actual instruments of the Devil? How could Liszt conjure up such frightful evil?*

Winifred's eyes rolled left and right, frantically seeking reassurance; was Adolf succumbing to Liszt's perplexingly faithful rendition of Dante's fiery *Inferno?* She had to know. Impulsively, she reached over and tenderly touched his leg.

Her timing couldn't have been worse. With Hitler caught up in pounding his thighs to the tempo of the ominous climax, it was like disturbing a deranged caveman in the midst of bashing in the skull of a wild animal, or in Hitler's case, the skull of a loathsome Jew or Pole. He glared at Winifred with crazed eyes. His clenched fists, still giving his lap a deadly pounding, suddenly stopped, as the cataclysmic coda of the *Inferno* movement ended with its five hammering deathblows.

Hitler was emotionally charged, but now physically drained, as beads of sweat trickled down the side of his face. His wild and possessed eyes finally lost their red glow as they focused on Winifred's pleasant features, soothing the beast.

With the orchestra now paused, the sudden silence allowed him to regain his senses, as he said above a whisper, "My God, Winifred, I must say, that was absolutely invigorating! Brutal! Nasty! Simply magnificent!"

Winifred's soft complexion turned steely cold. She felt betrayed. Adolf's reaction seemed bombastic, just like Liszt's *Inferno*. Seldom, if ever, had she seen him so charged. She remained speechless.

Meanwhile, a distinguished-looking young man leaned forward to whisper over Hitler's shoulder, "Pardon me, but if you think the *Inferno* movement was spectacular, just wait until you hear Liszt's final *Magnificat.*"

Surprised, Hitler swung around. "Son, I surely doubt it could ever surpass this movement. After all, of the three parts of Dante's *Comedy,* the *Inferno* is the only one professors and the public fixate on, and rightfully so. No one cares about struggling do-gooders or the illusions of Paradise, my dear boy. In the real world, evil always mesmerizes the masses, like moths drawn to a flame. Look at the newspapers. Publishers and the public thrive on it."

Winifred's eyes twinkled. She had just recalled an anecdote about what Wagner said when Liszt presented him with the first draft of the *Dante Symphony*. She leaned toward Hitler, half anxious, half teasing, "Adolf, I think you should know, this piece doesn't even have a *Paradise* movement."

Hitler turned back to her, perplexed. "What do you mean no *Paradise* movement? Dante's *Divine Comedy* ends with it."

Winifred smiled. "Yes, I know, but Richard had told Franz that no human being is capable of writing music that depicts Heaven. So Liszt only wrote a *Purgatory* movement and then ended the work with a musical arrangement of the *Magnificat* prayer. Therefore, Liszt's work falls short. It's flawed."

The young gentleman smiled, as he whispered back, "Yes, but although some critics say the absence of a *Paradise* movement destroys the balance of this work, I must say, once you hear Liszt's *Magnificat* you'll be most satisfied. In fact, you'll probably be transported to Heaven."

Hitler rolled his eyes, as Winifred pompously lifted her nose and turned toward the stage.

Meanwhile, Weingartner had been waiting irritably for their rude murmurs to cease. Remaining erect, with his back still facing the irreverent ones, he raised his baton—the *Purgatory* movement then commenced.

Having faithfully reconstructed Dante's immortal allegory, Liszt deftly portrayed Dante's ascent from the lowest circle of Hell, as he eventually rose to the surface to view the peaceful, healing waters of redemption. The soft and serene melody evokes the arduous travels of souls striving for atonement, which then leads straight into the glorious *Magnificat*. Although not Paradise, Liszt offers the mortal listener a spiritually moving glimpse of the luminous transcendence awaiting those granted access into God's Heavenly Paradise.

Evidently, Hitler found Liszt's *Purgatory* just as insufferable as the ludicrous concept of Purgatory itself, and the staunch atheist almost dozed off. Now, with the equally insufferable "Christian" coda rising up, with the aid of a chorus, no less, Hitler's patience was tested almost beyond his limits. Although initially shocked by the heavenly voices that appeared out of nowhere, since Liszt ingeniously called for the chorus to remain hidden to heighten the spiritual revelation, Hitler soon began squirming in his seat and then irritably scanned his playbill. He flipped through the pages, but only grew more restless. His piecing blue eyes rolled up to scan the ceiling, veered over to the ornate bas-reliefs, and then ran back down along the fluted pilasters until they reached the audience again. All he saw was a stupid throng of brainless pigeons all being spiritually seduced by a chorus of Christian claptrap. Oh, how he had grown to hate the absurdities of religion over his years of struggle. In fact, just before entering the hall, Hitler had told Winifred of his intentions once he seized full control of Germany—he would abolish monasteries and confiscate their property.

Driven to distraction, Hitler's wandering eyes suddenly beheld a peculiar sight: amid the stagnant sea of mediocrity, he saw an elderly gentleman with thick, grayish-black hair and olive-colored skin, wearing a herringbone suit. It wasn't so much the man's appearance that captured Hitler's attention, but rather his mystifying behavior. The man's head was turned sideways with his right ear toward the orchestra; but stranger still, he appeared to be writing in a notebook nestled on his lap. Intrigued, Hitler's eyes instinctively zeroed in closer. The mysterious fellow was clearly straining to listen intently to every note of the music, yet he continued scribbling, without even looking down at his hand to guide it. Perplexed, Hitler searched his mind for an explanation, *Well, he's certainly not drawing anyone. And he doesn't appear to be deaf. How peculiar. Whatever could he be—?*

Just then, Hitler's thoughts were diverted when the audience erupted with a thunderous round of applause, further fueled by enthusiastic shouts of, *"Bravo!"* The *Magnificat's* gloriously triumphant coda had ended.

Hitler, however, sat morosely fixed, with a cold, blank stare chiseled on his face. It was now clear to Winifred that Liszt's Christian *Magnificat* did not resonate with her Adolf. Filled with internal delight, a subtle grin cracked her porcelain skin. Meanwhile, Eva, the bubbly young sprite, seemed not even to have comprehended the profound piece of art that had just transpired.

All the while, Hitler remained outwardly stiff but inwardly fluid. Thoughts of the mysterious old scribbler quickly faded as a far more serious issue flooded his troubled mind. How could his fellow Germans be so lacking in artistic taste? Sure, he thought the *Inferno* movement was absolutely terrifying and oddly sublime—although he loathed the fact that a non-Aryan trumped even Wagner. But he couldn't grasp what they saw in Liszt's insufferable *Purgatory* or in the childishly Christian notion of longing for a vaporous illusion called Paradise. Hitler had grand visions for his beloved Deutschland, and the Christian religion not only posed a roadblock to his ultimate mission of winning the upcoming election and one day seizing full control, but it also deflected their idolizing worship toward God, when it should have been aimed at the Nazi Party and, of course, at its infallible leader.

Rising from their seats, Eva and Winifred each leaned toward their man of the hour. Waking Adolf out of his rankling reverie, the two prideful peacocks helped their Nazi idol to his feet, and then tepidly applauded Weingartner's conducting—more so for performing the illustrious works of their Germanic God, Richard Wagner, than for the Hungarian gypsy-warlock, Franz Liszt.

As the maestro exited the stage, the audience dutifully retook their seats. Then, with a mild round of applause, they signaled for his return. Taking the stage once more, Felix bowed and mounted the podium. With but the subtlest wave of the baton, he engaged a most beautiful encore, rendering the audience spellbound. The enchanting piece was soft and luring—so much so, that even Hitler seemed transported to another realm. Upon its magical conclusion, the audience burst into an enthusiastic roar of appreciation.

As Hitler and his two companions rose once again, he turned to Winifred. "Winnie, what was the name of that piece?"

Winifred was startled, just like a young schoolgirl caught daydreaming by a questioning teacher—especially since her Adolf had called her by the old pet name, *Winnie.*

She demurred, "Actually, Adolf, I'm not sure. I wish Siegfried were still alive, he certainly would know."

"Well, surely it must be one of Wagner's?"

Winifred remained quasi-paralyzed. "Well, uh, actually, Adolf…it very well might be…but, uh—"

Without hesitation, the young Eva seized the moment. "Yes, it *must* be. I know I've heard it somewhere before. It must have been at a Wagnerfest, somewhere."

Hitler glanced at her and smiled. "Yes, I'm sure of it. It was most beautiful. A true picture of perfection, one that only a true master of sound like Wagner could paint."

Overhearing their conversation, the young gentleman behind them once again leaned forward. "Excuse me, but you're all mistaken. That, too, was by Franz Liszt. It was the symphonic poem *Orpheus*."

The two women cringed, as Hitler's face reddened.

Unwittingly, the young man went on to describe the piece, lauding how beautifully Liszt had captured the ancient legend of Orpheus, the greatest of all musicians and poets—capable of charming even the rocks and trees—who used his sublime art as a seductive lure to lift and elevate mankind.

Hitler's humiliation, however, had quickly turned to smoldering disgust. He was in no mood to hear of a Hungarian, or a Greek, elevating mankind and civilization with his sublime art. That task could only be accomplished by Germans of good blood, and with Hitler's blood now rushing through his veins and radiating racial disgust, the young man prudently recognized the red-faced warning signs, turned away, and sheepishly slipped into the shifting crowd.

As the audience shuffled toward the open exits, Hitler, quite unexpectedly, caught a glimpse of the old scribbler in the herringbone suit. He was standing alone in a dark recess chiseled into the chamber wall. Suddenly the elderly man turned and looked Hitler straight in the eye. Then, quite unexpectedly, his hand rose, wielding a pistol, and took aim. Hitler's eyes bulged—*he* was the target!

Somewhere in the crowd, a woman screamed, "Gun! That man has a gun!"

Two shots rang out, as the pistol belched smoke and fire. Hitler heard the bullets whiz by his left ear, as well as the two thuds behind him where they buried themselves in the plaster wall. Seeing the man take aim again, Hitler veered to the left and grabbed Eva to pull her down. Three more wild, rapid shots rang out, as Winifred still stood in shock. Reaching over, Hitler pulled her down and used his hands to shield both women's heads.

As screams echoed throughout the chamber, Hitler peered over the top of his bullet-pierced seat and located the chiseled alcove. To his relief, the firing stopped, but he noticed that the recess was an emergency exit, and the thick metal door was now ajar. The mysterious old man, however, was gone.

✠✠✠

Meanwhile, five miles away from the Berlin Opera House, the preeminent physicist, Albert Einstein, stood at the front door of the Kaiser Wilhelm Institute for Physical Chemistry and Elektrochemistry. It was the home of some of the greatest scientific minds of the day, including its illustrious president, Max Planck, and the Nobel Prize laureate for chemistry, Fritz Haber.

The Kaiser Institute had been built twenty-one years earlier in 1911 and featured a modest but dignified façade. Quite aptly, it also featured a turret with a tapered roof that mimicked the Kaiser's characteristic Pickelhaube. The Institute had been built with the express purpose of promoting scientific research, and the project even received funding from several foreign entities, including the Rockefeller Foundation.

The fifty-three-year-old Einstein, with his classic wild hair and mustache, radiated anticipation as he awaited the arrival of the Institute's newest team member.

Walking up to give him a warm greeting was the strappingly built and rather handsome mathematician Angelo Di Purezza Jr. Standing at about five feet ten inches, Angelo had a well-defined jaw with cleft chin, and a thick mane of jet-black, wavy hair. He had gotten into a strict regiment of exercising, having first been influenced by his father and then more recently by the world's most popular muscleman, Angelo Sciliano, who changed his name to Charles Atlas. "Albert, my friend, it's good to see you again. I do hope you managed to make room for me?"

"Most certainly. I'm pleased to have you back, Angelo. Your brief visit last year wasn't nearly enough time for you to learn much about our facility here."

Angelo smiled. "Yes, but those few hours with you and Max were enough to win anyone's approval, so I'm elated to be accepted." Glancing around, he added, "I'm looking forward to my new home here."

Einstein shrugged his shoulders. "Well, we all have to follow our gut instincts, and leaving Italy because of *Il Duce* is a wise move, but—" Einstein looked around cautiously, then whispered, "Germany is equally unstable these days. No one knows what direction the government is heading, and I sense it is *not* good, once again."

"No matter," Angelo said confidently, "perhaps we can change that." Angelo's attention was drawn to the building's unique façade, as he relayed the fact that he was now fifty-two and had procrastinated long enough. After working in Pisa and then Bologna for a total of thirty-two years, it seemed fitting that 1932 would be a perfect time to make a move. On top of that, his wife had left him for another man. With a sigh, he acknowledged that she had every right to leave him, being that he was a workaholic and had neglected her. Then, with a rejuvenated smile, he looked at Einstein, and added, "So, it's time to focus on positive things, Albert, and that I'm here with some of the brightest minds on earth, I know greater days lie ahead."

Einstein smirked as he grasped Angelo under the arm and escorted him into the vacant lobby. It was furnished with rich, walnut paneled walls, ornate bronze wall sconces, several oil paintings, and two red pleated couches. "Listen, Angelo, brilliant scientists are not always the wisest people."

Angelo squinted. "What do you mean?"

Einstein leaned close. "You must know that I have been quite vocal about promoting my pacifistic beliefs."

"Why, yes, your *Manifesto* in 1914 created a stir, but—"

"But, let me tell you," Einstein interjected, "there are many great minds, right here in this building, that have mindlessly and shamelessly sold their souls for the benefit of the state to create horrible weapons of unthinkable destruction. And my old, former friend Fritz Haber just so happens to be the most honored and heinous of the lot. He developed—"

"Ah!" a deep, raspy Germanic voice rang out. "Talking behind my back again, ay, Albert?"

Einstein spun around, his face pale. "Oh, hello, Fritz. No, no, I was just telling Angelo that—"

"Never mind," Fritz snickered. "We here all know you're a passive lamb."

Fritz Haber was an imposing figure. He was stocky with a thick mustache, sported round clip-on glasses, and was bald. Looking at Angelo with his enlarged round eyes, he asked, "And whom do we have here?"

Before Einstein could answer, Angelo assertively pronounced, "I am Angelo Di Purezza Jr., a mathematician."

"Ah, an I-talian. I see our première institute lets anybody in here these days."

Angelo wasn't quite sure if Fritz was being comically welcoming or just downright racially sarcastic. But picking up on Einstein's earlier comments and Fritz's fencing skills, Angelo boldly countered, "Well, I wasn't aware they accepted thick-headed xenophobes here."

"*Mutig!* Or perhaps I should say *Bravo,* Angelo. I see you're not a pansy like Albert here. But, remember, tough talk is cheap. You had better produce around here, or I'll make sure you're turned around and booted right back to that big I-talian boot of yours."

"Oh, don't worry about me, Fritz. I'll hold my own. And in the event *I* decide to leave, I'll just rub that shiny, crystal-ball dome of yours to find out where I'd like to go."

Haber's lower lip curled, not accustomed to or relishing having his sarcastic wit outmatched. "I see we share certain traits, Mr. Di Purezza, *Junior*. So, for now, I'll offer a truce. Fair enough, *il mio amico?"* Fritz extended his meaty hand and grinned unconvincingly.

Angelo smiled diplomatically. "Certainly, *mein Freund.* After all, if we're going to be working under the same roof we might as well make the best of it."

As Angelo shook Haber's hand, Einstein courteously leaned over to pick up Angelo's valise. As he did, a small, gold pendant fell off and hit the ground. It was a stylish G clef with the name 'LISZT' written across a musical staff.

"Ah," Einstein said, "I see you like the Hungarian composer Franz Liszt?"

Haber looked quizzically at Angelo. "I may be a proud nationalist, but what's this, *you* don't like Italian composers?"

Angelo bent down and picked up the pendant. He explained that it happened to be a special gift from his father, who had the good fortune of not only studying under Liszt, but was also a very dear friend of the Master. They had lived in Rome together and had indeed studied Italian greats, like Paganini and Palestrina, which Angelo admired.

Haber smirked as he proclaimed, "Listen, Angelo, there might be a few 'good' Italian composers, but the only 'great' ones are German."

At this, Einstein irritably shook his head. "This has become a disease, Fritz. All I hear in Germany these days is Prussian-German nationalism. When will any of you wake up? You do realize that beyond our borders there is a vast world brimming with rich cultures and music that can broaden our horizons, don't you?"

Haber simply waved Einstein's remark away, while Angelo rallied to buttress Einstein's global perspective, which he shared. With a final breath, he added, "And as far as Italian composers, Fritz, do you seriously believe that Verdi, Puccini, Rossini, Vivaldi, Respighi and others are not great?"

Haber laughed disdainfully. "You could never compare that cheap laundry list to the sacred scrolls of high German art. Although we have many to boast of, all I need to say is BWB! Bach, Wagner, Beethoven. They're the Teutonic Trinity. Sacred and divine."

Einstein sniggered. "What would you know about things that are sacred and divine, Fritz? In the domain of your heart and soul I've only witnessed a vacuum."

Before Haber could fire a retort, his tall and attractive associate, Rudolf Hein, approached the trio. Hein had always been a puzzle to many at the Institute. There was no disputing he had drive, but Rudy also possessed a wily and secretive disposition that many found strange or unsettling. Towering at six feet five inches, the sixty-six-year-old chemist never appeared to be as bright as he claimed, being even older than his former mentor, Fritz. But Hein looked forty and was fabulously fit, and he knew it.

After a brief but formal introduction, the foursome resumed the musical debate. Hein, with his odd staccato-styled speech, jumped into the fray and defended Haber's patriotic stance, which Angelo couldn't help but notice contained ample doses of Aryan supremacy. Hein then whipped his head back to remove the dark brown hair from his sparkling blue eyes and leaned toward Haber. The two briefly whispered an inaudible conversation, as Hein, with his peculiar gaze, scanned Angelo from head to toe. Then the two scientists abruptly said their goodbyes and coldly departed.

Einstein exhaled with relief. "Do you see what I mean? This place is teaming with brilliant minds, yet they have all been swept up in a growing cult of national fanaticism, on a scale that seriously concerns me."

Angelo shook his head. "I don't get it. My country has already gone down the tubes with *Il Dunce* and his fascist regime, and it appears yours is following right behind. What in God's name is going on?"

Einstein grimaced. "God? I abandoned the childish notion of a divine being governing human affairs long ago. There's absolutely no intelligent or scientific data to support it. Yes, I think there is a 'god' in the sense that something, or rather some *force,* created this vast and puzzling universe. But with all the death and destruction that keeps recurring over the centuries, history proves time and time again that mankind has not changed one iota, nor do we have a single shred of tangible and logical evidence as to who or what really is *The* one and only Creator."

Angelo's back stiffened. "Well, I beg to differ, Albert. Granted, mankind does make many mistakes, but when you focus on the other side of the coin, namely how great minds and godly people rise up to help their fellow man strive for a better world, that can only inspire us to believe that there is a God watching over us. Just as our mission here to uncover wondrous advancements for the betterment of mankind also coincides with God's plan. It's simply a matter of making the right decisions, Albert. But unfortunately many leaders today are brainwashing the people to follow their own demonic course—" Angelo briefly gazed at his musical pendant, and continued, "and speaking of demonic, I've been meaning to ask you, are you familiar with Franz Liszt's *Dante Symphony*?"

Einstein looked baffled. "No, not really. To be honest, Angelo, I don't care much for Liszt's modern music or all that *Sturm und Drang*. I much prefer the elegant and refined music of Mozart."

Angelo smiled. "Well, yes, most people gravitate to pleasant music, Albert. Meanwhile Liszt explored many new directions, far beyond the catchy melodies and beauty that lulls and lures the masses."

Einstein shrugged his shoulders. "I never really understood that man. Obviously he was very talented, but it appears he composed many pieces of ghastly visions of Hell or of mankind's unseemly destructive side. And, quite plainly, some of his music just seems undignified. What could he or his listeners possibly gain from such endeavors?" Einstein rubbed his chin. "Furthermore, if memory serves me, didn't Liszt lead a scandalous love life and then join the Church?"

Angelo rose to the Hungarian's defense. He explained that it was unfortunate that many people couldn't understand Liszt's artistic versatility. Besides his visions of Hell (which spawned from great works of literature and the ravaging wars of his age) or his dazzling virtuosity, Liszt also composed some of the most romantic melodies ever dreamt of, not to mention countless religious pieces that truly lift the soul." Angelo smiled unexpectedly. "But, yes, Liszt was indeed a man of many contradictions. He was a world famous virtuoso and leader of the Romantic Movement, yet became somewhat of a recluse; a flamboyant showman, yet was a profound thinker committed to the highest ideals of art; and, yes, even a hedonist who became an abbé. But despite his sensationalized love life, he remained a bachelor. And, let's face it, Albert, many have engaged in numerous romances or unconventional bonds. Even *you* married your cousin Elsa."

Einstein's face twisted with a painful grin. "Yes, indeed. And the castigations about our union have not ceased. But I married one woman, Angelo. Liszt, they say, had many women."

Angelo nodded as he adjusted his Italian silk tie. "Yes, women were a vice for Liszt. But even Adam fell from grace right from the very beginning of time, Albert. Women *can* be bewitching." Glancing at his crucifix tiepin, he added, "You see, redemption and forgiveness are important tenants of the Christian faith. No matter how bad we falter, if we truly apply ourselves to the purity of the good Word, we shall overcome our deficits and gain salvation. So Liszt's minor faults didn't blemish his lifelong deeds, deeds that in some instances surpassed every other composer in history."

Einstein's left eyebrow rose in doubt. "How so?"

Angelo explained that Liszt not only formed a school to promote his avant-garde Music of the Future, but he also taught his students free of charge. Moreover, Liszt's school became the Mecca of the music world, to the utter frustration of Brahms, Clara Schumann, and the traditionalists. But their old world would indeed fade as Liszt's new progressive music radically changed the course of history. From his impressionistic and atonal innovations to his improvisational paraphrases, Liszt's roots can be found in most forms of modern music, even, quite shockingly, in American Jazz.

As a child prodigy, Liszt had made his initial impact on the world as a virtuoso of the piano. Many attempted to rival his skills, but by unanimous consent, Liszt ruled supreme. Yet while his early piano compositions were revolutionary in their own right, as Liszt matured, he embraced orchestral music, which became even more radical and innovative. And while Liszt did indeed explore the darker side of human nature, just as many works offered unique impressions of nature, character portraits, various nationalistic tributes, dreamy evocations of love, and even sublime masterpieces that glorified God, despite the fact that critics only seemed to focus on, and deride, Liszt's darker works.

While Angelo deplored the ignorant critics who colored the minds of millions, he admired Liszt's genius, which he said, "Apparently streamed out of his fertile mind like the waters of Baptism; blessing all those who truly listened to his works."

At this, Einstein irreverently raised a cynical brow, which Angelo keenly noticed, as he added, "But, unfortunately, too many people have condemned Liszt's music without ever truly listening to it. Meanwhile, others simply refuse to remove the dark blinders of tradition—seeing only what others wish them to see, or in this case, hear."

Einstein grinned as he acknowledged Angelo's not-so-subtle point. "Well, you make a valid point, my dear friend. Society does mold us. And, yes, I am unfamiliar with Liszt's works, so I'd do well to be more objective."

As scientists and administrative personnel arrived for work and weaved around Angelo and Albert, Angelo straightened out his fashionably new, double-breasted suit jacket, then pinned the Liszt pendant onto the lapel of his jacket. "And that leads to my second point," Angelo said, as he expounded further.

Liszt's music, he firmly believed, reflected not only the man, but also the world. Liszt had travelled extensively and even visited hospitals to aid the sick or those wounded in war—being the first person to use music as a therapy to battle depression. He also moved among royalty, peasants, priests, poets, artists, and politicians. Basically, Liszt experienced all facets of life. And those rich worldly experiences, Angelo believed, allowed him, in certain works, to express himself more authentically and effectively than any other composer in history.

Einstein's lips twisted with doubt as several technicians walked through the lobby. "Just a minute, Angelo," Einstein said as he stepped closer. "I must challenge you on that. Mozart composed some of the most splendid music ever written and was versatile enough to write such spirited pieces as his *Marriage of Figaro Overture* or his quite gloomy *Don Giovanni*. And—"

"Listen," Angelo interjected, raising his hand. "I am not insinuating that Liszt was superior in every regard or flawless; in fact, he wrote a few duds, as did Mozart. But, as I said, the variety of music he composed was far more diverse and, in many cases, far more radical, advanced and prophetic than all others, including Mozart or even Beethoven. Yet, quite sadly, people have been groomed to believe that no one else can rival such gods, and the ignorance prevails. Do you realize that neither Mozart nor Beethoven ever devised a new musical form? Yet Liszt did. His symphonic poem broke the long-held tradition that all others obediently adhered to with their multi-movement symphonies."

As Einstein listened intently, Angelo continued, "But, propaganda also plays a role in all of this, and Liszt did have many adversaries. They admired and lauded how he played the piano, but deplored his innovative compositions, some being jealous peers, some biting journalists, and others were huge political movements." Having noticed the two huge paintings of Kaiser Wilhelm I and II on the lobby wall, Angelo added, "After all, your Prussian-German machine here would never allow a Hungarian to rival a true-blooded Aryan like Wagner, and the records prove it. Yet, despite the bigotry, I'm convinced that Liszt's influence shall one day prevail."

Einstein paused a moment as he rubbed his mustache, then nodded thoughtfully. "Well, I do know that Tchaikovsky openly praised Mozart, yet his works clearly revealed the influence of Liszt, as do the works of many others. However, as for me, I still prefer Mozart—our temperaments, by some grand design of nature, are harmoniously in sync." Einstein glanced at the royal portraits. "But as for the topic of Prussian propaganda, I certainly agree, Angelo. As I told you, there's a hellish fire beginning to rise here in Germany, which has been smoldering for decades."

"Yes, hellish, indeed. And that returns me to my initial question, namely about Liszt's *Dante Symphony*."

"Oh, yes, but as I mentioned, I'm not familiar with it, nor am I with most of Liszt's works. So I doubt I can be of any assistance."

Angelo bent over and opened his valise, pulling out an old leather-bound booklet. He gazed at it pensively, then looked at Einstein solemnly. "This is a score of Liszt's *Dante Symphony*. It was found in my father's hands the night he was murdered, back on January 29, 1914."

Einstein's eyes widened. "Murdered!"

"Yes, but the newspapers of the time said he died of a ruptured appendix. However, I no longer believe that. Even before my father died, I knew he had a peculiar obsession for this enchanting symphony. And for the past eighteen years it's been like a hellish thorn burning in the back of my mind. I somehow know that this devilish score has something to do with his demise, although I have yet to figure it out. And with you being the ultimate savant of our age, I'm truly hoping that you can help me solve this deadly riddle."

Einstein's face couldn't conceal his innermost feelings of doubt, as he murmured, "Angelo, you're going on a hunch, and eighteen years is a long time. So even if we invest a good deal of effort into solving this mystery, there is no guarantee that the killer is still alive."

Undaunted, Angelo shook his head. "Albert, this was not some petty local dispute gone wrong. Rather, I believe it's somehow tied into a massive web of royal, political, and possibly even religious intrigue. And, if so, there's certainly going to be more than one person involved."

Einstein's head recoiled. "I thought you said your father was a pupil of Liszt?—a humble musician, an artist. How in the world could he or Liszt have had ties to such high levels of intrigue?"

"Well, as I told you, Liszt was an extremely versatile and famous man, and he moved among almost every royal court, be it in England, France or Germany, as well as taking minor orders in the Catholic Church. So he had far more important connections than just your average musician."

Intrigued in spite of his skepticism, Einstein's bushy eyebrows rose. "Fine, I'm impressed. The man was evidently far more multifaceted and successful than I had thought, but I'm still a bit perplexed. What exactly does his score of the *Dante Symphony* have to do with all of this?"

Angelo reached back into his valise and pulled out several old newspaper clippings. "Here, look at this. There are numerous accounts of people and clergymen deriding Liszt's music, for not only being grotesque or menacing but also for spewing out the vile and corruptive words of the Devil."

Einstein briefly surveyed the headlines, then looked squarely up at Angelo's face. "Surely, you *must* be kidding? Do you really expect me to believe that Liszt conjured up the demons with his music? That's insane. Infantile! And I won't be a part of a silly witch hunt, or any—"

"Hold on!" Angelo interjected. "Of course that's not what I'm suggesting. It's just that those reports simply led me to assume that Liszt very likely could have relayed hidden messages within the score."

Angelo returned to the *Dante* score and flipped through several pages, then stopped. "See here? Look how Liszt instructs the conductor to play this section of the *Inferno*. He states: *This entire passage is intended to be blasphemous mocking laughter, very sharply accentuated in the two clarinets and violas.* Meanwhile, he offers other indications throughout the score that—"

"Wait just a minute," Einstein moaned. "Instructions to play a piece of music with a crystal clear idea of what the composer is trying to convey is a very wise move on Liszt's part. But to what avail is it to make music that sounds like blasphemous mocking laughter? That's of no use to a secret agent, unless he wishes to transmit mocking laughter to his fellow operatives or rivals. And at this rate, you might just be ridiculed with mocking laughter *by me!*"

"Hold on!" Angelo pleaded. "Once again you're missing the point. I'm merely showing you that Liszt did include unconventional instructions but *also* some very unique proprietary markings. Being that his music was so radically new, Liszt had to invent his own musical symbols to instruct musicians how to play certain passages." Angelo pointed to one of the glyphs. "See, look here."

Reluctantly, Einstein stepped closer and looked down at the score, as his weary eyes struggled to focus. Yet once they did, they sprang wide open! With a jolt, he grabbed the score from Angelo and drew it closer. "Hmm, you do have a point, Angelo. I've never seen anything like it. There are some very odd symbols here. And, oh my, look at some of

Liszt's notation. What was he thinking, or doing, with all these wild configurations?"

"Well, as the famous phrase goes, 'Liszt hurled his lance into the future.' He was easily a century ahead of his time, was he not?"

"Indeed," Einstein concurred. "It's clear where Mahler, Richard Strauss and Sibelius acquired their ideas." Running his fingers along the score, he then began to sight-read the music. Humming the tune while following Liszt's dotted script, Einstein bobbed his head to the aggressive *Inferno* melody. But suddenly, he stopped. "Hmm, I wonder what these symbols here mean? I have no clue as to what Liszt was seeking, but perhaps you're right. Maybe these symbols do have dual meanings. This indubitably is most fascinating."

Angelo's face beamed. "Does that mean you'll help me?"

Just then, an uproar of anxious voices emanated out of all the nearby offices and laboratories. Rudolf Hein suddenly re-appeared, alarmed and bellowing, "Did you hear the news?"

Einstein and Angelo both turned with blank stares, as Hein excitedly continued, "There has been an assassination attempt on Adolf Hitler! It just occurred about twenty minutes ago!"

"What happened?" Angelo inquired, as employees began streaming out into the hallways.

"He was at the Berlin Opera House," Hein said with a gasp, trying to catch his breath. "And the assailant, apparently an old man, pulled out a pistol and fired off several shots. Thank God, Hitler ducked and emerged unscathed." Hein shook his dazed head. "I shudder to think of Germany's future if that deranged madman killed Hitler. He's our only hope and savior."

"Yes, of course," Einstein uttered tepidly, trying to comprehend the mindless fervor over a blustering upstart.

Meanwhile, questions filled Angelo's mind. "So who else was with Hitler? And do they have any leads as to whom the assailant might be?"

Hein swallowed hard, his eyes wide. "Hitler was with Winifred Wagner and his new lady friend, Eva Braun. I hear she's a photographer's lab assistant. It's a damn shame she didn't snap a photo of this failed assassin."

"Well, I doubt she'd bring a camera into the opera house, or if they would even allow it," Einstein deduced calmly.

Angelo seemed to be thinking out loud. "Winifred Wagner, huh? Then I assume it was a Wagner fest or opera, correct?"

Before Hein could answer, a deep voice rang out behind them, "Actually, no!"

As the three turned toward the voice, they saw Fritz Haber plodding toward them, his baritone voice booming, "After some overtures by Wagner the concert ended with Liszt's *Dante Symphony*."

Angelo's head snapped towards Einstein's, their astonished eyes connecting. After a chilling, brief moment, of seemingly reading each other's thoughts, the two turned back toward Fritz.

As Haber approached, wearing his lab-issued smock and rubber gloves, he noticed the silent exchange, and queried, "Why the shocked looks?"

"Oh, it's n-nothing," Einstein stammered. "We're just alarmed by the assassination attempt."

Haber adjusted his round spectacles and focused in on Angelo's face. "Well, I know why *you're* startled."

Angelo looked puzzled. "What do you mean?"

"You know darn well," Haber said, with a suspicious twang. "I just did a little homework on you, *Signore Di Purezza*. I thought your name sounded familiar. Your father was Angelo Di Purezza Sr., who died some eighteen-years ago. The newspapers said he was found with the score of the *Dante Symphony* in his hands. How very interesting."

"How so?"

"Well, your father died with the *Dante* score in his hands; Hitler almost gets terminated after a performance of it; and *lo!* What do we have here?" Peering at the score in Einstein's hands, Haber commandingly snatched it, and flipped it open.

Angelo reacted instantly, forcefully pulling the precious booklet from Haber's hands. "Just who the hell do you think you are? This was my father's score. It's highly treasured and priceless. Furthermore, it is none of your business. So just what the hell are you getting at?"

"Hmm. Testy, testy, aren't we?"

"Never mind the cute sarcasm, Fritz. What's your beef?"

A sinister grin etched Haber's round, meaty face. "Oh, nothing really. I just find it interesting that you happen to have a score of the very same piece of music that was played at Hitler's assassination attempt, a score, no less, that was also found in your dead father's hands. It seems this *Dante Symphony* truly is the work of the Devil. No?"

"No!" Angelo retorted coldly, as he hurriedly stuffed the newspapers and score back into his valise.

Haber stepped closer. "Well, my suggestion is don't get too intimate with that damning *Dante* score of yours. It clearly leads to trouble...or even *death!*"

Angelo turned and faced Haber—his coal-burning eyes menacingly scanning the German ox from head to hoof. Meanwhile, Angelo's tense jaw and flexed biceps were receiving cerebral commands to simmer down, and they slowly began to comply. Angelo didn't want to make a scene on his first day; worse yet, the startled employees were now filling up the lobby, all chattering about the assassination attempt. Angelo gazed over at Einstein. "Would you be so kind as to show me to my quarters?"

"I'd be delighted," came the relieved Einstein's jovial response.

The two began plowing through the crowded lobby, when an attractive secretary, standing near the main office, elbowed her female colleague. The two women gaped admiringly at Angelo as he strode by. His virile good looks and muscular physique didn't quite seem to fit the laboratory setting, but they certainly didn't mind, especially Mildred, as she brushed the hair away from her radiant face.

Oblivious to the admiring glances, the two scientists exited the plush lobby and walked down a sterile, white corridor with black-and-white checkered floor tiles.

Einstein gazed blissfully at Angelo. "I'm so glad you're here. I finally have an ally—one with backbone to boot!"

Angelo smirked. "Well, let's not get back into that *boot* business. But I can certainly see now what you meant about the brilliant minds in this place. I think it's going to be a rough ride here. But, more importantly, what do you think about the assassination attempt on Hitler today?"

Einstein shook his head, a pained look marring his matured face. "The world is truly going mad. What can I say, I think it's a shame."

Angelo turned. "But I thought you despised Hitler?"

"Yes, I mean it's a shame the old man missed."

As they both chuckled, Angelo grasped Einstein by the arm, firmly stopping him in his tracks, his face now dead serious. "But, I must know, Albert. Will you help me decipher the mystery that lies in the score of Liszt's *Dante Symphony?*"

Einstein hesitated only but a moment before nodding. "After what just transpired, of course I will, or at least I'll try. All these events appear to be more than coincidental, Angelo. My only question is: If Liszt and your father are both dead, how could this score still be transmitting messages? And don't tell me it's because Liszt could summon the spirits or some crazy mumbo jumbo.'"

Angelo laughed, but then paused. "I'm not sure. Evidently someone has carried on the tradition. But to be quite frank, I'm not too pleased with this Fritz Haber of yours either. He's already gotten under my skin."

Einstein grimaced. "Yes, I noticed. As I was about to tell you—before Fritz rudely interrupted—he and I used to be friends. In fact, I even lived with him for a while many years ago. But our opposing ideologies and political viewpoints tore us apart. What I was also trying to get at is this; Fritz Haber is the father of chemical warfare. He worked directly for Kaiser Wilhelm II and it was his ghastly poison gas that killed thousands during the Great War. Fritz even received a medal for his loyal service, a service of coldly and cruelly exterminating humans en masse like insects."

Angelo's face turned pale. "My God, I knew you Germans were competing with the French in the production and use of poison chemicals, but I had no idea that I'd land right here in Lucifer's Lair."

"Yes—" Einstein suddenly paused as a group of colleagues were heading back to their laboratories, still upset over the shocking news. Exchanging cordial nods, Einstein waited for them to pass, then cautiously continued, "As I said, my aims at scientific research are at polar odds with the vast majority of those walking these halls. And that's why it's a stroke of good fortune that you decided to come here."

Angelo grinned, yet his mind drew him elsewhere.

Einstein tapped his arm. "What? What is it?"

Angelo answered slowly. "It may be nothing…but I just don't like how Fritz needled me with his ominous warning. He seems to know something. And it certainly felt more like a lethal threat than friendly advice. Don't you think so?"

Einstein peered around them before drawing Angelo in closer. "Listen, I think we should just focus on decoding the score and steer clear of Fritz. In fact, getting too close to Haber can yield deadly results, too. His charming wife Clara was also a chemist; but like me, she abhorred his efforts to aid the Kaiser with his poison gas. In a moment of utter despair, Clara took Fritz's military pistol and shot herself right in the chest. She died in her poor son's arms."

Angelo breathed out sharply, his head dropping. "My God, that's awful."

"Indeed. Worse yet, the coldhearted Gas Man returned to work the next day, delivering his poison to the Russian front."

In dismay, Angelo shook his head, as the two friends resumed walking. Angelo's mind was churning—trying to piece together all the loose ends.

Einstein then took a giant step forward and grasped the brass handle of the heavily varnished lab door. He swung it open, pivoted Angelo's body around, and extended his arm into the room. "Here we are! One of the finest laboratories on the face of the Earth, if not *the* finest."

Angelo was overcome with a flood of emotions. He felt a deep sense of accomplishment for being accepted into such a prestigious facility, yet he was deeply saddened that his father and mother were no longer alive to share in his success—his mother dying when he was only twenty and his father when he was thirty-four. Yet, his mind still kept returning to the vexing score of the *Dante Symphony* and the string of coincidences, or calculated plots, that caused his father's death and may nearly have caused Adolf Hitler's. Then there was this new irksome irritant, Fritz Haber, which posed another layer of complexity. It seemed his plate was overloading and that didn't even include his new mathematical workload.

Angelo shook his head, then looked over at his new colleague. "So, Albert, where do we begin? Quantum mechanics, electromagnetic fields, laws of gravity…what?"

Einstein strode right past him towards the blackboard, which was densely populated with a dizzying array of mathematical equations. Pointing at the longest and most complex numeric sequence, he said, "No sense fooling around, Angelo, so—" his arm suddenly flung down and pointed at Angelo's valise. "Break out that darn score and let's see what the hell Liszt was up to!"

With their eyes connecting, the two scientists laughed in unison, as Albert grasped a chair and joined his new colleague at the desk. Angelo patted Albert on the back, then promptly pulled out a hefty sandwich from his valise. "I hope you don't mind, but I'm famished from the long train ride. Care for a bite?"

"No, no," Einstein said. "But, please, do go right ahead." His nose wriggled. "What is it?"

Angelo took a bite and said, "Salami and provolone," as he wiped the oozing mustard off his lips.

The two scientists then morphed into sleuths. Opening up the precious score, they began scouring all the scales, notes, time signatures, and symbols in Liszt's mysterious *Inferno* movement. Amid their cryptanalysis they found themselves also reflecting upon the turbulent world in which Liszt had been immersed.

SCENE II: ROME & PARIS [1866]

The ornate walls and marble floor of the Sala Dante in Rome only seemed to amplify the menacingly bleak, dark and turbulent rumblings of Franz Liszt's *Dante Symphony*. Windowpanes rattled and chairs vibrated as the room filled with blasphemous mocking laughter. Directing from the podium was one of Liszt's many former, and now successful, students, Giovanni Sgambati.

It was 1866, and Italy had been almost a vacuum in regards to professional musical performances, save, of course, for Italian opera. Despite being musical innovators in so many ways (having bequeathed to the world the inventions of the violin, cello, piano, and other instruments, as well as instating Italian as *the* official language for musical notation), Italians only focused on opera, religious chorals, or street songs. There were no symphony orchestras, salons, or concert halls, and as such, this inaugural performance was of major historical importance.

It was merely just one more important contribution Liszt made, for he had performed in the Sala Dante many years earlier making a huge impression. However, those were solo performances on the piano during Liszt's heyday. The handsome and flamboyant youth had dazzled all of Europe with his electrifying shows, which even prompted the German poet Heinrich Heine to coin the term 'Lisztomania'.

But to the world's utter shock and dismay, Liszt retired from the stage to devote himself to composition and teaching. Nevertheless, his sparkling performances had whetted the Italians' appetite for more; and like the true lovers of great food that they were, the Italians began to serve up and devour these public performances as if lasagna with growing enthusiasm and delight.

However, the famous Hungarian was now fifty-five, and he and his artistic visions had matured. His trademark mane of long, straight brown hair was now mostly whitish-gray and he often wore a black cassock, having taken minor orders in the Catholic Church a year earlier. Meanwhile, the maestro's music had changed even more dramatically. Liszt's thrilling virtuosity on a solo instrument had now morphed into a huge symphonic beast; one that not only featured a standard orchestra, but also harps, tubas, gongs, and other instruments that were now bellowing frightful evocations of the torments of Hell. Although some were awed by Liszt's radically innovative soundscapes, others were horrified. One such horrified spectator was Monsignor Waldo Inganni.

Inganni was a twenty-eight-year-old hybrid; his German mother being Lutheran and his Italian father a fanatical Catholic. His mother's early death allowed his overbearing father to pursue his ultimate goal—that of practically horsewhipping Waldo up the ranks at the Vatican.

Sitting in the back of the moderate-sized chamber in the Sala Dante (which was part of the Palazzo Poli), Inganni was smoldering as he feverishly tapped his fat, stubby fingers on his short, stubby thighs. He would have much preferred washing his hands and ears of this rabble—and could have done so just outside in the Trevi Fountain, which consumed one massive side of the Palazzo Poli—but he had come here today to quench his burning curiosity, which indeed he did, even if with brimstone and fire.

As Liszt's blistering *Inferno* movement assaulted his fanatically rigid ears, Inganni clenched his rosary beads, lifted them to his mouth and kissed them, swearing to make sure such evil rot would never contaminate the public again. Inganni then tapped the shoulder of his skeletal and rather odd-looking childhood friend, Kiel Leiche—with his cadaver-like face and large yellow teeth—and motioned to leave.

As the two exited the Palazzo Poli, the monsignor put on his broad-rimmed galero and vented, "What a profane insult to the art of music! Bach and Palestrina must be turning in their graves. It's simply deplorable!"

Kiel shook his boney shoulders. "Well, Wally, I don't care much for music, except for the rollicking folk songs we sing at Oktoberfest, but Bishop Matessa—who is pretty darn smart—told me Liszt is just expressing what Dante spoke of in his *Divine Comedy*. And I think he said that poem is considered a masterpiece. So what's the big deal?"

Inganni's eyes burned like lava, as he retorted, "It's a shame you never learned to think for yourself, Kiel! Or at all! And what's the big deal? First, he insults the great name of Dante right in the Sala Dante. Second, his blasphemous torrent defames the art of pure and glorious music. Third, his infectious noise spews the venom of Satan!"

Kiel squinted, then snickered. He was used to Waldo's biting insults and similar crude core, which his vestments poorly concealed, but his religious obsession had become unbearable.

Waldo snapped, "Laugh if you like, you mindless brick, but this is serious. I must tell the Pope, *immediately*. Follow me!"

Inganni swiftly hailed a carriage and the two rapidly took flight. They breezed past the ancient and majestic Pantheon, crossed over the Tiber, and promptly arrived at Bernini's immense circular colonnade.

Constructed to symbolically form a grand welcoming entrance, the colonnade enclosed a large, round piazza. In the middle of the piazza stood an eighty-one-foot-tall Egyptian obelisk. It was transported to Rome in the first century AD by the deranged and coveting Roman Emperor Caligula to decorate his racetrack. Over a millennium later, in 1586, Pope Sixtus V coveted the pagan obelisk, allegedly to mark the spot where Saint Peter was crucified. Yet for some it has remained a constant reminder of the power plays between regimes, religions, nations, and the corruption that afflicts both the temporal and religious realms.

With a pious wink, the monsignor instructed Kiel to wait for him by Caligula and Sixtus' stolen Egyptian obelisk. Impatiently, Inganni turned and stormed feverishly through the Belvedere Courtyard, past the Swiss guards (in their blue and orange striped uniforms), and into the Vatican Palace.

Pushing his way through a group of cardinals, Inganni managed to catch sight of the Pope strolling down one of the palace's lavish hallways. Propelling himself up to the Holy Father and his entourage, he boldly queried, "Your Eminence, may I have a moment of your time?"

The Pope's retinue huffed and rolled their eyes, being very familiar with *Wild Wally,* as they called him in private. As they entered the Basilica, Pope Pius IX graciously waved his hand, signaling the young cleric to join them. "Monsignor, I only have but five minutes until I reach my destination downstairs, so I suggest you make it quick and succinct."

"Thank you, Holy Father. But I must relay a matter of the utmost importance. The very Devil is among us in Rome. He now speaks directly to the public in his foul and cryptic tongue, but I understand his secrets and motives."

Pius came to an abrupt stop and spread out his arms, thus firmly halting his two flanking bishops and in turn the small train. With a look of the utmost gravity, His Holiness turned and gazed at Inganni. "This better not be some silly hoax, Monsignor. Just what are you insinuating?"

Inganni ran his stubby finger around the edge of his stiff white collar, which was now choking his fat sweaty neck. With an unwanted rush of adrenaline, his vocal chords strained to sing his words. "Well, uh, ah, actually I don't mean to sound impertinent, as I know your Eminence's powers of deduction exceed all others, but I'm telling you that Franz Liszt is in the Sala Dante right now and, I swear to you, his music is the very vessel of evil!"

With a sigh of relief, Pius said, "Monsignor, you *are* aware that I am on personal terms with Abbé Liszt, are you not?"

Inganni's meaty head began beading up with sweat. Nervously, he wiped his forehead with his forearm. "Uh, naturally I know you know *of* him, Holy Father, who doesn't? He gets more press than God. But did you say *personal terms*?"

"That's correct, my impetuous young inquisitor. So what is this nonsense about him speaking with a forked tongue?"

"Holy Father, I have not only heard his satanic rabble with his new *Dante Symphony,* but I've also heard that his score contains hand-written notes instructing the players to produce evil mocking laughter. And I must say, such impressions and communiqués to the innocent public will only corrupt their weak constitutions. Can't you see? Liszt is laughing and mocking *us.* We will lose our parishioners to this evil madness. This I assure you!"

"Hogwash!" Pius retorted. "As I told you, I know Franzi very well. We have spoken countless times on numerous subjects, and even engaged in delightful musical recitals in his private chambers, where the maestro graced me with his glittering talents on the piano while I sang some of Bellini's luminous arias." Then gazing at all those around him, he said, "I'll tell each and every one of you this, Liszt is far more magnanimous and selfless than some of you in this Basilica." As the clergy either bowed their heads in shame or frowned with resentment, Pius continued, "Granted, some of his music is wild and untamed, but he has also given birth to some of the most ethereal and gracious music ever created." Then staring directly into Inganni's eyes, he queried, "Are you not aware of his beautiful *Liebesträume?* Or *Un Sospiro*? And what about his masses and oratorios? Do you realize he is currently writing a grand, three-hour-long oratorio entitled *Christus,* which glorifies the life of Jesus? Are they not highly venerable and glorious attempts by a humble and loving soul to honor our Lord God?"

Inganni felt the massive weight of the Pope bearing down on him as if Bramante's entire Basilica were collapsing on his fat little shoulders. Nevertheless, his deep repugnance for Liszt emboldened him to fire back a retort that he never thought possible. "Well, go ahead, rattle off your string of works that beautifully seduce and deceive, but I can name just as many that blatantly spew sacrilegious bile. What about his *Faust Symphony*? His *Mephisto Waltz?* Or even his diabolical *Totentanz?* And now this damned *Dante Symphony* of his even begins with a telling notation by Liszt to 'Abandon all hope ye who enter here!' The man is obsessed with the Devil, I tell you, and is overcome by the Devil. Maybe, Liszt even *is* the Devil!"

Pius bristled. "Monsignor! First, you will *not* address me in such a tone. And as for your ignorance of art, the Faust legend, for your information, is one that emanates from the fictitious pages of literature, composed by such great writers as Goethe and Marlowe. And the phrase *Abandon all hope…* as you must know, is not Liszt's; it's Dante's. Liszt simply added it to the score to clarify the ominous mood dictated in Dante's poem. So if writers can engage their imaginations to tell tales of Satan, then why can't composers? My poor misguided and over-zealous child, even our own Bible contains ugly passages about Satan. Neither our Holy Scriptures nor Liszt's music endorses evil, Monsignor; they both simply address the issue. After all, stifling the truth only breeds ignorance. *Capisca?*"

Inganni remained painfully mute, while Pius finally expelled a sigh of frustration. He then concluded, "Listen, Monsignor, Liszt is perhaps the most multifaceted and complex creature I know; and bear in mind that he is an artist, an artist of the highest magnitude, despite his flirting with undignified music or with infatuated women. Despite his human flaws, Liszt is truly endowed by the Creator. He is a gift to humanity, Monsignor, and I suggest that you listen to the remainder of Liszt's symphony to fully appreciate the spiritual scope and sublime Christian message it imparts. And, please, I'll hear no more of this nonsense. Utilize your free time more judiciously and productively. May the Lord be with you."

Grudgingly, Inganni lowered his head and crossed himself. Meanwhile, Pius turned abruptly, and he and his two flanking bishops marched off as a train of cardinals followed.

Inganni's heart felt like a blast furnace full of rage. He knew the Pope was dead wrong and nothing would stop him. His plans would now have to change, but the mission remained the same. He immediately turned about and darted to meet Kiel, who, to his surprise, was still standing near the obelisk. Kiel was unpredictable—and, lo and behold, as Waldo approached, there he was, throwing pebbles at the pigeons.

"Kiel! What the hell are you doing?"

"These damn birds are disgusting," Kiel belched. "All they do is eat and shit. What the hell good are they?"

Inganni shook his head. "Just put the rocks down and pay attention. Let's head back to the Sala Dante. I want to—"

"Oh, spare me," Kiel moaned, his cadaver-like face screaming *boredom.* "You're not going to force me to sit through the rest of that crap, are you? Hell, Liszt is like these damn pigeons, all he does is eat and produce—"

"Yes, I know, I heard you!" Inganni retorted. "But, no, I have no intentions of listening to any more of Liszt's sinful ranting. My plan is to shadow his every move, because I know I'll find something tangible to ram down the throat of that pompous fool, Pope Pius. And I know you'd enjoy doing something like this."

Kiel smiled, his half-rotted yellow teeth emitting a creepy specter of his inner core. "Sure, I'm game, Wally," he said, just now beginning to realize other possibilities for the mission. "But if this trail leads nowhere, I'm out!"

With a peculiar gleam in their eyes, the two sealed the pact with a solid handshake, and returned promptly to the Sala Dante midway into the performance. Inganni sighed with relief—Liszt was still in attendance. But his soul soon twisted with revulsion—unwilling to suffer Liszt's *Purgatory*. Irritably, Inganni nudged Kiel, and the two made their way out to the antechamber. Some fifteen minutes later, upon the symphony's conclusion, the chamber doors swung open and the audience began to file out. It was then that they spotted Liszt exiting the building, surrounded by a team of dignitaries and friends. Inganni and Kiel tailed the group as they traveled along the unadorned wall of the Palazzo Poli. Liszt's entourage then came upon the magnificent Trevi Fountain, where they stopped to marvel at the famous landmark.

At the center of the fountain stood the commanding statue of the Roman god Neptune, flanked by two winged horses, one calm and the other restless, symbolizing the ocean's oscillating nature.

Filled with delight, the entourage gazed at the refreshing streams of falling water as they poured into the massive basin, then began tossing coins as they made their wishes.

Meanwhile, Inganni and Kiel crept closer. Stopping about twenty steps behind the group, they could hear Liszt imparting his plans. He would be leaving tomorrow for Paris to visit his Old Italian friend, Gioachino Rossini.

Inganni grasped Kiel's arm and walked him away. "Did you hear that?"

Kiel nodded. "Yeah, but when we leave tomorrow you better ditch that big black galero and silly mantelletta."

Inganni's eyes rolled. "Yes, I know, I know! Let's go, I have to make arrangements. Tomorrow we ride to Paris."

Liszt caught an early train and arrived in Paris by the afternoon. The ride had given him time to contemplate the unrelenting turmoil that plagued Europe, as well as his covert plans. But as his carriage rode along the streets of Passy, his attention turned to the pleasant scenery, thus clearing his weighted mind. Passy was an exclusive area on the Right Bank of Paris and home to the city's wealthiest residents. Up ahead he spotted Rossini's posh villa.

As Liszt entered the crowded and impeccably decorated vestibule, Rossini immediately dropped his plate of lasagna, braciole, and bread. Eagerly, he brushed the semolina crumbs off his massive vest, then barreled his way through the crowd to greet his dear friend. "Franzi! How good to see you. But what's this? Don Juan ditched his cassock?"

Liszt grinned. "Ah, I see your tongue still matches your wit—razor sharp!"

Rossini smiled as the two embraced. "Well, why shouldn't it be razor sharp?—my ancient Roman ancestors invented the illustrious razor. I believe Livy said it was King Lucius Priscus. But I use them to not only shave, but also to fillet fish and slice up some of my meats—it does a splendid job. You know how I love to cook these days."

Liszt patted Rossini on his hefty shoulders. "Indeed I do. And I see you haven't changed a bit since you retired from the operatic world as a disgustingly rich man." Liszt chuckled as he glanced around at the opulent furnishings.

Rossini laughed. "Ah, your jealousy delights me and only makes my ripe old age all the more sweet. Can you believe I'm seventy-four years old?"

Liszt shook his head. "If only we could control time the way we control tempo in a score. But alas, we cannot. And to think, in two years hence, you will have lived half your life as a fruitless, partying *bon vivant*."

As Rossini and Liszt laughed, their talented group of friends overheard Liszt's playful raillery and began to converge. Huddling together were the brilliant composers Hector Berlioz and the budding Camille Saint-Saëns, the eminent writers Victor Hugo and Alexandre Dumas, and the trendy artist Jean Ingres.

They all exchanged pleasantries for the better part of an hour, when Saint-Saëns eventually walked over to Liszt. "So, I'm curious, how did the *Dante Symphony* go over in Rome?"

Liszt rolled his eyes. "Well, as you know, blazing a trail into the unknown realms of the future always elicits fear from the indolent masses. But a pioneer I shall remain."

Saint-Saëns smiled. "Yes, ever since my music has taken on some of your Lisztian qualities, I've noticed a rise of opposition, too. The price we pay for innovation, I suppose."

Overhearing his fellow Frenchman's remark, Hector Berlioz—with his wild rooster hairdo, three-piece suit, and a fluffy, red silk cravat—meddled his way closer and turned toward Liszt. "*Oui*, and that brings to mind someone who has blatantly stolen your inventions, yet vehemently chastises anyone who attempts to reveal that fact, namely your good friend Richard Wagner. You know, that depraved viper who benefits from your esteemed clout, mind, and wallet, yet expresses his gratitude with a knife in your back."

Liszt shook his head calmly. "Tut, tut, Hector. All artists borrow ideas to some extent. Moreover, I cannot concern myself with how others conduct themselves in private, nor do I care if they deny me credit. All I care about is the ultimate goal, which is promoting and elevating *art*. And that goal, I believe, should be achieved with selfless dedication, not only to that glorious pursuit but also to helping one's fellow artist—for the objective is not personal glory, Hector, but to collectively enhance culture through our art. That is why I expended great effort, eighteen years ago, to establish my school for modern music at the Altenburg in Weimar."

Berlioz grimaced. "There goes the Abbé Liszt side of you again. You are too damned generous. And in Wagner's case, too damned forgiving. Many have learned from you, yet Wagner goes beyond learning—he steals! His now famous chromatic chord from *Tristan und Isolde* is really yours! And his entire being has practically been transformed, as if by metamorphosis. The ugly Wagner Worm has become a flying Lisztian Lepidoptera. Influence and plagiarism are two different things, Franz. And, as I said, the man only uses you for his own personal gain. That man is one of the most unethical, arrogant, racist, and vile parasites I know!"

"I strongly beg to differ!" a strident voice sounded.

As they all turned, Hans von Bülow approached along with his wife Cosima. Hans' appearance was oddly striking, being that he had a bushy goatee and a predominantly round baldhead with thin strands of hair wrapped around.

However, Hans was a gifted former student of Liszt's, a virtuoso pianist, and currently a preeminent conductor.

Cosima was Liszt's daughter, of average looks with a prominent nose, who, to his dismay, was ensnared in an adulterous relationship with Richard Wagner. Worse still, their tryst had become extremely hard to conceal, since Cosima had given birth to a love child a year ago, which they had flagrantly named Isolde. Von Bülow, however, was a rare specimen, one willing to conceal the sins of two people he now cherished most, despite all the heartache and gossip, which he suffered in stoic silence.

With conviction, Hans continued, "Listen, Hector, it is foolhardy to judge the earthly traits of others while being blind to their higher lofty deeds. Wagner, despite any flaws as a man, is going to prove in short order that he is a god among us. Even Liszt is wise enough to separate the man from his music and has rightfully praised and firmly championed his works, even against great financial odds and fierce critical opposition. And that's why I will dedicate my craft and life to aiding Wagner's rise to world acclaim. Wagner will dwarf all—mark my words!"

Hector crossed his arms and snickered. "Hans, what is it with you Germans and Prussians? You all have the innate defect of mindlessly rallying behind monsters!"

"Hector, your problem, like most Frenchmen, is that you're too much of a woman. Just like a woman scorned, you maliciously attack and disparage others who are brilliant rising stars, all because you're *Fantastique* star has fallen. Face it, Hector, you're a has-been; and not only does no one care to hear your music anymore, no one cares to hear your pathetic whimpers of woe or nasty invectives."

Berlioz grimaced, then burst out laughing. "And what do *you* know about a woman's true feelings and motives, Hans?" As the faces of both Hans and Cosima turned crimson, Hector bellowed, "And as for your god, Richard Wagner, I will never forget what he told me two years ago after he met King Ludwig II for the first time. And we mustn't forget that Ludwig had rescued Wagner from debt and arrest while providing him with an estate and ample funding. Naturally, Richard sponged clean his golden goose to buy himself extravagant silk and velvet clothes and decorated his living room with the finest ornamentation and reams of satin. Still, your dear Richard said: 'Ah, Ludwig is so handsome and wise, soulful, and lovely, that I fear his life will surely melt away in this vulgar world.' Yes, a world made vulgar by the likes of slimy German leeches like Wagner. He's a monster!"

Unexpectedly a voice chimed in, "Just like the Prussian monster Otto von Bismarck, who recently incited the Austro-Prussian War."

Turning around, they saw one of Liszt's pupils, the seventeen-year-old pianist and firebrand, Angelo Di Purezza.

Liszt's face lit up. "Angelo! I'm delighted you made it."

As the group exchanged their brief—and mixed—greetings, Liszt warmly patted Angelo on the back, signaling that he'd return, as he walked over to shake von Bülow's hand. He then turned and kissed Cosima. Gently, he grasped her hand and escorted her away from the gathering. "Cosima, my dear, I see that my taking you and Hans to Pest last year did little to persuade you to stop this embarrassing escapade with Wagner. It's becoming far too unbearable!"

Cosima grimaced. "Father, please! I am not a child. I am a mother and a wife, and—"

"An unfaithful wife!" Liszt interjected.

"Oh, stop it! Is the pot calling the kettle black?"

Liszt rubbed Cosima's arm tenderly. "Please, I don't wish to fight, especially here. But, as a parent, you must know that we always wish the best for our children, and we don't wish to pass on our mistakes. Although my union with your mother yielded three children, I've always remained a bachelor, rather than complicate things. I never pledged myself before God to do what I knew I could never fulfill. Yet, you have taken that solemn Christian vow to be Hans' wife, *till death do you part!"*

Cosima gazed down and then back up at her father. "I'm sorry, but you just don't understand. My love for Richard is not a frivolous whim; and unlike what everyone believes, including you, he did not woo me. The attraction was mutual."

Liszt shook his head angrily. "Enough! I don't care to hear this. What about your daughters Daniela and Blandine? How will *they* process Isolde, this new Wagner love child? You are married, for Christ's sake! Hans is a good man and deeply devoted, perhaps too devoted. And as you know, Cosima, you are now my only surviving child. The deaths of your brother Daniel and sister Blandine have torn a gaping hole in my heart. Therefore, my zeal for your well-being has naturally been amplified to fill that gap. And that your mother has always been, well, you know, battling her own demons and never really there for you, only makes my job as a parent all the more difficult."

Cosima politely removed her father's hand off her arm. "Well, your job here is done. I am a woman now. I, too, have suffered the losses of my brother and sister and have honored their memory by even naming my two girls after them. But time moves onward and we all must move forward with it to follow our own destinies. So you're relieved of your parental duties. Focus on all your musical children, or rather disciples. Your family is far larger than just I, Papa." Cosima gave her father quick pecks on each cheek, then strut coolly toward the buffet table.

Liszt's head dropped. After a brief moment, he turned and walked back to the friendly gathering; which, evidently, wasn't too friendly—Hector and Hans were still at it. Worse yet, the others were caught up in a fiery debate over the Austro-Prussian War, with Angelo dead-center fueling the flames. Most of Rossini's international guests rallied behind Angelo, and his charge about Bismarck's devious tactics in his quest for hegemony. Yet those of Prussian and German descent adamantly defended their chancellor as well as Kaiser Wilhelm's pursuit to unite all the various Germanic states, and Austria was a part of that imperial vision.

Meanwhile, Liszt shook his head and walked over to Angelo. He cordially grasped his muscular arm and escorted him away from the vitriol and out onto the veranda. The Master then brought their bodies to a halt so that his young protégé could take in the spectacular view. To one side was a clear view of the cosmopolitan city of Paris, while the other offered a panoramic vista of serene pastoral charm—each world offering the artist a respectable, yet disparate, slice of life from which to draw inspiration.

As they strolled down the stairs and onto the well-manicured lawn, Liszt peered around the perimeter, then turned toward his young disciple. "Listen, Angelo," he whispered, "it is fine to speak of political matters in public, but it is vital to keep it light and non-confrontational. We mustn't give anyone the slightest notions of our covert activities."

Angelo nodded respectfully. "Yes, understood, Master. But when I heard Hector calling Wagner a monster, I couldn't ignore how this calculating bastard, Bismarck, is bullying his way to conquering all of Europe. And I fear that Wagner's new handsome and effeminate patron, King Ludwig, is now placing his Bavarian principality in jeopardy by siding with Austria. Because, if Bismarck (with his political cunning), and von Moltke (with his strategic military prowess), win this war—which I now believe they will—King Ludwig might lose his Bavarian kingdom."

Liszt gazed despondently at the ground, then up into Angelo's eyes. "Yes, the Prussians are, and have been, hell-bent on devouring all the independent German states to create one massive Prussian Empire. And with this recent power play, we could lose not only critical territory, but also a Catholic stronghold. I know Pope Pius is also very anxious about the outcome of this conflict, quite naturally. In fact, I'm pleased you managed to get the score of the *Dante Symphony* into Sgambati's hands in time for the inauguration in Rome. Although its reception met with mixed reactions, at least its coded message scored another success."

A furtive grin etched Angelo's face. "Yes, you devised one *Hell* of a system, Master. Pun intended!"

Liszt smiled, but suddenly frowned. "I must say, Angelo, although I'm fairly pleased with how Sgambati conducted—since even the best conductors find my music too complex, which, in turn, distorts the true intent of my work—I am disappointed that he didn't realize the subtle cryptic changes I made to the score. I would have at least expected pupils of mine to realize these alterations."

"Well, actually, Sgambati did ask, Master. He noticed notation changes, but had no clue as to its hidden cipher. So I told him that you did what you so often do. Revise, revise—from sunrise to sunrise—that's no surprise."

Liszt laughed, knowing very well that he often would revise works many times or even create alternate versions, as his imagination was an endless font of ideas that made finalizing a work difficult at times. He looked at his protégé. "By the way, nice little rhyme."

"Well, I learned from the best."

Liszt patted Angelo on the shoulder. "You are too kind, my boy. But, yes, I'm relieved that Sgambati didn't suspect a thing. After all, I don't wish to jeopardize the lives of innocent conductors who are unwittingly performing my encoded symphony, especially a dear pupil of mine, like Giovanni."

Just then, an attractive woman appeared, wearing a puffy, pink satin dress, partially covered by a delicate, black lace shawl. As she approached, her brownish-blonde strings of hair gently wafted in the breeze.

Angelo's eyes widened as they connected with her seductive gaze. But the spell was broken when her eyes suddenly turned towards Liszt, and the two embraced.

"Angelo, let me introduce you to Virginia, or rather, Countess di Castiglione."

Angelo cracked a satiated smile. "How pleasing—I mean, how pleased I am to meet you, Countess. I'm Angelo Di Purezza."

Virginia giggled as Angelo kissed her extended hand. As the threesome exchanged pleasantries, Rossini burst out onto the veranda and made his way down onto the lawn. As he barreled over, he bellowed, "Ah, there's my buxom beauty!" As he approached the trio, he added jovially, "My dear Countess, it's been quite some time—like a decade, I believe." Then, playfully direct, he queried, "So, tell me, my dear, are you still flirting around with Emperor Napoleon III?"

Liszt shook his head with a smile, knowing well Rossini's penchant for bold remarks, while the tough-skinned Countess hardly blushed. "Oh, Gioachino, you haven't changed, not in couth nor girth." Proving to be just as quick-witted, Virginia garnered some chuckles of her own, then continued, "But, no, I have not seen the Emperor since that time. Evidently, dear Old Napoleon got too caught up in his quest to regain a portion of the Holy Land during the Crimean War." Knowing of Liszt's religious devoutness yet not his deceptive actions, she glanced at Liszt, and added, "It seems some people have a desire to regain lost Christian territory."

Rossini smiled. "Yes, I'm sure our dear abbé here would agree. But, at least you weren't with Napoleon when Felice Orsini bombed his royal carriage."

The Countess nodded. "Yes, many died. It's a miracle the Emperor survived unscathed."

Felice Orsini was an Italian patriot/activist seeking independence for Italy from foreign interference, and a follower of Giuseppe Mazzini. Mazzini was a politician, lawyer and prominent protester whose rhetoric and revolutionary faction caused disruptions throughout Italy in their quest for unification. Although hailed as a great leader in the Risorgimento, his followers' methods, such as Felice Orsini's, didn't always resonate with everyone, including the Countess.

Her eyes then twinkled. "But come to think of it, Orsini's assassination attempt almost prevented Napoleon from attending your fabulous opera, *William Tell*. I imagine that worried you more than my safety."

Rossini waved his hand. "Balderdash! You know I care about you, Virginia. And you also know I couldn't care less if the Emperor attended my opera. After all, that was many years after I had already retired."

Liszt laughed. "As I've said before, Rossini is the world's most lovable lazy genius. He dominated the world of opera, then left them wanting more—as they continue to sing his famous aria, *Figaro, Figaro, Figaro*—while he dedicated his life to *Food, Fun* and *Festivities*!"

"*Geloso,* Franzi, you are just jealous. Actually you underestimate my new activities. I am a dedicated specialist, a connoisseur, a master chef, and a perfectionist—if you will—in the Art of Partying. That is a most difficult profession, my dear friend; one that is often slighted by critics. So, please, may I tantalize your palates with one of my finest Tuscan merlots?"

As his guests all chuckled agreeably, Rossini fetched his precious bottle of wine and poured each of them a round.

"*Saluto!*" he cheered, as they all clinked glasses. Then after swallowing half of his prized *vino* in one gulp, Rossini bowed cordially. "*Scusimi*, but my other professional duties entail my being an attentive host. So, please, enjoy yourselves, and don't forget to try my delicious gourmet invention, Tournedos Rossini. It's filet mignon, *foie gras* and other tasty delights, the likes of which your senses have never experienced."

As his four guests laughed, Rossini jovially took a bow and reentered his resplendent villa, booming with revelry.

Abruptly, the Countess also excused herself, having caught the eye of a prominent statesman on the veranda.

As she floated away across the lawn, Angelo watched her intently. "My God, she certainly is a beautiful piece of work."

Liszt put a paternal hand on Angelo's shoulder. "Take my advice; don't get mixed up with a woman like that. And spare me the *'I should practice what I preach'* speech!"

As they both chuckled, Angelo replied, "Yes, I imagine Don Juan has conquered many such beauties."

Liszt shook his head, his eyes closing briefly. "No, no, my dear boy, the rumors and tabloids have it all wrong. Don Juan lustfully, and rather mindlessly, consumed women only for sexual gratification. I, on the other hand, am no conqueror, but rather the conquered. Many women have shamelessly thrown themselves at me, not because of any genuine interest in me, but because of my fame and their greedy hopes for riches. The women that I find hard to resist, however, are those with beautifully deep minds; the challenging ones that offer intellectual exchange and have that nurturing flare for genuinely inspiring a man, for all great artists need a muse. However, beautiful women, like Virginia, often have an agenda. They're either gold diggers or Donna Juanitas!"

Angelo laughed. "Actually, Master, I just like to observe objects of beauty. As I've told you before, I'm a very happily married man, and I meant that. Lisa means the world to me. When I was faced with the decision about which woman I would spend the rest of my life with, superficial looks played a miniscule role. Not that Lisa is unsightly, mind you. But she's just not a stunning beauty like Virginia. I much prefer a warm compatible heart over a cold beautiful shell."

"Then you're a wise and fortunate young man, Angelo. And since Lisa is pregnant, I truly hope you stay together. One of my regrets is that my three children, for the most part, had to grow up without their mother, Marie. That poor woman still suffers from serious mental afflictions, so I've learned to be very forgiving of the scornful things she's said and done. But I thank God my dear mother Anna stepped in to help out by truly raising my children. She's an amazing woman. Anyhow, I would hate to see you stray like my daughter Cosima. I failed in trying to keep her and Wagner apart and now she has inflicted so much pain, humiliation, and disgrace on poor Hans. I pray she comes to her senses, but I believe it's too late. The von Bülow love nest has been defiled, and I can no longer speak to that old, chick-snatching hawk, Wagner."

Angelo smiled at how Liszt phrased his last comment, but remained solemnly mute, knowing very well that Wagner was practically Liszt's age, and that grated his Master to the bone. However, Liszt suddenly caught his own witticism, and chuckled, breaking him free of his despair. "Ah, laughter is a much needed tonic, Angelo. We need it to get us through the trials and tribulations of life. Always remember that."

Angelo nodded with a giggle. "Yes, much like your other favorite tonic—cognac."

Liszt smiled. "Yes, but one must not overdue either, or else the laughing drunk becomes the laughingstock."

As Angelo chuckled, Liszt smiled and looked at him with endearing eyes. "So, tell me, do you and Lisa have any names picked out?"

Angelo's face beamed. "Yes, we do. If it's a girl, we'll name her Angela, and if it's a boy, Angelo Jr."

A warm smile etched Liszt's face. "Sticking to angelic names I see. Nice idea."

"Yes, especially since I feel just as strongly about our Catholic agenda as I do about our political one."

Liszt gazed at Angelo like a son. "That's why I chose *you*, Angelo, to be an integral part of my covert operation. I never would have asked you if I thought for a moment you might ever prove disloyal. Entrusting our lives to one another has made our already firm relationship even stronger. You truly have become like a son to me, since my son Daniel died in my arms at the tender age of twenty."

Angelo was deeply moved and empathized with Liszt's loss, compounded by the more recent death of his eldest daughter Blandine. Angelo had lost his parents two years ago and was taken in by the good graces of Abbé Liszt, along with a Dominican priest, all three residing at the Monastery Santa Francesca in Rome. Liszt introduced Angelo to great works of literature and music while the librarian priest acted like a big brother—drilling him with religion and history. Angelo had come to respect Liszt as a father figure, and hearing him finally acknowledge this connection made Angelo feel even more alive somehow. However, despite their bond, Liszt was an extremely busy man; being summoned by the aristocracy, royalty, the Pope, publishers, impresarios, and even countless students and new applicants all demanding a moment of his precious time. Moreover, Liszt split his residency between three different cities—Rome, Weimar, and Pest. As such, there was much that was never said between the two, and Angelo now felt this was the ideal time to ask. "Master, I know *why* you engaged in this secret mission, but you never told me *how*?"

Liszt scanned the grounds, spotting several guests on the patio, then escorted Angelo to the property's perimeter where a row of tall cypress trees lined the yard. In front of the thick wall of conifers stood an ornate, baroque-styled marble bench. It featured carvings of a barber, a magpie, Queen Semiramis, and an apple pierced by an arrow—all images from Rossini's many operas.

As the two sat, Liszt turned and spoke softly, "Naturally, I need not remind you that everything I'm about to tell you is of the utmost secrecy and never to be spoken of again."

Angelo genuflected, like an altar boy before the pope, as Liszt began his tale. "Back in 1853, a new student of mine joined us in Weimar at the Altenburg. Her name was Agnes Street-Klindworth. She was an attractive and very talented woman who could speak fluently in several languages, and was actually quite good at the piano. Unfortunately, Agnes also radiated that special charm that I find hard to resist. I need not go into details, but let's just say we got on rather well. And as I would soon find out, her father Georg Klindworth was Prince Metternich's top secret agent who gathered intelligence for the Habsburgs in Austria. At some point he worked for the Stuttgart Court, and he conversed with statesmen such as Disraeli and even Emperor Franz Joseph, among others."

"I see Georg got around—almost as much as you."

Liszt grinned. "Yes, I may have rubbed shoulders with more royalty, statesmen, and aristocrats, but Georg has been putting his life on the line for many years longer than we have, and has been part of some very high-level activities."

"But it appears we're approaching his plateau, as our latest code allowed us to dupe and repel the Prussians at Hanover. And that brings to mind another burning question. How did this whole *Dante Symphony* scheme come about?"

Liszt leaned back, grasped the lapel of his jacket, and pulled out a cigar from his inner pocket. Lighting up the stogie, he took three deep drags of the brown beast and blew out three puff clouds. As he watched them ascend toward the heavens, he said, "Well, I was working on the three sections of my *Dante* score, when Agnes and her father beckoned for my help. Being engrossed in Dante's work, I decided I had to act, for I, too, could see the Hell that was brewing. Europe has seen a great deal of unrest in my lifetime, Angelo. Britain, France, Russia, Hungary, Italy, and the German states have all been like a river of lava, boiling and flowing from place to place, scorching and blurring the borderlines. However, I could sense the horror of a worldwide volcanic eruption on the horizon, and there comes a time when a man has to take action. While penning those fiery notes of the *Inferno* movement, it dawned upon me that I could transmit encrypted messages right in my score. So I devised an algorithm whereby musical notes represented certain cantos found in Dante's poem. I then used Morse code, as short and long notes on the trombone, to direct them to specific lines in the text of those cantos to locate a specific word. So, signaling (4,3), for example, meant the fourth line down, and the third word in. Hence, piecing together all these words formed the message. Once Georg saw the prototype, he immediately put me in contact with Napoleon III. Naturally, I had known the Emperor beforehand, yet we've become much closer ever since."

Angelo coughed from the smoke, and said, "Well, I'm honored you began teaching me how to encode these messages rather than just delivering them. I was beginning to feel like a delivery boy. And Lord knows; I couldn't decipher the darn things, even knowing that they contained encrypted messages. There's no way anyone could ever figure out your mixture of Lisztian and Morse codes, especially since they'd need Dante's poem as the key."

Liszt smiled. "If there's one thing I've learned over the years, Angelo, it's never say never."

Just then, Saint-Saëns called out from the veranda, "Paging Orpheus and little Caesar! Please come in and join us. Rossini has some music planned for us and, of course, some scrumptious-looking Italian pastries."

As the two smiled and stood up, Liszt extinguished his cigar on the bench's arm, then tossed it into the cypresses.

Recoiling from the advancing cigar butt, Inganni fell from his stealthily, crouched position (on the other side of the cypresses) and onto his back.

As Kiel began to chuckle, the monsignor quickly shushed him. "Quiet!" he whispered. Then with a gloating smile, he added, "You see? I told you Liszt was up to no good."

Kiel's piercing blue eyes sparkled, as he whispered, "Yeah, I never would've guessed it. I knew Liszt mingled with royalty, but holy mackerel. The idea of Liszt being a secret agent for that fop, Napoleon, turns my stomach. The Emperor's been nothing but a royal pain in the ass to the Kaiser and Bismarck."

Inganni put his hand on Kiel's shoulder. "Now hold on. We may have grown up together in Leipzig, but I never bought into that Prussian bravado nonsense."

Kiel abrasively removed the monsignor's hand from his shoulder. "Oh, yeah, how can I forget? You abandoned Luther for a pompous Pope who thinks his stupid Catholic Church owns every Christian soul."

Inganni's meaty face turned red. "I will *not* tolerate you speaking about the Pope or my religion that way!" he scolded quietly. "I may have my differences with Pius, but the true faith is what calls me to action, and that's why we're here."

Kiel's boney jaw jutted forward as he gritted his teeth. "Well, get this, *I'm* not here for *your* stupid religion!"

"You really are an obstinate fool," Inganni huffed. "Just be quiet!"

Meanwhile, Liszt, still speaking to Angelo, turned curiously toward the cypresses. He paused, then turned back to Angelo. "Did you hear something?"

"Hear what?"

"It sounded like voices."

Angelo shrugged his shoulders. "No. But your hearing is a hell of a lot sharper than mine, Master. Then again, maybe it's that Romantic imagination of yours."

"Yes, perhaps the cypresses are calling out to me. They *are* beautiful specimens of nature. I must remember to treat the subject one day." Liszt grinned and turned around. "Very well then, let's see what Gioachino has in store for us."

As the Master and his pupil strolled up the stairs, they glanced up at the restless sky, with its darkening hues and stormy clouds, and reentered the boisterous party. Rossini had platters of sfogliatelle, cannoli, zeppole, gelato and other goodies for his guests. With a mouth full of cannolo cream, Gioachino introduced Liszt's friend and violinist, Ede Reményi.

Ede smiled and waited for the guests to simmer down. Then he picked up his bow and thrust it across the catgut, as his Stradivarius squealed a scintillating caprice by Niccolò Paganini.

Liszt's foot tapped to the rapid trills as he recalled how the great Paganini himself first awakened him to the possibility that he could bring the same virtuosic vitality to the piano. That inspiration truly kicked off Liszt's glittering career as his new dazzling works for the piano—utilizing eighty-eight piano keys in lieu of only four violin strings—propelled musical complexity to astronomical heights.

Upon Ede's concluding strains, the crowd applauded politely, as Rossini then looked over at Liszt. "No party of mine would be complete if I neglected to ask the King of the Piano to play a tune for us."

As the guests extended their applause, Liszt walked past a row of arched windows, which bathed the crowd in an amber glow, and he sat at the Bechstein with its beautiful, richly carved wood exterior. The maestro then raised his hand, to signal quiet, and the crowd eagerly complied. Liszt's head tilted back as his eyes closed, his mind summoning the heavens to enter his soul. His eyes then slowly opened as he raised his hands and lowered his head. Looking at the keys as a mere extension of his voice, his fingers ripped into the ivories as the piano exhaled Liszt's musical breath. The crowd was stunned into silence as the trampling assault of Liszt's *Wilde Jagd* (Wild Hunt) filled the room. In awe, they watched Liszt's hands feverishly run up and down the instrument, then slow for a regal mid-section, and resume again with a roar. His fingers appeared to move like a hummingbird's wings—so fast as to be almost invisible. It was mindboggling, impossible, intensely poetic—it was Liszt.

After the triumphant finale, the crowd shook their heads in amazement and clapped just as wildly. Liszt gave a humble nod, then honored his good old friend with a sparkling performance of his galloping transcription of Rossini's famous *William Tell Overture*. Once again, Rossini's guests' burst out with applause, this time honoring both great men. Liszt was about to rise, when they beseeched him for an encore. As they suggested a glittering assortment of vigorous warhorses, Liszt once again waved for silence. With bated breath, they awaited another storm, yet the first tranquil strains of Liszt's beautiful *Consolation #3* emanated from the Bechstein instead. As his slender fingers softly cascaded across the keys, the guests were transported into an ethereal realm where time and space serenely vanished. The entire room floated as if into another dimension—the sojourn was tantalizing, paralyzing, beautiful.

Upon the lovely piece's conclusion, a round of applause broke out. As Liszt stood up and graciously nodded, Victor Hugo turned toward Ingres. "The man is not of this world. Liszt has the mystical power to penetrate beyond the empyrean."

Ingres nodded. "Indeed he does. My dear friend has an unparalleled touch of phrasing and inimitable execution. I only wish I could move the soul with paint the way Liszt does with sound."

Rossini graciously thanked all his guests for visiting such an old man, only to find himself showered with loving praise. Liszt was clearly the King of the Piano, but Rossini was the King of the Party. With that, the matinée began to break up, as all the guests bid each other farewell.

Liszt's Good Samaritan heart, however, was still troubled, and he made it a point to bring von Bülow and Berlioz together. Preaching his maxim—that it was crucial for art to take precedence over one's personality or race—Liszt diffused their clashing war over Wagner and won his son-in-law's pledge to perform Berlioz's *Symphonie Fantastique*. He then patted Berlioz on the back, offering the once brilliant composer words of encouragement. Despite the music world's neglect of the flamboyant, and now floundering, Frenchman, Liszt would use his influence to somehow ensure that his old friend's works would see the light of day.

With his charitable duty done, and both great men left smiling happily, Liszt joined up with Angelo, and the two made their way down to the cobblestoned street. As a line of carriages gathered, horses snorted and stepped in place, awaiting their next delivery run. Rossini's guests began filling the coaches when, seemingly out of nowhere, one of Liszt's students ran up to him. "Master Liszt, I heard you'd be here. I hope you don't mind my dropping by?"

Liszt smiled, knowing very well that the eager youth was seeking an opportunity to brush shoulders with greatness. "Kristian, you're a bit late. As you can see, everyone is leaving. Furthermore, as I told you, you would be much better off pursuing a life in the Church with your love of the faith and your organ skills. But I am heading to Gustave Doré's residence, and due to your special status, perhaps you should join us."

"Glory be!" Kristian rejoiced. "Doré's my favorite illustrator."

Camille Saint-Saëns approached Liszt from behind. "So are we ready?" he whispered in his dignified French accent.

Liszt turned and whispered, "Yes, and our newest recruit, Kristian, will be joining us, along with Angelo."

Saint-Saëns put on his top hat and nodded. "Very well. Do you wish to walk or take a carriage?"

"Rue Bayard is only a mile or so away, and it doesn't look like it will rain, just yet. So let's roll the dice and walk."

As the foursome made their way down the narrow sidewalk, Inganni and Kiel slipped out from behind a hedgerow. Inganni gazed up at the sky. Dark clouds were rapidly mounting and twilight appeared to be coming much faster than it should. He looked at Kiel. "Excellent. So now that we know Liszt uses his *Dante Symphony* as a cipher, let's see what else we can uncover at Doré's abode."

Kiel's shifty eyes suddenly stopped and peered at Inganni. "Fine, so we heard Liszt say he's encoding messages, but we couldn't hear exactly how he does it. So that still doesn't give us any concrete proof."

Inganni irritably tucked his white collar under his shirt. "That's why we need to follow him to Doré's place, you concrete-headed fool." As Kiel rolled his eyes, Inganni continued, "And if, by chance, we can't get our hands on anything tangible, I'll try to get my hands on his precious *Dante* score. I'm sure I can decode it, and once I do, I'll have two splendid options. I can shove that proof in Pius's face, thereby adding his *personal friend,* Abbé Liszt, to the list of souls who fell from grace. Or, I can hand over that subversive document to the police in Weimar, who will then bind the wrists of their famous, yet troublesome, old Kapellmeister in shackles for espionage. Either way, Liszt is mine!"

Kiel's skeletal face cracked with a creepy smirk. "That sounds swell. But I must say, his little Kapitän, Angelo, really gets under my skin with his crass remarks about Bismarck. I'd love to run *him* through. And now it looks like the abbé Crusader recruited some more apostles."

A pensive look washed over Inganni's face. "Yes, for once, you're right—his apostles. The bad seed *is* spreading. They, too, require serious attention."

Meanwhile, Liszt and his retinue walked past the Seine River and down a series of narrow city streets. The ever-darkening clouds blotted out the setting sun, casting a foreboding veil of deep purplish-brown hues. All around them, Parisians cleared the streets, anticipating the coming storm. To the relief of Liszt's party, they entered Doré's apartment building just as a deluge of rain crashed down, mercilessly pounding the pavement and creating gushing streams that rushed along the gutters and flooded the sewers.

The foursome flicked the droplets off their jackets, as Liszt pointed to the stairs. "His studio is on the rooftop."

As they walked toward the base of the stairs, they gazed up the tall, hollow shaft of the atrium. The flights of stairs squarely wrapped around the central vault with a huge square skylight above. Yet with the murky clouds above, the shaft unnervingly faded into a dark void. As they continued up the five flights, Liszt suddenly turned and looked down the stairwell as he reached the fourth floor.

Angelo stopped and likewise looked down. "What is it?"

"I don't know," Liszt replied, as he turned his ear to the cavernous well below. "I suspect I'm just hearing things today."

Just then, a voice echoed from above, "*Bonjour*, my friends."

Liszt looked upward. "Gustave! *Bonjour!* How *good* to see you…"

That last 'good' comment, however, turned ominous as a flash of lightning illuminated the skylight above Gustave, turning his colorful flesh into a burnt silhouette. As the menacing flashes of light flickered, Doré appeared like the Grim Reaper, sending an awful chill down Liszt's spine.

A loud rumble of thunder shook the building, as Gustave's face finally regained its color. Liszt closed his eyes and shook his head, then slowly looked back up. The ghastly image of the Grim Reaper was gone, but Liszt's heart shuddered when he suddenly saw a terrifying vision of *Hell!*

As he squinted, Gustave's voice rang down, "I know you've been yearning to see this. So what do you think?"

Gustave was holding his astonishing rendition of the Malebranche from Dante's *Inferno,* a group of winged demons wielding wicked rods in their claws. Their duty was to batter and submerge corrupt politicians in a putrid lake of boiling resin.

"What can I say, but utterly *fantastique*!" Liszt's emotional reply rang out, as it echoed through the cavernous atrium.

Gustave beckoned his visitors to come up, who, upon arriving on the fifth floor, sighed, as if having climbed out of Dante's nine terrifying circles of Hell. Doré escorted them into his spacious studio, outfitted with a string of huge mullioned windows, providing him with not only the much-needed sunlight to draw his famous illustrations, but also with a splendid view of Paris. However, both were now blotted out by a turbulent swirling mass of dark clouds, intermittently illuminated by flashes of lightning.

Gustave excitedly directed his guests to look at his complete set of illustrations for Dante's *Inferno*. As he turned up the wicks on several oil lamps, Angelo and Kristian scanned each glowing illustration with awe, as Saint-Saëns and Liszt stopped to examine them closely, savoring the intricacy of Doré's finely crafted strokes.

After several minutes, Liszt turned and commented, "Gustave, these are tremendous. You have given Dante's grisly visions of Hell life."

Doré smiled graciously. "Coming from you, that is truly the greatest compliment I could ever receive. After all, I know of no other artist who has brought to life Dante's grand vision like you have."

Liszt shook his head. "I appreciate your sentiments, Gustave, but a musician has a most difficult and humiliating task when trying to compose an aural interpretation of a literary masterpiece. Unlike an artist, who can draw an infinite number of illustrations depicting all the various cantos in Dante's *Inferno,* I was forced to simply express the fear, torment, and terror in sound. And due to time restraints, I could only give impressions of several cantos while focusing on one canto specifically."

"Yes, and you wisely chose the love-torn, tortured souls of Francesca da Rimini and Paolo Malatesta from Dante's Second Circle of Hell. After the menacing whirlwind that launches your *Inferno* movement it was sheer perfection to have its calm middle section evoke Dante's phrase: *There is no greater sorrow than to recall happiness in times of misery.*"

As Liszt's pupils nodded in agreement, Doré concluded, "While I may have the advantage of creating numerous visions, they fall drastically short of the utter terror and painful sorrow that your *Inferno* movement evokes. Not only has no other artist in the entire course of history ever created such terrifying sounds from an inventive array of instruments, but music, in general, has the ability to strike deep emotional chords in people's hearts that a painting or drawing simply cannot muster. What's more, the full impact of that experience can be recreated in perpetuity without losing an ounce of its vitality. Meanwhile, a painting's impact does wane slightly with each successive viewing. So in that regard, I humbly bow to you."

"As do I," Angelo chimed in, as Kristian and Saint-Saëns echoed similar words of praise.

"I do thank you, but unfortunately the majority, at least thus far, do not share your opinions," Liszt replied.

Angelo shook his head. "I'm sorry, Master, but all of us are keenly aware of your prophetic phrase. You are indeed *hurling a lance into the future.*"

"Unquestionably," Saint-Saëns added. "The most radical advances rarely, if ever, take root within their own time. So it appears the majority of people today will never comprehend this work. But rest assured, it will transcend our time, and *will* resonate with future generations."

With that, a bolt of lightning flashed, illuminating the entire studio.

Gustave laughed. "You see? that prophetic statement was even validated by God Himself."

Just outside—with their ears pressed to the door—Inganni and Kiel crouched awkwardly, as their drenched clothes created pools of rainwater on the floor.

Back inside, Liszt was keen to notice Doré's two uprights. Motioning to Angelo, Liszt and his protégé mounted the instruments and began playing his *Dante Symphony transcription* for two pianos. As the two virtuosos roared through the *Inferno* movement, flashes of lightning and rumbles of thunder outside seemed the perfect accompaniment. However, as they reached the final *Magnificat,* the jarring fireworks somehow dampened the piece's ethereal glow, as if a bad omen. Nevertheless, their friends gave the two pianists a hearty round of applause.

With Dante being on their minds, Kristian and Doré beseeched Liszt to play his *Dante Sonata.* The revolutionary sonata had been Liszt's first artistic treatment of Dante's *Comedy* some six years prior to his full-scale symphony, and it proved to be a spellbinding precursor. As Angelo stood up and joined his comrades, Liszt, once again, immersed himself into the piano, as if fusing into the instrument, while the strings miraculously became his vocal chords. The piano rumbled and sighed, taking his fellow artists on a stormy stampede through Hell, with brief moments of forlorn beauty—thus showcasing the Master's unrivalled ability to orchestrate on the piano.

Upon its conclusion, the cultured secret agents began discussing a variety of topics, including literature, religion, art and, inevitably, politics—with Liszt making the segue from art, "It was most apropos, Gustave, that you greeted us with your illustration of the wicked *Malebranche* from Dante's Second Circle of Hell. As we here all know; Kaiser Wilhelm I and his cunning right arm, Otto von Bismarck, have Emperor Napoleon III and Pius IX in a frightful stir. And it is wicked politicians like those two cagey Prussians that will one day suffer the wrath of God."

Kristian nodded fervently, while his blonde curly hair bounced. "Yes. And I'd love to be one of those winged demons pushing those two sinners into a vat of boiling pitch!"

Doré grinned at the passionate youth and then gazed at Liszt. "I'll have you know that I've taken your advice. Now that I've finished my series of the Bible and *Paradise Lost,* I intend to begin illustrating the vile effects that the Prussians are having upon France and Europe."

"That's splendid news, Gustave. It's imperative that we all dedicate our God-given talents not only to our art, but also to the crucial task of preserving our rich and precious culture. Unfortunately, the Prussians have only focused on the barbaric and militant aspects of Europe's past. This has become much more troubling for me. As you know, I have now divided my life between living in Rome (the home of my faith), Hungary (the home of my ancestors), and Germany (the home of my new school). And this last home poses both fatal threats and opportunities. Prussian eyes are constantly on my activities and my precious flock, yet being close to one's enemies does have its advantages."

Angelo interjected, "Yes, and that barbaric Prussian, Herr Bismarck, deviously lured Austria into a dispute over the governing rights of Holstein and Schleswig, which Austria rightfully countered. And that gave Otto exactly what he wanted, this current Austro-Prussian War so he can add Austria to his growing Empire."

Liszt nodded. "Exactly, and with each aggressive step the Prussian beast takes, the larger and more deadly he becomes." As Liszt spoke, Doré was sitting quietly, his pen moving deftly across a drawing pad. Meanwhile, Liszt posited a disturbing prophecy, "For many years I have seen this ugly beast in my mind's eye. But unlike Dante's winged demons with fangs and claws, the monster I envision is human, albeit having small signs of the beast marking his face. And although we may not be able to see the wings and claws, he and his winged demons *will* cause great havoc and worldwide destruction."

After several long minutes of ingesting Liszt's chilling vision, Doré boldly held up his drawing to a sea of bulging eyes. His fellow agents gasped at his alarming rendition of Liszt's eerie premonition. They turned toward one another, then back at the enigmatic portrait.

"That's simply astounding!" Liszt exclaimed. "Now, you see, you have just revealed to us, in the matter of minutes, a vision of mine that no piece of music could ever produce."

Doré smiled. "Well, I suppose visual art does have its advantages in some respects." He extended it toward Liszt. "Please, take it. After all, it is *your* menacing vision."

Liszt gratefully received the illustration, while Angelo peered over his shoulder to take another look. "Hmm, that's a devious looking fellow all right, Gustave."

Kristian squinted, as he, too, took a closer look. "Yes, but who in God's name is it?"

Saint-Saëns interjected, "Its certainly not Bismarck."

"I must confess," Doré replied, "I had no cognitive input into this sketch whatsoever; my hand simply followed Liszt's line of thought. So even I cannot help you in that regard."

Liszt shook his head, as he once again gazed at the startling sketch. "That's all the more intriguing, especially since this so eerily captures the visions in my nightmares." He then looked over to his comrades. "But as I've mentioned, I see far greater pain and suffering upon the horizon. Therefore, it is imperative that we stay resolute and diligent in our efforts to undermine and defeat the beast. So, please, stay focused, and it is crucial that we stay in touch."

With an emotional round of goodbyes, the foursome bid Doré farewell. As Gustave opened the door, Liszt glanced downward, spotting the puddle of rainwater just outside the door. "It appears you have a leak."

Stepping outside, the two looked up at the ceiling, yet found no signs of breach.

Pensively, Liszt gazed down at the puddle once more. "Odd, very odd indeed."

"Well, never mind that," Doré said. "Just make sure that sketch doesn't get wet in the storm outside."

"Yes," Liszt replied solemnly. "Otherwise it would vanish into a pool of black ink, foretelling a more personal omen, namely that our divine efforts will vanish into a Prussian pool of dark evil. So I will indeed safeguard and treasure this sketch with my life, my dear friend. Again, I cannot thank you enough for gracing us with your presence, and me personally with this sketch."

Walking his friends toward the stairs, Gustave looked up at the skylight, as rain pounded the glass and thunder rattled the walls. He looked down at his departing friends.

"Listen. It's one hell of a storm out there. Are you sure you don't want to stay here for the night?"

As a searing flash of lightning illuminated their faces, Saint-Saëns gazed at Liszt. "Perhaps he's right. My place is some distance from here, and it would be hard to hail a carriage at this late hour."

Liszt nodded, submitting to Camille's sound advice and Gustave's generous offer. Re-entering the studio, they all decided to have a nightcap, as shots of vodka and cognac were gulped down. With another round of small talk, and additional shots, they enjoyed the extended evening, then made their makeshift sleeping arrangements and turned in.

The dark and turbulent night raged on, making sleep particularly difficult for Liszt's young apostle, Kristian. Tossing and turning under his blanket on the floor, Kristian couldn't remain wrapped up any longer. He stood and gazed out of the tall windows. Violent discharges webbed the sky with spidery veins of electricity, prompting him to cover his eyes and turned around. Growing more anxious with each jarring flash, Kristian tiptoed quietly to the door, gently unlocked the latch, and stepped out into the corridor.

As Kristian gazed up, blinking at the flickering skylight, he noticed a small flash of light out of the corner of his left eye. Peering to his left, he saw a dark hallway that receded into total darkness. His head was still slightly numb from the vodka but he knew he wasn't seeing illusions. He stood and waited for another flash of lightning to repeat the occurrence, but none came. Curiously, Kristian strolled unsteadily down the dark corridor. As he proceeded, he thought it odd that it was windowless. He wondered *where did that confounded flash of light come from?*

Just ahead he could see that the hallway terminated, intensifying both the mystery and his pulse. Suddenly, a brief flash of lightning revealed a smaller hallway branching off to the right. With his heart thankfully returning to a calm, steady beat, he contentedly approached the corner. Yet as he turned, his heart stalled! A menacing dark face was inches away, as another flash of lightning illuminated the figure from behind. Kristian recoiled and tried to scream, but his vocal chords were literally severed by a blunt metallic object. Kristian fell backward, his head smashing on the cold marble floor. All was truly black.

As the rising sun's rays pierced through small apertures in the densely clouded sky, one beam of light shone through Doré's studio window landing on Liszt's face. As he squinted, the beam of light was suddenly blocked when a figure rushed toward him. "Oh my God!" Angelo cried. "I just found Kristian down the hall. He's *dead!"*

Liszt sprang to his feet, along with the others. Shock marred their faces, as Liszt painfully queried, "What do you mean, *dead!?* What happened?"

"Well, I awoke early," Angelo's voice struggled, "and I didn't see Kristian anywhere in the studio. So I decided to take a look outside. When I opened the door, I noticed the narrow hallway to the left. It was then that I saw a body lying on the floor at the far end. And as sure as Hell, when I got there, it was Kristian. But worse yet, Master, Kristian was murdered!"

"Murdered!?"

"Yes," Angelo wailed, with a mixture of grief and rage. "Someone rammed a bronze crucifix right into Kristian's throat! It's horrible, Master, and absolutely infuriating."

"Show me where he is?" Liszt implored.

The team anxiously followed Angelo, only to gasp as they gazed at the grotesque mutilation of Kristian's throat. Liszt kneeled down. He grasped the cross and pulled the bloody chunk of sacred metal out of his protégé's neck. A tear welled in his eye. "This was a cruel and horrific death, not to mention dreadfully profane to our Christian faith." He looked up, and uttered, "Someone call the police."

Saint-Saëns was about to comply, when Angelo placed his hand on Camille's chest. "Wait! Do we really want the police involved? You know they'll ask a million questions. And, personally, I don't like the idea of police hounds poking their wet noses into our covert business."

Doré shook his head. "This is not the kind of death that we can keep quiet, Angelo. How could we ever explain such a death to his family or the undertaker?"

Liszt nodded. "Gustave is right. Besides, we owe it to Kristian and his family, as the police might find this deranged villain. Remember, Angelo, our mission is to aid Napoleon and Pius by providing them with intelligence and transmitting their messages. We are *not* policemen nor are we armed secret service agents. We are clearly out of our element here. I will, however, implore Napoleon to appoint a special team to handle this unfortunate tragedy. This way we can speak freely with them and keep this as discreet as possible."

As Liszt stood up, footsteps could be heard back near the staircase. A young male suddenly appeared, then looked down the hallway—trying to decipher the silhouettes.

Saint-Saëns whispered to Doré, "Do you know him?"

Doré zeroed in on the illuminated figure under the skylight. "No, and he's not anyone that lives in my building."

The young man squinted, as he called out, "I'm looking for *Monsieur* Franz Liszt. Can any one of you help me?"

Doré looked at Liszt, then back at the stranger, as he called out, "Who are you, might I ask?"

"I'm a messenger, *monsieur*. I was sent by *Signore* Rossini. He said that his friend might be here or at Camille Saint-Saëns's house. But no one was there."

"I am Franz Liszt," the maestro replied. "What does my good friend Gioachino want?"

As the youngster walked toward them, Liszt vaguely remembered seeing the gangly lad at Rossini's party. However, his face was now glaringly solemn. "I'm sorry to report this, *Monsieur* Liszt, but your mother died last night."

Liszt almost collapsed, as Angelo and Saint-Saëns readily grasped an arm to steady him. White with shock and wracked with grief, he uttered, "Oh, dear God. How did she die? Please tell me of natural causes?"

The young messenger twitched, perplexed. "Yes, *Monsieur* Liszt. Natural causes. Did you fear otherwise?"

"Oh, no, dear boy," Liszt replied. "It's just that we—"

Before the Maestro could say another word, the teen spotted Kristian's tortured corpse lying in a pool of blood. He cringed, then covered his mouth. "Oh, my Lord! What happened? Is there anything I can do?"

"Thanks, but no," Angelo replied quickly, as he stepped forward. "It was just a terrible accident. We'll handle this."

The teen crossed himself, and was about to leave, when he turned and added, "Oh, yes. I almost forgot. I was also told to inform you that *Signore* Rossini received a telegram. Signora Di Purezza gave birth to a girl—Angela."

Angelo's solemn face cracked with joy. "Oh my God! I have a daughter! It appears Lisa was early."

His comrades briefly purged the horror from their minds and congratulated Angelo. Meanwhile, the young messenger keenly took that opportunity to say goodbye, as he scurried down the hall and then down the stairs.

Liszt turned back toward his dear friends, his face lugubriously marred with pain, yet struggling to release a glimmer of joy. "Well, I'm truly delighted to hear that you have a daughter, Angelo. Congratulations."

As Liszt rubbed Angelo's thick crop of black hair and pulled him in for a hug, the others all stepped over to pat

Angelo on the back. Liszt's moist eyes could no longer restrain the surge of tears that now forced their way over his lower lids and trickled down his face. The mixed emotions were cruel and torturous. He took a deep breath and stepped back to face his brood. "One arrival—two departures. Last night was indeed one Hell of a night."

A remorseful look washed over Doré's face. "I'm so sorry, Franz. I somehow feel responsible for these catastrophes. Perhaps you never should have come here last night?"

Liszt shook his head. "Don't be foolish. These events have no bearing on my location; they were somehow ordained. Let us all just say a prayer for my dearly departed mother, and for our young lost brother here."

As they all hung their heads and finished their prayers, Liszt looked up at his small band of brothers. "Well, I obviously have a lot of plans to make for my mother's funeral, as her death has just torn a gaping hole in my heart and soul. Yet, by the grace of God, my children and I were very fortunate to have her for so many years, a gift that Cosima and I will cherish until the end of our days. On the other hand, Kristian, as you know, was far too young for such a fate, and too pure and kind for such a gruesome demise. But this only brings to light a chilling new fact. Someone or some entity is on to us. So not only must we proceed with far more caution, but we must also be far more vigilant and aggressive."

As time would tell, Liszt and his covert team would face even more adversity—increasing their need for Liszt's coded messages. For, alas, Europe's problems had only just begun.

SCENE III – BERLIN & BASEL [1932-33]

It was now August of 1932, and Angelo Jr. and Einstein spent a month scouring Liszt's cryptic infernal score of the *Dante Symphony* to no avail. Inside Angelo's laboratory, Einstein sat at a large, maple lab table with its brand new, black epoxy top. The score was opened, and his eyes oscillated left and right as they scanned the staves.

Meanwhile, Angelo was pacing and livid. "Albert, this is simply amazing. All that we've managed to gather from this score are instructions by Liszt on how to use his proprietary symbols for dynamics, or play with various emotions of angst or sorrow. How could Liszt baffle not just me, but even *you*, of all people?"

Einstein barely heard a word, as his eyes remained glued to the score. "Angelo, this Liszt fellow was truly an astronaut among charioteers. Nothing like this ever existed before. The sheer brutality and terror of his *Inferno* movement is unprecedented. Meanwhile, his central passage is equipped with advanced sequences, imaginative instrumentation, and an audacious 7/4 time signature—it's incredible!" Glancing at another passage, he continued, "And look here, his use of the harp is ideal for evoking the whirlwinds of Hell, yet also quite apropos for the two torn lovers, Francesca and Paolo, who are entrapped in a swirling gust of eternal misery. Liszt's music skillfully portrays Dante's words; *'There is no greater sorrow than to recall happiness in times of misery.'* And the way this sequence swells into a profoundly sad love melody is beyond words. I'm truly—"

"Albert!" Angelo interjected. "We have been working on this score for a month, and all you can do is get ecstatic over skillful passages? Have you lost your focus?"

Einstein looked up, somewhat startled. "Angelo, I apologize for my rapture, but, as you know, I've been remiss in giving Liszt proper attention or credit. While the violent part of his symphony clashes with my personal tastes, I do recognize his genius. And why his beautiful passages are rarely if ever mentioned, I find quite baffling. But, no, I have not totally lost my focus, Angelo. In fact, I've noticed something here that's quite odd."

"Odd! What do you mean odd?"

"Well, don't get too excited, Angelo, but—"

"Go on!" Angelo prodded, as he rushed to his side, peering down at a dizzying array of notes and symbols splattered across staff lines. "Tell me, what's odd?"

Einstein gazed up at Angelo, then back down at the score, pointing with his finger. "You see, right here."

"Right here, where?" Angelo asked impatiently. "You're not even pointing to a musical note or symbol?"

"No, no! Not *in* the score. I'm talking about this stain, right here on the edge of the score."

Angelo's tense shoulders collapsed, as he stood erect. "You must be kidding! You're asking me about a stain on an old score from the nineteenth century? Are you serious, or just being playful?"

Before Einstein could even respond, Angelo continued, "And you know how I hate when you're playful at the most inappropriate times, Albert. And this *is* a most inappropriate time. Do you hear me, Albert?"

"Calm down, for heaven's sake, and please listen for a moment. This is no ordinary stain, Angelo. I've noticed this stain only at the bottom of this page and again on the booklet's cover. The stain on the cover is much less visible due to the dark brown leather, but these stains warrant closer scrutiny. They don't appear anywhere else on the score and the discoloration seems odd."

"There you go again with that *odd* business. I told you this score is a relic. Liszt gave it to my father in 1866. So what's so odd about a historical document having a stain?"

Einstein smiled, wisely, patiently. "Angelo, most liquids or oils make materials darker and even get darker with time. But haven't you noticed? These stains are a pale, yellowish-brown color; and even though the stain on the cover appears slightly different from the one on the page, don't let that fool you—it is the same organic compound all right."

"Organic compound?"

"Yes, Angelo, while we've been working on this score I've noticed an ever-so-slight scent of either garlic or mustard. And I'm embarrassed to say this, but I always thought it emanated from you, since you use a lot of garlic on your pasta and spread an awful lot of mustard on your salami sandwiches. However—"

"What can I say," Angelo interjected, "I'm Italian. I enjoy good food and love garlic and mustard. And so did my father, so that scent can be from either one of us."

"No, Angelo, that's my point. These stains are *not* garlic, *nor* are they mustard. They appear to be an organic man-made compound called sulfur mustard, or (Cl-CH2CH2)2S."

Angelo squinted. "Just what are you saying?"

"I'm saying that it is very likely your father was poisoned with mustard gas or, rather, some liquid variant of it. After all, you did say your father died with this score in his hands, correct?"

Angelo suddenly felt lightheaded; he grasped the seat next to Einstein and slumped into the chair. Einstein placed his hand on Angelo's forehead. "Relax. I'm sorry if my bedside manner is not up to snuff, but, as you know, I'm not a medical doctor. Anyhow, I think we should run some tests on these stains, just to make sure."

Angelo's dizzy spell passed quickly, as thoughts flooded his head. His body suddenly sprang upright. "No! It all makes sense. Like I told you, he died in 1914, right at the outbreak of the Great War. I'm sure some German bastard found out about his coded messages and silenced him with poison mustard."

"Or some liquid variant of it," Einstein corrected. "But I will run some samples just to verify my hypothesis. I suppose I'll use Fritz Haber's lab to—"

Albert and Angelo suddenly looked at each other, as Angelo blurted, "Fritz Haber. Of course! The Gas Man. That son of a bitch worked with this damn poison."

Einstein rubbed his chin. "Are you also thinking what I'm thinking?"

"Yes!" Angelo scowled. "Haber must be the man that murdered my father. He even said my name was familiar the day I arrived here. Remember?"

Einstein nodded. "Yes, I remember, but that's not what I'm thinking."

"What do you mean?"

"Angelo, these sulfur mustard stains might be from Fritz's hands when he grabbed the book out of mine. Remember when he confronted you about your father's death and Hitler's assassination attempt? At that time he pulled the book away from me, and it's quite possible that his fingers may have contained some poison residue. As such, these stains may only be a month old."

Angelo began to think out loud as his mind raced, "But even if these stains were just made by Fritz a month ago, the premise that he is the killer still makes complete sense. My father was found dead right here in Germany, not Italy, and the dates and methods all fit. Haber must be the man!"

Einstein raised his hand. "Hold on, Angelo. Please, it's imperative that we be guided by logic and scientific research, not raw emotions. Even if these stains were, in fact, made by Fritz's poison-laden fingers from a month ago, this does not necessarily condemn him. He may have accidently touched the poison and contracted the deadly toxins, as well. Furthermore, the circumstantial evidence that he was in Germany at the time of your father's death is useless in a court of law."

Angelo's face grew tense. "Court of law? This crime was inevitably authorized by this very same corrupt German government. More importantly, this is my father's death we're talking about. He did not simply die, Albert. He was murdered! And the circumstantial evidence that keeps mounting against Haber is dreadfully compelling and extremely hard to label as mere coincidence. This screams of being calculated; something a scheming chemist like Haber would do. His wife may have committed suicide because of his deplorable actions, but I won't! I'll expose this madman, or do more, if need be. But I'll give you the benefit of the doubt, Albert. So, go ahead, analyze the stains all you like. I'm sure they'll be sulfur mustard *or* some liquid variant."

"Angelo, there are still some things that don't add up. Mustard gas is a vesicant, or blistering agent. It causes painful skin rashes and, naturally, *blisters*. So even the mild residue on this book should have caused some minor irritation to Haber and us. Yet it didn't. Additionally, it is also a mutagen, which means it actually alters or mutates genes. This can cause any number of side effects or fatal diseases to occur. It is, therefore, inconceivable that Fritz would be walking around with poison on his fingertips—he'd be dead! As you know, we do have strict protocols here for all scientists that handle such lethal agents."

"I understand, Albert. But if you'll recall, Fritz was wearing rubber lab gloves that day. So if these stains are recent, they could have been intentionally meant for us!"

Einstein's eyes widened. "My, oh, my! You're right, that could be another possibility. At this juncture I think it would be wise if we stop extrapolating and start analyzing these stains immediately."

Angelo wondered aloud. "And is there a way to determine exactly how old these stains are?"

"Not exactly, but I will try," Einstein replied, as he delicately slipped the tainted booklet into a plastic case.

Suiting up with their lab coats and rubber gloves, Einstein then opened the door and peered down the hall. He motioned to Angelo to pick up the booklet, and then checked his watch. "Haber should be heading out to lunch in ten minutes—that should leave us an hour and twenty-three minutes to do our testing."

Angelo grasped the booklet and looked at Einstein, confused. "And *twenty-three minutes?* How on earth can you be so precise?"

Albert shook his head. "Not me—that's the Nazi German in him; Haber, and Hein, run like clockwork."

As Angelo chuckled, Einstein's expression suddenly turned solemn, as he added, "And speaking of these damn Nazis, I've been meaning to tell you—"

"Tell me what?" Angelo interjected warily.

"Well, I didn't wish to upset you or make you feel like I was abandoning you, Angelo, especially since you've only been here a month, but—"

"Abandoning me? What? You're leaving?"

"Angelo, I never would have considered the thought, but, you must understand, the Nazis have been gaining tremendous ground, and I simply do *not* trust Hitler, nor his Aryan henchmen. I also refuse to believe that his massive military buildup is for peaceful relations. War is inevitable."

"Look, Albert, I know you and Freud just co-authored that pamphlet *Why War?*, denouncing war and offering solutions, but—"

"Yes!" Einstein cut in assertively. "You must know how vile and despicable war seems to me. I would rather be hacked into pieces than take part in such an abominable business. And that's why—"

"Listen, I understand your repugnance for war, Albert, but fleeing the country? Where to?"

Einstein's face drew solemn. "I'm not a hundred percent sure, but I must tell you. Three months ago, I was offered an appointment to head the Institute for Advanced Study in Princeton, New Jersey."

"What? You're going to sail across the Atlantic to the wild frontier, where a bunch of unruly cowboys are in the midst of battling a deep depression?"

"It's a distinct possibility, yes. And they are no longer wanton cowboys, Angelo. In fact, the Americans have just built the world's tallest skyscraper—the Empire State Building. I hear it's truly a marvel of engineering. And their universities, as you must know, are nothing to scoff at. However, I am considering traveling to Scotland first, as it might not be so easy getting out of Germany these days."

Angelo smirked. "Running away is rarely the answer, Albert. But I wish you had mentioned this sooner, so I could have started making plans myself. I came to this facility because of you, not only for my career, but also to win your assistance in solving this *Dante Symphony* mystery."

Einstein nodded. "Yes, I know, and that is why it was difficult for me to break the news to you. I guess I was sheepishly putting off the inevitable. I'm sorry. It wasn't my intention to hurt you, but rather spare you."

"But, Albert—*fleeing?* That's why bullies like the Nazis flourish." Angelo shook his head. "Never mind. Let's just make the best of the time we have left together. Deal?"

"Deal," Einstein replied. "But I *have* spoken out, Angelo. When you've been here longer you'll understand the fear and paralysis that grips the German people, especially Jews. After all, you did flee Italy, so you must have some idea of what we're up against. But I assure you; things are a hell of a lot worse here. Phones are tapped, SS agents eavesdrop on conversations in cafés, arrests are made, and ruthless beatings and one-way trips to camps take place. Anyhow, I shall do whatever I can to help you. I promise." Einstein glanced down at his watch. "In fact, Haber must be leaving for lunch right now." He turned and opened the door slightly. Peeking out, he whispered, "And there the Nazi robot goes, just like clockwork."

The two sleuths crept down the vacant corridor and carefully made their way to Haber's lab door. As Angelo's eyes vigilantly darted from one end of the hallway to the other, he whispered, "Are you sure his peculiar pal, Rudolf Hein, isn't in here?"

Einstein boldly swung open the door to an empty lab, gazed back at Angelo, and winked. "Hein leaves for lunch five minutes before Haber. Like I said, Nazi clockwork."

Angelo breathed a sigh of relief, as they slipped into Haber's laboratory. Einstein closed the door behind them and pointed to the lab table in the corner. As Angelo walked toward the table, he curiously examined Haber's bizarre apparatus. Huge chrome canisters with rubber hoses and aluminum tubes radiating outward sat alongside Bunsen burners, test tubes, and beakers of colorful boiling solutions. The noxious odors stung his lungs, as he set the book down.

"My God, this place stinks like Hell," Angelo whispered. "No wonder he was able to kill my father—he's brain dead!"

"Remember, Angelo, we cannot accuse him just yet," Einstein cautioned, as he set up the optical microscope. He then slid a few books near the microscope to support the large score and carefully slipped the *Dante Symphony* booklet out of its plastic case.

Propping the score up next to the microscope, he slid the stained page onto the scope's stage and under the lens. As he peered down into the microscope, he turned the focus adjustment wheels, bringing the molecules sharply into focus. As he scrutinized the compounds, Angelo anxiously peered out the window through the venetian blinds. The minutes seemed to pass like hours, when finally Angelo turned around. "Dear Lord, Al. How much longer?"

Einstein glanced at his watch, then waved his hand. "Don't worry, we still have time. Just keep a look out."

Nervously, Angelo peered out the blinds again, while Einstein rummaged through the lab drawers in search of a pair of tweezers and three Petri dishes. Opening the wall cabinets, he pushed bottles around and grasped the solutions he needed, then walked back over to the book. Angelo strained to watch from his post as the great Einstein delicately scraped off a minuscule amount of leather particles, which he carefully placed in each of the dishes. With the same diligence, he began mixing the solutions.

"I prefer calculus to chemistry," Angelo said. "What's up?"

"As I had learned from Haber's research, I need to test the particles with these different solutions so I can see their reactions and, with a little luck, discover their properties."

"Ah, yes, like a pH test?"

Einstein nodded. "Exactly, but these solutions will tell me more than just acidity. They'll also tell me—" Einstein's head popped up. "Bingo!"

"Bingo what? Bingo bad or Bingo good?"

"Well, you be the judge of that, but this chemical is unequivocally a variation of the mustard gas poison, yet it contains some additional Haber-like properties. Judging by these reactions and my earlier tests, I'd say there is no way that this was a recent stain. That's for sure."

Angelo smiled. "That's actually a 'good Bingo'. Because that means we weren't infected by any contaminants or agents, correct?"

"It appears so," Einstein replied. "But we cannot be totally sure, because, as I said, this is not the exact strain used during the Great War. And if it is a mutagen, it could have a lethal mutating effect on our genes at any time, be it now or ten, twenty, or even forty years from now."

"Well, despite your warning of gloom and doom, I'll bet the farm that it's not a serious mutagen. After all, if this stain is from the time of my father's death, and I've handled this booklet over the past eighteen years, I really can't be too concerned about it."

"True," Einstein replied. "At least that takes care of the ten-year factor, but you have yet to make the twenty or even forty year marks."

"Fair enough, but I prefer to look at the glass as half full, thank you. And although this exonerates Fritz from poisoning us, we are still left with the very distinct possibility that he might have poisoned my father. So one lethal riddle has safely been answered, but I still have a lot of homework to do."

Just then, Angelo spotted a skulking silhouette through the translucent glass of the lab door. His heart raced as he turned toward Einstein. "Oh, Christ! We're done for."

Yet, as he gazed back, his pulse subsided. The silhouette was gone. He exhaled, and peered back at Einstein. "You clean up, and I'll go see who that was."

As Angelo crept toward the door, he suddenly heard a jarring metallic sound. His shoulders rose up to his ears, as he pivoted around. Einstein had dropped the tweezers, his eyes now bulging. Angelo shook his head, as his shoulders lowered—his index finger now over his lips. "Shhh!"

Einstein shrugged his shoulders. "Sorry. Now, go on!"

Angelo turned and tiptoed to the door. Cracking it open a notch, he took a quick peek, and then quietly closed it.

Einstein looked over. "Who was it?"

"Mildred, the secretary; she walked down the hall and she's now talking to our Nazi Adonis, Rudolf Hein. But I don't know how long she was standing by the door, or what she might have seen or heard."

Albert had finished cleaning up and had the score in his hand. He walked over, beside Angelo, and cracked open the door. He peeked out and then turned back. "They're gone. Let's go!"

"But, what if she heard us, and told Hein?"

Einstein nudged him. "Forget them. Come on, let's go before Haber gets back!"

The remainder of Einstein's limited days at the Kaiser Wilhelm Institute seemed to fly by faster than either he or Angelo ever expected. Yet, with the heightened tensions of political instability and anti-Semitism, Einstein had no recourse but to flee while the going was good. It was an emotional sendoff, as Angelo hugged Albert and then his wife Elsa to bid them farewell.

As the weeks passed, Angelo couldn't help but think about the vexing *Dante* score that still kept its code a secret, and its deadly stains that caused his father's death. Adding weight to those perplexing matters was the burning question of who tried to assassinate Hitler. That question became all the more pressing after the New Year was ushered in.

On January 30, 1933, President Paul von Hindenburg unhappily swore in Adolf Hitler as Reich Chancellor. Hindenburg was part of the Old Prussian regime—dating back to Kaiser Wilhelm I and Otto von Bismarck—and he found this rabble-rousing upstart wholly unworthy of the rank now bestowed upon him. Hitler came from peasant stock, was a drop out, had failed twice to gain entrance into the Art Academy, and never managed to get beyond the rank of corporal in the military. The latter truly added to Hindenburg's disgust. But Hitler cunningly forged a name for himself, as his radically stirring speeches cultivated a growing cult of militants who now forced Hindenburg's hand to lend support.

Standing at the window of the Chancellery building in Berlin, Hitler received a thunderous ovation from a sea of deceived and deluded spectators. Hitler's Nazi power play had paid off, the propaganda worked, and the pact was now sealed; the Old World Orders of monarchs or liberal republics were irrevocably dead and the future of Germany, and the world, now lay in his sulfuric hands.

Angelo felt the brunt of these spiraling events, as well as Einstein's absence, as five lonely and distressing months passed. Yet one morning, upon arriving earlier than usual at the Kaiser Institute, Angelo discovered a letter in his mailbox from his sorely missed friend. A smile etched his face, as he cautiously peered around the mailroom. He knew Einstein's flight from Germany did not resonate well with many at the Institute, so he had to be vigilant.

It was still semi-dark, as some lights in the lobby and corridors were not yet switched on. He peered out the mailroom doorway and looked both ways, only seeing two colleagues walking to their dark laboratories and the janitor beginning to switch on the lights.

When the coast was clear, Angelo stepped out and walked quickly to his new office; it had formerly been Einstein's. Stepping inside, he flicked on the light, and closed the door behind him. The room looked rather unchanged from the days his former colleague occupied the space, except for Angelo's precious new bookcase that filled one entire wall. Proudly, Angelo scanned his lifelong collection of books on mathematics, physics, and chemistry, as well as his fine selection related to art, history, and music. These subjects had consumed much of his life in Italy. Whether he was teaching mathematics in Pisa or doing research in Bologna, Angelo had always tried to visit art museums or attend concerts and operas on his free time. He smiled as his eyes then shifted down to his walnut desk. It was painfully stark; save for three photos, one of his father, mother, and sister—all of whom were dead. Angelo's head dropped—heavy. His heart—empty. His eyes, at first glassy and aimless, then spotted the envelope from his dear old friend in his hand. Angelo smiled as a warm feeling filled his heart. He felt comforted just by seeing Einstein's sloppy handwriting. Eagerly, he flipped it over to slice it open, when his eyes noticed something peculiar. He drew the envelope closer. It appeared as if the flap had already been opened and resealed.

Just then, his office door swung open! Startled, Angelo spun around, as Rudolf Hein boldly stepped in. "We have a meeting at ten-thirty."

"Uh, s-sure…no problem," Angelo stuttered. Regaining his vigor, he added, "By the way, do you know who handles our mailroom?"

Hein's eyebrow curled with suspicion. "Why do you ask?"

"Oh, I'm just curious. You see, my uncle said he wrote me a letter, but I never received it—that's all."

Relieved, Hein calmly shrugged his shoulders. "Not sure. I suppose one of the secretaries, perhaps Mildred."

As he turned to leave, Angelo added, "Did *you* get your mail today?"

Hein spun around, perturbed. "*Yes.* Fritz brought it to me. What's with all the questions?"

"Oh, nothing. Well, I guess I'll see you at ten-thirty—right, Rudy?"

"For sure," the Teutonic giant replied, as he squinted and slowly closed the door.

Angelo looked back down at Einstein's tampered letter. Rudolf's suspicious reactions to his questions didn't make Angelo any more comfortable, but neither did the fact that Fritz Haber evidently handles other people's mail. He slipped his index finger under the loose flap and easily slid it across; it practically opened itself.

Pulling out the letter, he unfolded it, and began to read:

May 9, 1933

Dear Angelo,

I hope all is well for you at the Institute, and that your studies and research, *in all regards*, is moving along with *sound* results.

As for Elsa and myself, we already miss home and our many dear friends, like you. I recently told her, as we left the shores of Scotland, "Take a good look at it; you will never see it again." But I now know my wise decision to leave was timely and justified. I hear that, back in March, a band of Nazi Storm Troopers raided my house like a pack of German Shepherds. And just this month, Hitler's Minister of Propaganda, Joseph Goebbels, has initiated his Nazi book-burning campaign. My book *Why War?*—which had just been published—met with the flames, as did many other greater works. And who is now in charge of educating the youth in Germany with vile thoughts and idol worship toward the Führer?—Baldur von Schirach. The Nazi regime is turning back the clock of human progress 3000 years! Adding insult to injury, I hear their anti-Semitic campaigns have also escalated to feverish levels, and I now fear for all the lives of my Jewish friends there who failed to heed my warning.

As you know, I've lived my entire life as a pacifist, wishing that one-day mankind would learn to live in harmony. I am opposed to the use of force under any circumstances, except when confronted by an enemy who pursues the destruction of life as an end in itself. And these barbaric overtures by Hitler's Third Reich appear to be only the beginning of far worse destruction among all peoples of Europe and the world. As such, I have already taken action by renouncing my German citizenship and I resigned from the Prussian Academy. My home is in America now and I bid you safe tidings, my dear friend. So please accomplish all that you wish to achieve and get out of Germany before it's too late!

Your friend,

Albert Einstein

Angelo leaned back in his chair, as his hand holding the letter fell to his knee. He gazed emptily into space, contemplating the grim reality that had now gripped Germany. It now seemed imperative to accelerate the pace of his investigations, but which one to focus on had always plagued his judgment. However, as he gazed back down at the tampered envelope, that dilemma was instantly resolved. He had never trusted Haber, so the Gas Man was now his top priority. The cryptic *Dante* score would have to wait.

Angelo attended the 10:30 meeting, trying to secure a lead, but came up empty-handed. To his further frustration, seven more months would pass as Angelo increasingly made a nuisance of himself, trying to irritate Haber or Hein into divulging incriminating evidence. However, the one good break was that Haber was showing signs of weakness, both in constitution and health, yet still he revealed nothing tangible.

All Angelo managed to ascertain was that it would have been extremely rare for any of Haber's colleagues to get their hands on his poisonous concoction, as he had been far more stringent in sharing his discoveries in his youth. Haber was hungry to prove himself the brightest butcher in Kaiser Wilhelm's war machine, and the Gassy Galoot did just that.

It was now late November 1933, and on this particular morning Angelo managed to confront Haber once again, as they simultaneously entered the Kaiser Institute.

"Good morning, Fritz," Angelo said with a pseudo smile, barely concealing his contempt.

"Yeah, so it is," Haber grunted, without turning. Yet as he took another step, Haber's face flinched—he quickly grabbed his chest.

"Chest pains again?" Angelo jabbed, now barely concealing his apathy.

Haber managed to reach the main lobby and took a deep breath. "Yes, the old ticker again." Then turning towards Angelo, he added, "I'm sure that makes *you* happy."

Angelo decided to play good cop. "Listen, Fritz, I know we both started off on the wrong foot, but be realistic, you must know that your days are numbered here in Germany. Hitler is not like the Kaiser. He only sees black and white; good and evil; and of course, Aryan and Jew. And *you*, Fritzy, are a Jew. The Nazis have already begun expelling and deporting Jewish scientists; and regardless of your past service to the war effort, or even your medal from the Kaiser, you *will* undoubtedly be shoved onto that train. So why not set your priorities and loyalties straight?"

Haber pivoted about and plopped down on the lobby couch. Angelo followed and stood before him, feigning concern, as Haber's eyes cautiously veered left and right, then slowly upward. "As much as I really don't like you, and it pains me to say it, you're absolutely right."

Emboldened by the breakthrough, Angelo tactfully replied, "Of course I'm right. I think it's a damn shame the way they treat us scientists. They dictate what we can and cannot develop, and when a regime change occurs, they discard some of us like old cattle—and, in your case, just because you're an old Jewish bull."

Haber rolled his eyes. "Actually, I converted to Christianity a long time ago, in an effort to assimilate. But, here it is, this Hitler maniac only fixates on pedigrees. And now his bloodhounds are hunting down anyone with Jewish blood. It galls me to give up my German heritage and my chemical discoveries to a racist pig like Hitler."

Angelo saw the opening and took it. "I can fully understand that, Fritz. Hitler's a swine, and I'd be damned if I'd hand over the kind of great discoveries you made. The Kaiser certainly made good use of your talents, didn't he?"

Haber gazed at the floor, his mind drifting into a sullen fog as he massaged his chest. "Yeah, he sure did," Fritz mumbled. "He was a good man. It was an honor to work for him, as well as for Hindenburg, and for my country."

Cunningly, Angelo stroked him further. "So, tell me about that wonderful invention of yours—poison gas?"

Upon hearing the word *gas*, Haber's gloom miraculously evaporated. "Oh, yes, it *was* wonderful. But it wasn't only gases I invented; I also developed gas masks to protect our troops. Then there were a few liquid poisons that I toyed around with. After all, chlorine and mustard gas may have been extremely painful, causing rashes, burns and of course amazingly large blisters, but the mortality rate did not meet my expectations. But it sure did scare the hell out of the enemy. And, boy, did it disfigure them. What chemicals!"

"Yes, they sure were, nasty as Hell. But what about that liquid poison?" Angelo prodded.

"Ah, yes, like I said, mustard gas was mutilating, but unfortunately, not always fatal. So I secretly worked on liquids that could be lethal; and, indeed, this one compound I developed was. I called it Habercide."

"Nice touch!" Angelo said, with a convincing smile.

Emboldened by Angelo's apparent enthusiasm, Haber's blind and toxic self-absorption continued, "Yes, it was based upon the sulfur mustard compound but my special additives made it a very effective poison. Only a small dose could cause death within minutes. But the drawback we faced was how to distribute the solution. Since the liquid was not flammable, it would not explode upon impact in a mortar shell, it would only splatter it in a very small radius. Whereas, the toxic gas would benefit by the explosion, thus being carried on the breeze and inflicting greater pain and misery, and sometimes death, on thousands of troops. I tell you, it was truly amazing and historic what I accomplished back then. My poison chemicals actually defined the Great War!"

"Yeah, really *great*. What an amazing accomplishment, Fritz," Angelo retorted sarcastically. Angelo had heard more than enough of Haber's warped, diabolical madness, and was now more than happy to let him know it.

"Oh, I should have known you were playing me!" Haber snapped. "To Hell with you *and* Hitler! It appears there's no one left to trust in this mad world." With that, Haber rose unsteadily to his feet. "I can't wait...I'll be glad to not see your face when I—oh, never mind!" he blasted.

Haber fixed his glasses, then strode angrily down the hall. Angelo looked on with a grin, savoring the moment.

Just then, Mildred walked through the front door, sporting a stylish dress by the leading designer, Elsa Schiaparelli. "Good morning, Dr. Di Purezza."

"Oh, hello, Mildred," Angelo replied, as he turned and walked alongside her. "I hear Dr. Haber is taking a vacation. How fantastic. Do you know where he's going?"

Mildred smiled demurely. "Well, perhaps I'll tell you, if you take me along?"

Angelo was taken aback. *"Take you along?* Well… uh…besides, I don't even know where Haber is going. You see, I'm not going anywhere, all I want to know is where Fritz, I mean Dr. Haber, might be staying. That's all."

Mildred squinted, as she looked right through his clumsy charade. "Dr. Di Purezza, I've kept tabs on you since the day you arrived here. You two may have been tossed together here in this mixed salad of ours, but I know you're like oil and vinegar." Then peering around, she continued, "And I must confess, I never liked that man. He's a calculating murderer, just like Hitler. The only difference is—Haber doesn't realize it."

Angelo grinned. "What a relief. I thought you might have been one of the loonies around here. I'm glad to see that you have a good head on your shoulders and a human heart. You're comparison of Haber and Hitler was very astute."

Mildred's face illuminated with delight.

Angelo had noticed Mildred before—how could anyone not? Although middle-aged, she featured that utopian hourglass figure, and her face was magnificently carved, even giving Venus in the Louvre a run for her money. Yet, with all the distractions and secret agendas, Angelo barely had time to wash his face in the morning. But suddenly he felt wide-awake, as if his eyes were seeing for the first time.

Mildred poured on some more charm. "Yes, I may be *astute*, Dr. Di Purezza, but I must say, I think you're rather cute."

Angelo suddenly felt a prickly sensation, as a wave of testosterone surged through his loins. It had been well over two years since he'd been sexually active with a woman, and he had almost forgotten that he even had the apparatus. But it felt good to know it still worked, and even better yet, that he was the prey and not the predator. He had always found the chase most awkward. And this rousing conversation was looking quite promising, as he stuttered nervously, "Uh, t-thank you, M-Mildred. Please call me Angelo. And I, actually, k-kind of think you're pretty kind of cute. I mean, sort of kind of pretty yourself."

Mildred's luscious lips pouted playfully. "Well, Angelo. Is that just kind of cute? Pretty cute? Kind of pretty? Or what?"

Angelo chuckled tensely. "As you can s-see, I'm a *pretty* smooth talker. But all of the above, I guess. I mean, for sure. Pretty! Yes, definitely pretty."

Mildred laughed as she grasped his arm and stopped walking, halting Angelo in his tracks. "May I?"

"May you what?"

Mildred looked around. "Well, you wanted to know where Fritz is going, and I have access to his entire itinerary. Naturally, I don't have to remind you that I could lose my job for doing this, so how important *is* this?"

"Look, Mildred, this is extremely important to me, but I won't put you or your job in jeopardy. So thanks, but no thanks."

Mildred pulled Angelo in close, real close, and gazed deeply into his eyes. Her alluring hazel eyes and penetrating stare rendered Angelo euphorically paralyzed, like a love-struck deer in headlights, as she queried, "You said put *me* or my job in jeopardy. How would this information put *me* personally at risk? And just what kind of jeopardy are we talking about here? Financial jeopardy? *Fatal* jeopardy?"

Angelo blinked hard, scanned the corridors, then gazed back into her bewitching eyes. "Mildred, you seem like a really great gal, but I shouldn't be getting into details, at least not yet. But I won't lie to you. Yes, *fatal* jeopardy. So I cannot and will not drag you into this."

Mildred tightened her grip on his arm, as she turned toward the east wing and began walking. As she moved, Angelo's stationary body jolted forward like a car in tow.

"Where are you taking me?"

"Where do you think, silly?—to get that information."

"Mildred, I said I really don't want to drag you into this."

"You're not *dragging me*, I'm *dragging you!* I'm a firm believer that actions speak louder than words, Angelo. And there's no better way for me to prove to you that I'm loyal and willing to do whatever you need."

Mildred kept marching toward the Records room, as Angelo tried to regain eye contact. "My God, Mildred, stop and look at me! We hardly know each other. How can you be so sure you're siding with the right fella?"

As she ushered Angelo into the small windowless room, Mildred kicked the door closed and stopped in front of a metal filing cabinet. She turned and looked into his eyes. "Because I happen to know Fritz Haber better than you do. And like I said, he's a monster, just like Hitler. So you're the right man."

Angelo smiled. "Well, I can't argue with that logic."

Mildred grinned, then bent over to pull open the drawer labeled "H". As she did, Angelo couldn't help but notice her round, shapely rear. As Mildred unwittingly sifted through the manila folders, Angelo dreamily scanned every titillating inch of her beautiful body—it was screamingly sensual. And her choice of clothing was always classy, even if avant-garde. Then without turning her head, Mildred said, "I just want to tell you, we only have seven minutes in here, so get ready to go when I say so."

Hmm, seven minutes. That's all I'd need. I'm ready to go now. Angelo shook his head. "Ah, yes, seven minutes. Clockwork!"

"What was that?"

"Oh, never mind. Did you find it?"

"Yes! It's right here." Mildred pulled out the folder and quickly located Haber's itinerary.

Angelo leaned over and peered over her shoulder. "Hmm, very interesting. But never mind the Jerusalem part of his vacation, I just need to know where he's going in Switzerland."

Mildred turned and snickered. "*Jerusalem*. What a joke! Haber renounced his Jewish faith to embrace the Kaiser and his evil Prussian regime, only to find out that Hitler hates him. Now the poor old fool is trying to reconnect with his old faith. And scientists are supposed to be the smartest people on earth. Ha! What a yoyo—just like all the others around here."

Defensively, Angelo rose up and peered down at her. "I hope you're not insinuating that *all* scientists are yoyos?"

Mildred stood up and placed her hand on Angelo's chest. "Oh, of course not, silly. Don't take it personally. But, I do know everyone that works here, and let me tell you, it's appalling how ninety-eight percent of them don't even realize that they themselves are the blind little lab rats—dutiful and patriotic pawns of whatever system is in charge. And only Einstein and you stood out from the pathetic pack."

Angelo smiled. "Damn, you really are astute."

"And you're so—"

"I get it!" Angelo interrupted, warding off embarrassment.

"No. *Now* you'll get it. Here it is—" Mildred looked down at the sheet, and read it aloud: "January 22, 1934. Arrive at the Basel Hotel, in Basel, Switzerland. And, woe!" Her head snapped up. "It says here that Haber resigned."

Angelo's eyes widened. "Very interesting. I guess he couldn't handle Hitler's anti-Semitic persecutions anymore." He then shrugged. "Actually, it's not all that surprising."

As Mildred read Haber's file, Angelo's eyes dreamily drifted back to her beautiful profile. Her incredibly smooth skin entranced him, while her flawless eyes, nose, and lips clearly trumped any painting of womanly perfection he had ever seen. He marveled over how her close-fitting rayon dress clung to her shapely curves, from her breasts to her hips. But then Mildred turned and caught his gaping stare. "I hope you like what you see?"

Angelo was about to blush, but honesty somehow trumped embarrassment. "Well, actually I was going to hand you a cock-and-bull story that I was looking at your beautiful rayon dress, since we *are* working on that new cellulose fiber here, but I must be honest, Mildred. I sure do like what I see; I just wish I'd really seen it earlier. I guess I was blind, just like these blind lab rats around here."

Mildred smiled, elated. "No, not at all, Angelo. I could tell you had a lot on your mind. Like I said, they're all blind in the most horrendous and pathetic of ways. But I hope one day you'll feel comfortable enough to tell me what it is that has you so preoccupied?"

Angelo tried not to sing; yet, as his eyes consumed her beauty, far greater urges made him sing like Caruso spilling his heart out. He sang of his invective and indictment of Haber for poisoning his father and of the stained score, but he somehow managed to contract laryngitis when it came to Liszt's mysterious *Dante* code hidden within the score.

Nevertheless, Mildred's soft shapely face beamed, having won so much ground on their first intimate encounter. Yet, Mildred still had that proverbial woman's intuition nagging at her. "Fine, Angelo, I understand all that business with Haber, but the way I saw you and Einstein coddling that *Dante* score of yours leads me to believe there's more to it than just the poison stain. What else is it about this score that's so darn fascinating?"

Angelo tried not to give in, but finally relented, "Well, actually—"

The door suddenly swung open, as Rudolf Hein barked, "What the hell are you two doing in here?"

Mildred discreetly snuck the papers behind her back and slipped them in the filing cabinet. As she gently pushed the drawer closed with her rear, Angelo unexpectedly leaned into Mildred and kissed her hard on the lips. As their rapturous bodies banged into the cabinet, it suitably concealed the click of the drawer.

Angelo looked back at Hein, and smiled. "Well, it looks like you caught us, Rudy." Then, turning back to a pleasantly stunned Mildred, he added, "I guess the gig is up. Right, honey?"

Mildred seamlessly joined the charade, flashing a big smile. "I suppose so, sweetheart."

As they embraced for another kiss, Hein shook his head and waved them out. "Take this nonsense outside. Now! Or I *will* write you both up."

Angelo pivoted about. "As your friend Fritz would say, 'testy, testy, aren't we?'"

Hein didn't find Angelo amusing, as he stepped to the side of the door and pointed. "Go! Angelo. Now!"

Angelo shook his head. "I guess that promotion has really gotten to your head. You're finally the number two man around here. What was Max thinking?"

Hein's blood pressure was rising fast. "Max had *nothing* to do with it. And I'm warning you, Angelo. You best leave now, and quietly, before I pursue this further."

Angelo looked back at Mildred. Her face was now dead serious, her eyes oscillating toward the door. He grasped her hand, turned, then marched past Hein, out into the hallway. Hein followed them, angrily slammed the door and locked it. Abruptly, he turned, as his steely-blue dagger eyes pierced his prey. "Listen, Mildred, I intend to keep this door locked from now on, and *you* will need to ask *my* permission to enter. And that goes for the mailroom, as well. Is that understood?"

As Mildred nodded, Hein added, "So hand me your keys, right now!"

"Yes, of course. But I don't understand. What's the security issue? I've worked here since the Institute opened."

"Shush!" he blasted, as he militantly marched straight up to her and gazed down at her trembling face. "You seem to forget, *Fräulein*. You're just a damn secretary. Don't dare question me, *ever!* Is that understood?"

Mildred flinched, and obediently handed him the keys.

Meanwhile, Angelo's patience was dying fast. "Look, Rudy, this is a laboratory, not a prison. What the hell is going on around here?"

"It's quite simple, Germany has a new Führer. And his *Gleichschaltung* policy demands that we have strict new protocols around here. The world is changing, Angelo, and if you don't change with it you'll be left behind, or worse!"

"Is that a threat, Rudy?"

"Take it any way you like," Hein retorted, as he pivoted about and marched imperiously down the corridor.

Angelo exhaled hard, as he stared at Hein's uniquely animated gait. "That man is really an odd bird." Then turning toward Mildred, he added, "I know he has most people around here believing he's a vicious hawk, but somehow I suspect he's just a gutless chicken." His left eyebrow rose. "Speaking of which; I believe they have roasted chicken on the menu today. Are you available for lunch?"

Mildred laughed. "What an odd segue." With a coy smile, she added, "So, is this a date?"

Angelo's lips tensed up. "Well, I admit; after what just transpired, that invitation was a bit spontaneous, not to mention artless. It's just that I have a habit of always thinking about food. But if this had been under different circumstances, I certainly would have asked you to join me at a fine restaurant, like Borchardt's."

"Wow! I'm impressed. Only Berlin's elite dine at Borchardt's. It's a historical landmark."

"Well, you're an exceptional kind of woman, Mildred. So I humbly apologize for asking you to our chintzy little cafeteria, but I think there's an awful lot we need to discuss. However, I would be honored to take you to Borchardt's, perhaps this weekend…but, wait…I'm jumping way ahead of myself, aren't I? You haven't even agreed to meet me at our world-class cafeteria. So will you?"

Mildred grinned. "Why certainly. I'd be delighted to dine with you at our measly cafeteria or even at a picnic table. I'll meet you at 12:00." She gazed down the hall, and spotted Hein at the far end, staring. Nervously, she looked back at Angelo. "Actually, I'm one of those that thinks Hein is a vicious hawk, so we better get back to work, and *pronto!*"

Angelo sat at his desk for hours, trying to concentrate on the quadratic equations before him, but the only numbers that kept popping into his head were Mildred's possible measurements and the number 12:00. He looked down at his sheet of mathematical formulas, then pushed it aside.

Reaching down to the bottom drawer of his desk, he pulled out the *Dante* score. Leafing through the pages, he still couldn't fathom how Liszt managed to baffle both him and the century's greatest intellect. Then gazing at the poisonous stain, his mind once again shifted to his primary mission. The *Dante* score may have been for transmitting secret messages, but it was the poison that killed his father. Haber's poison!

Angelo peered down once again at his watch—the noon hour had finally arrived. He closed the score and placed it back in the bottom drawer of his desk. Taking a cue from Hein, Angelo reached in his pocket, pulled out his keys, and locked the drawer.

Eagerly, Angelo paced down the hall weaving between the bodies of scientists and technicians that now seemed like irritating obstructions. Reaching the cafeteria, his face suddenly lit up when he spotted Mildred standing against the far wall near the food line. Her blondish-auburn hair was cut medium length and styled in a loose finger wave, while her Schiaparelli dress beautifully accentuated every feminine curve she had, and there were many. Their eyes instantly connected, as a delightful charge enlivened every inch of his body. Angelo oddly felt like a teenager, as his heart skipped to a whole new beat as he danced his way toward her.

Angelo didn't even seem to notice how dry the chicken was or how bland the canned peas were, as his appetite was being visually satisfied by Mildred's charming face and emotionally satiated by her warm presence. For the first time, Angelo felt comfortable with a woman in a way he had never experienced before. Suddenly, the butterflies and clumsy tongue-tied moments that had always plagued him were gone. Miraculously, the two were bonding, just like the resin and hardener that Angelo's lab was experimenting with to produce the new wonder adhesive, epoxy. However, as their rapport was solidifying, with endearing smiles and little bursts of laughter, Angelo was discomforted by the mounting eyes turning their way. He leaned over and whispered, "Dear Lord, these people would all make horrible Nazi spies with those gaping stares, but I still don't trust many of them. So how about we take a walk?"

Mildred nodded, as they rose up and returned their lunch trays. Exiting the cafeteria, they each fetched their hats and winter coats, then met in the lobby. As they approached the main exit, Mildred gazed at the Christmas tree by the front window. "So what are you doing for Christmas?"

Angelo pushed the door open to allow her to pass, as a gust of cold wind hit their faces. "Well, my whole family is gone—has been for many years—and my extended family is still in Italy, so probably nothing."

Mildred frowned. "Oh, that's just awful. Nobody should spend Christmas alone."

Having walked down the short flight of frosty steps and out to the street, Angelo looked at Mildred and shrugged his shoulders. "Oh, it's no problem, really. I've been on my own for quite some time, and humans are far more adaptable and resilient than we give ourselves credit for."

Strolling along the city street, Angelo glanced at the snow that blanketed the parked cars and horse-drawn wagons, then at a young boy looking in the decorated window of a delikatessen—his mind now recalling older days. "But, I must admit, Mildred, I will miss the traditional seven fish Christmas Eve dinners that my mother used to make."

Mildred looked up at Angelo. "Well, my family does the seven fish meal, too. So why not join us?"

Angelo was taken aback. "That's awfully kind of you, Mildred. I might just take you up on that."

"Please do," Mildred said with a warm smile, as she slipped on her long, white leather gloves.

"That's odd," Angelo said, "I didn't realize that Germans celebrate Christmas Eve with seven fishes?"

Mildred smiled. "They don't." Angelo squinted, as Mildred continued, "I'm half Italian. My mother was born in Florence, and she simply loves to cook."

Angelo swerved around a window-shopper. "Well, I know many northern Italians have lighter features, but with your hair and skin coloring I never would have known."

"Most people don't know," Mildred replied, as she stopped in front of a closed store. The word 'Jude' and the Star of David were sloppily painted on the window—the door was nailed shut. Angelo stopped and looked, as Mildred continued, "And lately, I prefer to keep it that way. Not that I'm ashamed, mind you, but with this growing wave of Aryan fanaticism, who knows what Hitler and his Nazi goons will do next. I heard of a Jewish couple in Leipzig that was brutally beaten by Storm Troopers. The man barely survived; but worse yet, his wife was pregnant and lost her baby. So I prefer to be cautious. Besides, I hear it's better to get raises and promotions this way."

Angelo nodded. "Perhaps so, but it really is a colossal disappointment. I came to Germany with hopes for a better life, not only a better job, yet it seems Hitler is on the fast track for surpassing Mussolini. Scarier still, he's cultivating a far more demented cult of obedient worshipers."

Mildred's brow lowered. "That reminds me. Getting back to our little face-off earlier with Hein, I just don't get it. Like I said, I've worked at the Institute since day one and had access to all those records. But now that tall quirky Nazi has them all under lock and key."

Angelo began pulling his coat collar up tight against his neck. "I found that odd, too. After all, what could he or anyone else there possibly hide from *you?*"

Affectionately, Mildred interlocked their arms. They glanced at each other with endearing eyes as they entered the grounds of a picturesque park, accented with frost-covered trees and a shapely pond littered with swans.

Contently, Mildred scanned the peaceful view, then looked back up at Angelo. "That's just it, I know everything, and there's certainly a lot of dirt that they don't want to leak out. So when you said earlier that I'd be putting my life in jeopardy, it certainly has become a reality, now that they've seen me with you."

Wearily, Angelo lowered his head, appalled to have put her in this position. "I'm really sorry." Then rather abruptly, his head playfully sprang up. "But, hey, I did warn you."

Mildred smiled as she jokingly hit Angelo's chest. "Yes, you did." Her expression turned serious. "But it's strange. You were trying to protect me from the harm that *your* secrets might cause, yet those are *not* the secrets that have now put my life in jeopardy."

"Well, just what kind of secrets are you privy to?"

"Angelo, I know almost every transaction that has taken place at that insane Institute, from highly confidential records to catty gossip."

"Come on, cough it up. Like what?"

Mildred giggled as the chilly air turned her breath into vapor. "Fine. Let's take Rudolf Hein, for example. Besides the money he embezzles, the blackmailing he engages in, the payoffs for advancements, or the experiments that he stole from his Jewish co-workers—who he knew were going to be deported, so he could easily snatch their ideas and handsome contracts—good Old Rudy is a carnivorous homosexual."

Angelo chuckled. "Wow! What a mouthful."

"Yes, well said. And some of his affairs have been with top Nazi leaders, like Ernst Röhm and Rudolf Hess. In fact, Hein often takes morning horseback rides with Röhm in the *Tiergarten*. And just down the street from there is Aktion T-4. That's the Nazi code-name for their sterilization program, located at *Tiergartenstrasse* 4, that rids them of people with mental or physical disabilities. But there is plenty of dirt on just about everyone at our nasty old Kaiser Institute."

As they continued walking, Angelo turned—their eyes connected. "So, tell me, what kind of dirt is there on *you?*"

"Oh, you sly dog," Mildred said, her face twisting with surprise. "I should've seen that coming. Fine, you've been honest with me, so why not? But be prepared, and please don't judge me. I know you're not going to like this, but Fritz and I had an affair two years ago, and—"

"WHAT!? You and Fritz? Please tell me you're joking?"

Mildred burst out laughing. "Of course, silly!"

Angelo's stunned face morphed into a smile, as he rolled his eyes. "Damn, you nailed me good with that one."

"Well, speaking of being nailed, I know Fritz's health records. And if he doesn't take care of himself, *he's* going to be nailed…in a coffin."

Angelo stopped dead in his tracks, as Mildred bounced backward. Unclasping their arms, Angelo looked at Mildred with concern. "What's wrong with him? Is it the old ticker?"

"Yes, he had a stroke recently, and he begged Max not to say a word to anyone about it. So this quest of yours to convict him for murdering your father better happen soon, or he'll leave this planet believing he was an innocent patriot doing the Kaiser's bidding."

Angelo angrily gritted his teeth and stared at the ground. "Damn! It makes me sick to think that he's managed to live all these years, while my father was taken from this world prematurely. And now I might not even have the opportunity to avenge my father's death. What sort of justice is there in the world?"

Mildred grasped his chin and lifted it tenderly. "Angelo, very rarely does this world offer justice. Look how the Prussians caused one war after another, finally culminating into the Great War that killed over nine million people. Their brutal rise to power caused four empires to crumble: their own German empire; the Austro-Hungarian; Russian and Ottoman; along with the fall of several royal dynasties, thus paving the way for the peasant working class to stake their claim. And who became the spokesman for that destitute and dispossessed lower class? Adolf Hitler! So eject some of that idealistic ballast overboard, because if you don't, harsh reality will always find a way to sink you."

Angelo brushed the hair out of her beautiful, yet steadfast, eyes. "My God, you remind me of my father—always the strong mast that could weather the storm, while others snapped under pressure. Thank you, Mildred," then, looking up, he incanted, "and thank you, Pa!"

Angelo was deeply moved, not only by Mildred's profound and practical words, but also by her resplendent beauty, an enchantment that not only visually radiated out of her features, but also that elusive inner warmth that any man fortunate enough to have experienced knows when true love stares them in the face. And, boy, did Mildred have a great stare—one so entrancing that it sent Angelo's heart and mind spinning.

Impulsively, Angelo grasped Mildred and leaned in for a kiss. As they lingered for a dreamy, lovely moment, Mildred suddenly broke their *liebesträume,* when she curiously pushed him away. "Where did that come from?"

"From the heart," Angelo replied euphorically.

As warm smiles lit up their faces, they had all they could do to prevent their growing magnetism from drawing them into each other's arms for another loving embrace. They tenderly re-clasped their arms and started to head back toward the Institute.

As they walked through the chilly Berlin air, Angelo noticed a train belching black smoke in the distance. His eyelids lowered slightly, his mind pensive. "I guess you're right about life not being fair, because we only have four weeks to spend with each other. I intend to catch a train to

Switzerland, which should arrive two days before Haber gets there."

Mildred playfully bumped Angelo with her hip. "Well, who says I have to wait around here? I'd love to join you."

Angelo stopped and swung her around, his hands firmly around her thin waist, his eyes glued to hers. "Are you serious? But you can't."

"Why not? I'll just call in sick."

"Mildred, in two days we'll be off a whole week for Christmas vacation. So taking off in the New Year, with Haber gone and me being out, is not good timing."

Mildred shrugged her shoulders. "That might actually be better. With two less scientists around, I imagine there would be less paperwork. Besides there's certainly no one around here I wish to be with, and I've always wanted to visit Switzerland." Mildred smiled as she gazed warmly into Angelo's eyes. "Anyway, that's one of the beauties of life—it's unpredictable."

Angelo couldn't resist, and once more he leaned in for an ardent kiss. Mildred rose up on her tippy toes, keeping one hand on her fancy pillbox hat, while pulling him in close with the other. Even with one hand, Mildred relished feeling Angelo's muscular back through his woolen coat.

The next four weeks were the happiest Angelo ever experienced. He joined Mildred and her family for Christmas Eve, and immediately felt right at home. He was intrigued to find out that her father, Herman Krause, had worked for the Bechstein piano company. He explained to Angelo that eighty or so years earlier, Carl Bechstein was determined to develop a new piano that could withstand the greater demands of the new breed of virtuosos; thus, he befriended the leader of the pack, Franz Liszt, by building him one. Liszt loved the sturdy new instrument and recommended it to his star pupil, Hans von Bülow, who would publically debut the Bechstein grand in 1857 in

Berlin, playing Liszt's mighty *Sonata in B minor*. This instantly incited demand for the new pianos, and they became the standard in many concert halls, as well as eagerly sought out by the elite to grace their mansions. Herman explained how he had met his wife-to-be, Carmela, in Florence on a business trip to deliver one such piano to a Florentine magnate. The rest was history, as they say. Angelo felt a deep and genuine warmness that he hadn't experienced in many years. And beyond connecting with his charming hosts, Angelo enjoyed eating the seven fishes that Carmela prepared and laid out, very much like his own mother had so many years ago.

As the weeks rolled by, Angelo and Mildred grew ever so close, as the two lovers shared fond memories, and even their sweat in the heat of passion. They had celebrated the New Year, and spent many days and nights in Berlin, even enjoying an exquisite meal at Borchardt's.

Then on January 20, 1934, they boarded the train for Basel, Switzerland. As the train chugged along 450 miles of track through the Alps, traversing long wooden trestles and heading through tunnels gouged out of the Alpine mountains, it finally arrived at the Basel Bahnhof. As snowflakes wafted on the breeze, the enamored couple made their way to the Zartes Haus hotel, situated two blocks away from where Haber's hotel was located.

Entering their quaint hotel room, Angelo threw their luggage on the floor and his small plaid suitcase on the bed. As Mildred began unpacking, Angelo used his key to unlock his special suitcase and flipped it open. Unexpectedly, the *Dante* score slipped out and fell on the floor. Mildred looked at Angelo and leaned over to pick it up. As she did, she noticed the barrel of a revolver sticking out from under one of Angelo's shirts. Angelo quickly closed the lid and sat on the bed to obstruct her vision.

"Nice try," Mildred said.

"What do you mean?"

"Listen, Angelo, taking the law into your own hands is just plain stupid. I might as well tell you, I eavesdropped on you and Albert many times, and I heard him warn you to avoid being guided by raw emotions. He told you to use your head and to use logic. But more importantly, he implored you to not fall into the trap of becoming a criminal like Haber."

Angelo's admonished face suddenly lit up. "Wait! You naughty girl! So you were spying on Albert and me?"

Mildred smiled. "No, not Albert. *You!* I had a crush on you the moment I saw you. And, by the way, I opened your letter from Albert. I just had to make sure you were not a Nazi. So, you're clean in my book."

Angelo leaned back, grasped a pillow, and swung it around, bopping Mildred on the head. "Well, you're not clean in my book, you little sneak. I can't believe you!" he scolded, with a smile. "You better swear never to do that again. Do you hear me?"

As Mildred playfully nodded, Angelo couldn't help but chuckle. Gripping her arms, he hurled her on the bed, rolled her on her back, and entangled their legs, pulling one of his old wrestling moves. Looking down at her smiling face, Angelo couldn't resist. "Damn, how I love you."

"Damn? Am I a curse?" Mildred asked with a giggle.

Angelo's face turned serious. "Well, just like Eve was a curse to Adam, yet also the greatest gift God could have ever given him, I, too, have been blessed." He kissed her, then added playfully, "Or, yes, maybe cursed."

As Mildred laughed and tried to wriggle free, they both succumbed to the inevitable as they embraced. After a long and impassioned moment, Angelo sat up and ran his fingers through his wavy hair like a comb.

Meanwhile, Mildred grasped a brush and tidied up her hair. After forming a big curl on the side, she rolled over and picked up the *Dante* score. Sitting at the edge of the bed, she flipped it open and looked down at the dazzling array of notes. "So you mean to tell me that Franz Liszt has managed to outsmart you and Albert Einstein? How can that be?"

Angelo moved up beside her and wrapped his arm around her. "That's a good question; one that has plagued me for quite some time now. Perhaps we just can't see it because Liszt was a composer and we're scientists."

Mildred peered into his eyes. "But aren't there direct links between mathematics and musical composition? After all, some of these music scales look like the mathematical equations that I see scribbled all over the blackboards back at the Institute."

Angelo nodded. "Yes, that's why I thought for sure Albert and I could unravel Liszt's puzzle. But it seems only Liszt and my father knew the code."

Mildred looked back down at the score. "Too bad, and now both men are dead."

"Yes, and have been for a long time. So their secret seems destined to survive throughout the ages. Well, it's good to know that some things survive for all eternity."

Mildred looked at the infamous stain on the score. "So, what do you plan to do about Fritz Haber? And it better not be anything with that gun."

"Well, you pretty much talked me out of that. But I'll shadow him to see what I can find out. Meanwhile, feel free to examine the score. Maybe a non-mathematician will have better luck."

Two anxious days passed before Angelo finally found himself sitting on the train station platform awaiting Haber's arrival. The frigid wind howled, as the porter turned up the heat and peeked out the frosty window. He knocked on the glass and waved for Angelo to come in from the cold, but Angelo signaled 'no thank you'—remaining seated under the huge awning. A long row of benches lined the platform, with only one other person sitting at the far end. And just as Mildred's gleaned information stated, Haber's train pulled into the Basel Bahnhof at 9:10 PM—actually ten minutes late.

Lifting a newspaper to cover his face, Angelo watched as Haber disembarked, carrying his luggage. Angelo's adrenaline began to rush as Haber walked right past him. Out of the corner of his eye, Angelo watched as Haber's stocky body slowly began to fade into the dark chilly mist. Placing the paper down, Angelo put his hand on his coat, feeling the iron piece underneath. He closed his eyes and thought *what the Hell am I doing? Why don't you listen to Mildred?*

Angelo stood up and quickly began pacing in Haber's direction, when, suddenly, he stopped. Angrily, he watched Haber's silhouette vanish into the dark veil of flurries. He stomped his foot and punched the palm of his other hand, as his head dropped. Taking a deep breath, Angelo looked up and headed back to the Zartes Haus hotel.

Peevishly, he entered their room and stomped the snow off his shoes. Mildred looked up. "What happened? I've been worried."

"I don't even know why I came here," he huffed, as he ripped off his coat and threw it on the bed. "I'm no bounty hunter or secret agent. Hell, I haven't even been able to gather any credible evidence. After all these years, I doubt if there's anyone or anything that can help me convict Haber."

Mildred picked up his coat, snapped the moisture off it, then walked toward the coat rack. "I know it's easier for me to say this because it's not my father, but maybe you should just drop this whole undercover operation." Mildred hung up his coat and pivoted around. "After all, Haber is very ill now, and who knows how much time he has left. Besides, we could take advantage of the beautiful Swiss countryside. What do you say?"

"I say, you're right—"

Mildred smiled.

"It was *not* your father!"

Angelo marched into the bathroom and slammed the door on their conversation.

Several uncomfortable days passed as Angelo tried to enjoy Switzerland by day with Mildred, while slipping out at night to shadow Haber. He morbidly fed his melancholic addiction as he angrily watched Haber enjoying himself at taverns and taking long scenic walks. He cursed himself, feeling paralyzed and useless. He couldn't purge the vexing thoughts that wracked his mind. Haber had to be the killer; yet, here it was twenty years later and this evil hack was still roaming the streets. Finally, Angelo had had enough. *Screw the finicky legal process that requires every little link of evidence,* he thought. *Fritz is guilty!* He had shadowed Haber's every step while in Switzerland and, like clockwork, he knew Haber's every move. Angelo looked at his watch and then over at Mildred—she had fallen asleep an hour earlier. His mind raced *Come on, Angelo, it's 12:15 and Fritz takes his nighttime walk along the Rhine. Let's end it, now!*

Angelo slipped his revolver under his coat, then kissed Mildred softly on the head. He put on his black fedora and gloves, and slipped quietly out of the hotel room.

The frigid night air only seemed to freeze the tension in his face as he walked toward the icy river. Looking down at his watch, he knew he had seventeen minutes to reach the dark and densely wooded park. Angelo had earlier staked out the park as being the ideal location, since its three lampposts had burnt-out bulbs. Moreover, any sound would be muffled by the roaring turbulence of the Rhine.

As he approached the park, Angelo slipped behind a row of trees and bushes. Three feet away was a path that ran along the river and through the park. To his left, all was dead quiet. He then turned to the right. There was Haber in the distance, slowly approaching, wearing a green felt Alpine hat and long, black woolen coat.

Angelo's lips twisted as he checked his watch. *This coldhearted killer is just like a machine. Right on time, just like a ticking, time bomb—and it's time to make it explode!*

Haber was now a mere ten feet away, and Angelo's heart started racing. As Haber reached the kill zone, Angelo lunged out of the bushes and grabbed him. Haber's hat and glasses fell off as Angelo viciously whipped him to the ground and gagged his mouth with a handkerchief. Pinning Haber's arms to the ground with his knees, Angelo pulled out his revolver and shoved it into his fleshy face. Haber's eyes bulged, looking like two cue balls with black dots for pupils.

Angelo growled, "Listen, Fritz, I'm going to ask you one question, and one question only. Did you kill my father? And if you scream, I *will* kill you!"

Angelo removed the gag.

Haber began gasping for air, then huffed, "No! I swear. No!"

Angelo's eyes widened as he cocked the pistol.

Haber stuttered frantically, "What t-the hell are y-you doing? Are you nuts?"

"*Me,* nuts? You're the one who used your precious poison, Habercide, to murder my father, Fritz. So *you're* the one who is nuts!"

Haber's heart was giving his chest one hell of a beating, and he appeared to blackout. Angelo slapped the side of Fritz's head. "Don't you dare die on me before you confess."

Regaining oxygen, Haber uttered, "There's nothing to confess, except that I did invent Habercide."

"Do you mean to tell me that you never laced my father's score of the *Dante Symphony* with it or wiped it on him somehow?"

"No! A thousand times, NO!" Haber barked.

Haber's pathetic pleas were disturbingly dousing Angelo's rage, as he eased up the pressure on his arms and removed the gun from his cheek. "Fritz, my father died from Habercide. That's a proven fact. Einstein even analyzed it. And it's a known fact that you never shared your secrets back in 1914. You were too hell-bent on creating poisonous gas to impress the Kaiser. So how the hell do you explain my father being killed by it?"

Haber gasped as foam oozed out the side of his mouth.

Angelo slid off his body and pounded his chest with his left hand. "You better not die on me, you dirty bastard. Tell me! How did my father die? Did you order someone to do it? What?"

Haber's eyes rolled up into his head as he seemed to stop breathing. Angelo irritably dropped his gun and raised his clasped hands. Then swinging them down, he ushered a hammering blow to Haber's chest. Haber's body bounced as his eyes rolled back down. Wheezing and gasping for air, Haber motioned to sit up. Angrily, Angelo pulled his body upright, and as he did, Haber quickly grabbed Angelo's gun, pointed it, and fired off a shot. The fiery muzzle blast scorched Angelo's shoulder as the bullet went flying out into the night sky. Wrestling the gun out of Haber's hand, Angelo gave him a solid right to the temple; snapping Haber's head sideways.

"You dirty pig! Now you try to kill me? Well, I'm sorry Fritzy boy, you're not going to kill *this* Angelo Di Purezza!"

Haber had now regained his vigor, as he blasted, "You damn fool! How many times must I tell you? I did not murder your father, nor did I order anyone to do so. So, if you let me up, I'll promise not to press charges."

Angelo laughed. "Ha! *You're* the one that shot at *me.* No jury would buy your story, especially here in Switzerland. So if anyone here holds the cards, Fritz, it's me!"

Haber sat mute, glaring at Angelo with contempt, as Angelo stood up and threw the gun into the Rhine. "Get up, and get out of my sight. You're nothing but a damn liar. Am

I supposed to believe anything *you* say? You're just a deranged monster that's in the business of gassing and poisoning men, and not only one or two men, but thousands of men. You're a disgrace to Germany, a disgrace to your Jewish faith, and a disgrace to the human race!"

With that, Angelo picked up Haber's hat and glasses, and threw them on his lap. Just then, a young couple was strolling along the riverbank.

As they came within visual range, the young lad looked over. "Excuse me, sir. Do you need help getting up?"

Haber shook his head briskly, and spat, "No! Leave me alone, I just tripped." Rising to his feet, Haber brushed off his hat and then covered his shiny dome. Clipping his spectacles on the bridge of his nose, he then gazed at Angelo with his four hateful eyes—all screaming retribution. Without a word, he turned and marched down the path toward his hotel.

Angelo looked at the couple and shrugged. "Strange fellow. He didn't want my help either and just carried on like a madman. Quite odd."

The perplexed couple chuckled, as the lad grasped his girlfriend's arm and said, "He looked rather odd, too—a bit menacing. Well, have a good night, sir."

"Same to you."

As the couple faded into the frigid Swiss night, Angelo's nerve-racked head fell into his hands. After an odd, long moment, in which the swirling furnace in his head finally reached equilibrium with the serene frostiness of the night air, he looked up and put on his fedora. Brushing the snowflakes and dirt off his knees, he straightened out his coat and headed back to the hotel.

Angelo quietly unlocked the door, pushed it open, and crept inside. Seeing Mildred fast asleep, he closed the door as gingerly as he could. Mindfully, he waited for his cold body to thaw, then removed his outer garments and slid under the covers to join her.

As the dawning sun illuminated the white sheer drapes, Angelo opened his eyes. Mildred was already up and about, while he now wrestled with his conscience. Should he tell her about last night's jarring altercation? Angelo felt lucky and decided to roll the dice. "I'm glad I took your advice about taking in the scenery here. It's been wonderful, hasn't it? What do you say today we try—"

"What do you say today you tell me where you went last night?" Mildred icily demanded, turning his lucky sevens to snake eyes.

Angelo shook his head. "*Damn!* I see there's no way of getting anything past you, is there?"

"Angelo, I'll be *damned* if I'm going to get mixed up with a dirty, no-good, lying sneak. If we're to have a serious relationship, we must be open and honest with each other, especially in these scary, changing times. I cannot afford to risk my life like this."

Angelo rubbed his sleepy, creased face, and looked at Mildred. Her disarmingly beautiful eyes were just too much to bear, and his hands fell to the bed. "Fine, you're right. I'm sorry."

"Of course I'm right. And you should know by now that I'm no simpleton. I see that your revolver is missing. So what in God's name happened last night?"

Intuitively, Angelo slapped on his poker face and was about to bluff, when she added, "And if it's the worst that I can imagine, I'll be out of this room and your life forever."

Angelo opted to fold and ditched the dice, coming clean—his dirty tale gushing out in full. Mildred sighed, then sat down beside him. Grasping Angelo's ailing head, Mildred gently drew it into her soothing bosom. "Well, you're one hot-blooded Italian all right."

Angelo grinned in shame. "Yes, that's something my father wouldn't have been proud of. He always preached how I should *use* my head, not *lose* it. He knew very well my disposition for being wild and impulsive, and he honorably tried to channel my thoughts toward the order of mathematics and music. But, it seems I still can't control my anger—especially knowing that Haber somehow killed him."

Mildred pulled his head away and gazed into his eyes. "Angelo, we all have our flaws, but you admirably became a mathematician, and a darn successful one at that. And even though you say your father learned to use his head more than raw emotions, you still share his resolve to defend civilized and noble ideals. You're a good man, Angelo Di Purezza. As you know, your name even means *Angel of Purity.*"

Angelo smiled, and, as they embraced, she added, "So regardless of Haber not confessing, or possibly being innocent of your father's death, the man is still directly linked to appalling mass murder. And his day of judgment awaits him. So let it be."

It was now their last day in Basel. Spending the whole day touring the Swiss countryside, and later walking the cobbled streets to admire the snow-laden city, Angelo and Mildred confirmed what they already knew; they were deeply in love. Stopping in a local tavern, they enjoyed a warm meal and toasted to better days. However, on their way to the train station, they happened to stroll past a newsstand; Mildred's eyes froze in alarm. Angelo turned and followed her line of sight, as they both gazed at the disturbing headline

'GERMAN CHEMIST FRITZ HABER DIES OF HEART FAILURE IN BASEL HOTEL!'

Angelo then noticed the date on the paper: January 29, 1934. He looked at Mildred. "Oh, my God! How bizarre. I just realized. Today marks the twentieth anniversary of my father's death."

Mildred embraced Angelo and looked up into his eyes. "It seems the Lord has put this matter to rest. You can finally move on with your life."

Angelo hugged her tight, and peered right through her eyes. "Well, if Haber did tell me the truth, that only puts to rest the toxic inventor." He gazed uneasily toward the horizon. "So there might still be an assassin out there, somewhere."

SCENE IV: ROME & PARIS [1870]

Four years had passed since the tragic chain of events at Gustave Doré's studio in Paris, yet the tragedies did not end there. During those four turbulent years, Liszt was further pained by the gruesome murders of three other students. Two were also chillingly impaled with bronze crucifixes, while the other was brutally shredded with a jagged knife.

More troubling still, these apparent serial killings were committed in two additional countries, two in Rome, Italy, and the knifing in Weimar, Germany. Meanwhile the police of all three cities remained clueless, unable to find the killer or discern the *modus operandi.* Liszt and his growing secret brotherhood, however, all believed they knew the motive, even if they disagreed what that motive was.

Liszt and his righteous band of rebels—who named themselves the 'Altar Eagles' to denote their defense of the Catholic Pope and French Liberal Empire—were now at the Villa d'Este in Tivoli, just outside Rome.

The villa had become Liszt's new retreat while in Rome, offering a silent rural charm that his room at the Monastery in the city lacked. The beautiful villa, known for its astonishing array of fountains, had been built by Cardinal Ippolito II d'Este, son of the infamous Lucrezia Borgia and grandson of the notoriously corrupt Pope Alexander VI.

The Altar Eagles felt aptly at home at the villa, being that they were honorably defending their Catholic faith, yet Borgia-like intrigue and blood now seemed to follow them wherever they traveled.

"I still contend that the killer must be a radical Protestant on a twisted religious mission," Saint-Saëns proclaimed.

Angelo shook his head. "I disagree. That would account for the deaths of Kristian in Paris and the two in Rome—who were all devout Catholics—but it doesn't explain Johann's death in Weimar. He was Protestant."

Liszt raised his hand. "That's very true. However, my ex-son-in-law, Emile Ollivier, who is the French Prime Minister, has informed me that Napoleon III discovered that the Prussians have a secret service squad called *Stahlklinge* or Steel Blade. So I strongly suspect that their agents are not just gathering intelligence or transmitting messages, as we are. And I now suspect that our fellow Altar Eagles might have been killed by the Prussians' Steel Blade."

Contemplating their discussion was one of the group's newest members, Sophie Menter. As Liszt's musical pupil, Sophie had developed into a phenomenal pianist who had recently dazzled the Viennese with her performance of Liszt's demanding *Piano Concerto No.1*. And, despite her current silence, Sophie could be just as demanding. In fact, she wasn't thrilled that her compatriots spoke of a *brother*hood, thus pressuring them to concoct their Altar Eagles codename.

"Yes, Master," Sophie replied. "But the Steel Blade doesn't sound like the type of organization to use bronze crucifixes to do their evil bidding, as their very name suggests the weapon of choice."

"That's true, on the surface of it," Liszt acknowledged. "But who knows what evil rot lurks in their scheming minds? They might be using our beloved cross as an insult—namely, that Catholics will die by their own mistaken beliefs—or they could simply be trying to lead us off their trail, by directing us to fixate on a religious conflict, when it's actually political."

"And let us never forget the Prussian puppeteer," Angelo declared. "Bismarck pulls the evil strings that make all of those steel blades slash and slice."

Liszt turned about and looked at his young disciple. "Indeed, Angelo." Liszt stepped back to face his brood. "However, upon further contemplation, I find this most troublesome. As Sophie astutely suggested, I imagine a sharp Prussian steel blade would suit them just fine for killing us off. So, why the grisly charade with bronze crucifixes? Is there really a religious enemy out there, or are the Prussians just being cunning devils?" Liszt paused a moment, his mind searching for the answer. He then added, "I must say, with Bismarck's devious track record, I still suspect this is the work of the Steel Blade."

Saint-Saëns strolled over to the ornately carved balcony, which overlooked a panorama of rolling hills, cypresses, and fountains. Gazing outward at the horizon and toward France, he noticed dark clouds. "I think my homeland is in for some stormy weather, in more ways than one."

Liszt walked over and sat on the ledge nearby. His eyes, too, lingered on the darkening horizon, until his gaze dropped down to the flowing fountains below. Franz always had a fascination for water and, in fact, in seven years hence, inspired by these very fountains, he would write perhaps the most sparkling impression of water ever created when he penned *The Fountains at the Villa d'Este*. And, looking at the flowing water now—with its graceful power and endless motion—he was compelled once again to take action.

Liszt pivoted about, and addressed his band of agents. "We must mobilize and flood our enemies with a stream of espionage to stall the Prussian war machine. Although Kaiser Wilhelm I is the emperor, we all know that Otto von Bismarck is the Prussian Puppeteer, as Angelo so rightly pointed out. Therefore, I have plans for all of you to relay to our newest Altar Eagles in Rome, Weimar, and Paris. Angelo and I will draft three newly-encoded *Dante Symphony* scores for the performances scheduled in each of those cities. Let's act expeditiously, because we four will be traveling to Paris in three days to meet with Emperor Napoleon III."

Liszt and Angelo diligently encoded the three scores with messages that aided either the political agenda of Emperor Napoleon III or the religious agenda of Pope Pius IX. Their secret plans included trafficking supplies and armaments to underground rebels throughout the German states and Prussia as well as helping the defense of the Vatican's shrinking borders. By day three, Angelo, Saint-Saëns, and Sophie had mailed the scores to the appropriate conductors at the three cities, which in turn would alert their receptive agents. All that remained now was to catch the train to Paris.

As the Altar Eagles stood on the platform in the Roma Termini, they could see a black trail of smoke in the distance. The rumbling steam locomotive finally approached, when its metal spoke-wheels suddenly locked, bringing the train to a screeching halt. The Altar Eagles eagerly grasped their luggage and stepped aboard. With the blast of its whistle and a huge puff of black smoke, the iron engine slowly chugged northward over its bed of rails.

As the train rocked and swayed, Liszt pulled his gold pocket watch from his vest. On the cover was an etching of Pope Pius IX. As he gazed down at it, he affectionately rubbed the shiny memento. It had been a gift from his long-time companion Princess Carolyne von Sayn-Wittgenstein. They had even contemplated marriage ten years earlier, but those dreams were derailed when Tsar Alexander II of Russia pressured the Vatican to rescind her annulment papers. With a ripened smile, Liszt flipped open the cover, checked the time, and snapped it shut.

Being an aficionada of fineries, Sophie keenly noticed Liszt's exquisite timepiece, and leaned forward for a closer look. "That's a handsome engraving of Pope Pius."

"Thank you. In fact, we can thank Pius for riding on this train. He inaugurated the rail system here. He's a good man."

"Well, as you know, I joined up with you for political reasons, but I know Pius had a rough time back in 1849."

Liszt nodded. "Yes, Sophie, he sure did. But there were many revolutions during 1848 and 1849, as all of Europe was in utter chaos—and, as you say, even the Pope wasn't exempt. Garibaldi had led his famous Red Shirts to an apparently rousing victory when they subdued the Swiss Guard and installed a Republican government in the Papal State. Giuseppe Mazzini was appointed triumvir and became a leading figure for reunification, but he also wished to strip the Vatican of its temporal powers. Pope Pius had fled earlier to Gaeta, yet he appealed to my other good friend, Emperor Napoleon III, for help. In fact, I delivered that message personally."

Angelo looked at Sophie. "And that's when Napoleon came to the Pope's rescue."

Liszt smiled. "Yes, by June, Napoleon's French forces had indeed prevailed."

Saint-Saëns interjected proudly, "So, now you can see the Catholic-French connection that we've vowed to support."

Sophie looked puzzled. "But I always thought Garibaldi and Mazzini were good rebels, fighting for the unification of Italy?"

Liszt nodded. "Yes, the *Risorgimento*, or Resurgence, was a noble cause, inspired by the French Revolution and, oddly enough, even by Napoleon Bonaparte's conquest in 1800, as that yielded temporary unification. After Napoleon's demise, in 1815, the Italian peninsula was divided up between several European powers by the Congress of Vienna. The *Risorgimento* attempted to reclaim independence and unify all of Italy."

Now Saint-Saëns looked puzzled. "I recall you saying that Mazzini was your friend. How can that be if he was against Pope Pius and Napoleon III?"

Liszt smiled. "Actually, Mazzini's republican politics weren't bad, and certainly not evil, like this Prussian-German tyranny we now face." Liszt explained that Mazzini was a political thinker who favored a class-free republic with hints of socialism, which didn't resonate with all Italians. However, he also advocated educating the public about the importance of unification, since many Italians, especially in the south, were illiterate farmers. Liszt commended those actions, and was elated that Italy was finally unified in 1860 by Garibaldi's sweeping victories, which the famous general selflessly handed over to Victor Emmanuel II. As the train rocked, Liszt leaned over and partially closed the paisley curtain to block the sun from his eyes, as he continued, "However, as for Mazzini's earlier bid for power in 1848, that simply collapsed, as greater forces prevailed, namely, by Napoleon III. You see, the Bonapartes come from Italian stock and admire their heritage. In fact, Napoleon III helped the Italians to undermine Austrian rule, which eventually aided the process of achieving final unification, and he still has a garrison in the Papal State to protect Pope Pius. Some of our coded messages are designed to aid the Papal cause."

"I'm eager to meet the Emperor," Sophie said. "He sounds like a respectable man."

"*I* think so," Liszt replied. "His Highness certainly tries to be. In fact, I might just have you play for him."

"I'd be delighted. I think I'll play *The Blessing of God in Solitude* from your 'Harmonies poétiques et religieuses' set."

"That's a splendid choice," Saint-Saëns said in a dignified manner as he leaned over and stroked his beard. "It's utterly sublime. But, as for me, I'd opt for *Funérailles*. A funeral march is more apropos for these warring times." Looking at Liszt, he added, "It's truly a tour de force of lugubrious emotion. A masterpiece."

Liszt nodded graciously. "*Merci,* Camille. That was written as an elegy for my three rebel friends who failed to topple the Habsburgs in the Hungarian Revolution—which, by the way, also took place in 1848. As I said, there were revolutions all across Europe at that time, and they fueled Bismarck to be more aggressive." Liszt relayed what Otto later said, namely "The great questions of the time will not be resolved by speeches and majority decisions—that was the great mistake of 1848 and 1849—but by iron and blood!"

"That speech," Liszt continued, "is what earned him the moniker Iron Chancellor. And it is that iron man, wielding his secret Steel Blade, whom we are desperately trying to prevent from dominating all of Europe. So, as you see, Sophie, the world, as I said, was extremely restless then, but unfortunately, it still is."

Angelo had been gazing out the unblocked portion of the train window at ancient Roman ruins in the distance when he poignantly sighed, "Some things just never change. We rise, and then we fall."

Meanwhile, four train cars back, Inganni and Kiel were trailing along, yet not quite getting along.

"I get up for one minute, and you steal my seat?" Inganni acerbically barbed.

"What's the big deal? You can have the window seat on the way back. So, shut up!" Kiel snapped irritably.

Inganni rolled his eyes, then angrily squeezed his hefty rear into the aisle seat. Reaching down, he pulled out biscotti from his baggage and laid them on his lap. Picking one up, Inganni sniffed it, then bit into the delightful biscuit. As he did, crumbs fell all over his meaty chest.

Kiel gazed over with his piercing blue eyes and twisted his lips. "You're such a damn slob."

"Ah, you're just jealous, because stupid you never brings any food. Am I supposed to feel sorry for you?"

"This has nothing to do with you being sorry, Wally, it's all because you're pissed off that I took your stupid seat."

"Fine!" Inganni bellowed. "Take one! That's why you're so damn skinny. Learn to bring food next time."

Kiel grabbed one of the biscotti and bit into it with his crooked yellow teeth. "Hmm, these things taste better than they look. It tastes like nuts or something, right?"

"Right—you're nuts! Or something."

"Very funny, fatty!"

"Oh, that's intelligent."

"Well, if you're so damn smart, just tell me what's in this darned thing?"

Inganni's face softened. "Fine. Yes. It's made with pine nuts and almonds. In fact, Antonio Mattei won a special mention award at the Universal Exhibition of Paris three years ago. He's the one who made biscotti so popular. They're actually made with flour, eggs—"

"Christ!" Kiel rudely barked. "All I asked is what kind of nuts are in this stupid biscuit. Who gives a chicken's ass about the eggs in it, or about the complete history of biscotti? Are you going to write a book or something?"

"You want to know *something?* You're getting on my nerves," Inganni vented. "With each new mission, you become more and more like these ingredients—*Nuts!*"

"I'll tell you what's nuts," Kiel bellowed, "following Liszt for four years is nuts!"

"Shhh!" Inganni hissed. "You really are nuts! Keep your voice down, you moron." Anxiously, Inganni looked around.

Kiel wiped the long, greasy strands of blonde hair out of his eyes, then peevishly waved his hand. "Stop worrying so much. No one heard me." Out of the corner of his eye, Kiel spotted a ladybug on the train window and tapped the beetle's back with his thumb—taking delight in tormenting the little critter, before firmly squashing it. Looking at his kill, Kiel squinted and wiped the remains on his pants, as he nonchalantly continued, "Besides, like I said, we've been snooping and hunting for four years and we still have no clue how Liszt is encoding his *Dante Symphony*. And to be honest, I'm sick of hearing your crazy rants about how Liszt is the Devil. I told you I don't believe your idiotic religious superstitions, and I also told you that if this leads nowhere—I'm out of here! I do have a life and other interests, you know."

"You ungrateful jackass!" Inganni barked, now boiling with anger. "If it weren't for me, you'd be nothing but a worthless vagabond. Not that you're much more than that now, but I did get you the job at the stable, you dung-shoveling newt. So, what are you saying? You're bailing out on me?"

Kiel's upper lip curled. His patience was dying fast as his mind now fixated on his own secret agenda. "You think you know everything, Wally, but you don't. One day, soon, I'm really going to surprise you, so watch your step. But yeah, mark your stupid calendar, this is our last run together, then I'm out!"

The loathing in Inganni's eyes matched that in Kiel's.

Meanwhile the locomotive steamed across the Alps and finally pulled into the Gare du Nord in Paris. The huge and impressive terminal—featuring rows of pilasters and statues representing different destinations—had only been completed five years earlier and now welcomed the Altar Eagles and all the baggage that came with them.

Catching a royal carriage supplied by the Emperor, Liszt and his team rode past the famous Louvre museum and arrived at the Tuileries Royal Palace. Ordered to be built by Catherine de Medici in 1564, the grand sprawling edifice appeared to be a mile long and sported not only a stately exterior, but also an astoundingly ornate interior.

Passing through the main lobby, they proceeded down the central corridor. As they walked, some glanced down at the intricate designs of the parquet flooring, others up at the marble-trimmed walls with fluted columns, and still others at the colorful frescos in-between. All, however, marveled over the splendid collection of exotic and historic artifacts. The personal touches of many monarchs, from King Louis XIV to Napoleon Bonaparte, could be seen everywhere.

Arriving at the designated antechamber, they were instructed to wait until summoned. The foursome actually appreciated the twenty-five-minute wait, giving them pause to inspect and reflect on the historic frescos and relics.

Eventually, a stately-looking clerk beckoned them to follow, and led them into the emperor's private meeting chamber.

"Good to see you, Franz!" Napoleon said cheerfully, as he waved them to step forward. "And who do we have here?"

"These three are the top chain of command for the Altar Eagles," Liszt replied. "Here are Angelo Di Purezza, Camille Saint-Saëns and Sophie Menter."

Napoleon nodded, and turned toward Saint-Saëns. "Ah, my fellow Frenchman of whom Liszt has told me so much. He foresees great things from you, Camille. Yet I hear you are not his pupil, *per se*."

"That is true, Sire," Camille replied with a respectful nod. "I cannot claim the honor of having been his pupil, but I am a fervid admirer and champion of his work. And in twenty-four years from now, when I reach Liszt's current age, I hope to have composed at least half of the masterpieces he has, for then I will consider myself a colossal success."

Napoleon smiled. "Camille, you appear to be only in your thirties, so you have time to prove yourself. But you are, indeed, a humble and good friend to Liszt, and an honor to our country." As Saint-Saëns bowed graciously, Napoleon turned and continued, "And I see you now have a lovely lady among you. The pleasure is mine, *Mademoiselle*."

"Thank you, Sire," Sophie declared, as she assertively genuflected. "I can't wait to play for you!"

Bemused, Napoleon looked at Liszt, who winked with a paternal nod. "Yes, Sophie is the best woman pianist to ever emerge from my school. In fact, I consider her to be the greatest woman pianist alive. I'm proud to call her my daughter of the piano. So, please excuse her zeal, as I did tell her I would love to have her perform for you, *if* that pleases you?"

Sophie's shoulders sank, as her alabaster complexion blushed. Yet, to her glee, the emperor nodded. "I'd be delighted. Any student of Liszt's is worthy of my time, especially one garnering such high praise."

Napoleon then turned toward Angelo. "So, I assume you are the Altar Eagles' counterpart to Bismarck?"

Angelo bowed humbly, yet was somewhat perplexed. As his head rose, he said, "Well, in one regard, that is surely too great a compliment, since Bismarck is the shrewdest man on earth. But in another, I hope that in no way compares our moral fibers."

"Of course not, Angelo. It is just that your master has informed me of how resolute and resourceful you are, and I know how vital you are to your cause, despite your youth. Do know that I look upon the Altar Eagles with great affection, being keenly aware that you all willingly place your lives on the line for France and the Papacy. But before I go off into one of my monologues, help yourselves to a drink over there, then please have a seat. I must impart some *very* serious news."

The threesome filled their glasses with fine French wine, while Liszt grasped the bottle of cognac. As they took their seats, Napoleon sat on his massive, gilt-trimmed mahogany desk and pushed his calendar aside. "Ah, it is July 19, 1870, and I must be frank. Things are going dreadfully sour. Hence, why I instructed you to have a stiff drink first."

Taking the cue, Liszt downed a serious swig of cognac and firmly set down his glass. "I know that look, your Highness, and it's not good. What ails you and France now?"

"As you know," Napoleon began gravely, "Bismarck has been very active by instigating outright wars, such as the Austro-Prussian War, but he is also a conniving chess master. Over the past several years, he has managed to maneuver Tsar Alexander II of Russia to secretly stand against France."

"Ah!" Angelo interjected impulsively. "So if Prussia declares war on France, the Russians don't even need to join their effort or engage you on the battlefield. Just remaining neutral causes France enough harm."

"Yes, Angelo," Napoleon acknowledged. "Bismarck has managed to isolate France from all our possible allies. We stand alone."

Liszt shook his head reflectively, as he muttered, "I was never enthralled with Tsar Alexander II."

"Oh, yes," Saint-Saëns recalled. "He's the one that sabotaged your marriage to Carolyne ten-years ago."

"He certainly did," Liszt recollected painfully. "But, this time Alexander's cold shoulder presents far greater woes."

"Yes," Napoleon said. "And added to Russia's neutrality, which eliminates an ally to the east, is the other and more volatile chain of events going on in Spain, to the west. Two years ago, Queen Isabella II was dethroned, and Bismarck is adamant about instating Prince Leopold of Hohenzollern, a fellow German, to the Spanish throne."

Angelo almost leapt from his chair. "You can't let that happen, Sire! The noose is already too tight. My God! Have all our efforts been in vain?"

Liszt placed his hand on Angelo's arm. "Calm down. I'm sure the Emperor has a team of brilliant minds making plans."

As the foursome looked up at Emperor Napoleon III, regally decked out in his royal jacket of black velvet with bright red sash and gold ornamentation, his facial expression didn't match the authoritative power of his uniform, nor did his downward solemn gaze offer the least bit of comfort.

With a heavy heart, Napoleon gazed up, only to see four forlorn faces staring at him intently—making his task all the more difficult. "I'm pained to tell you that, eight days ago, I dispatched Count Benedetti to meet with Kaiser Wilhelm to settle this very issue of Prince Leopold assuming control in Spain. Benedetti informed my court that the meeting was not productive in any way, but certainly not a closed door, and—"

"And I'll bet a million francs," Angelo interjected, "that door is not only closed, but now locked shut by our iron-clad adversary, Otto von Bismarck."

Angelo's compatriots were mortified by his impudent outburst, but were even more fretful of what Napoleon's response might be.

The Emperor frowned, then sighed. "I'm afraid so. The conniving Chess Master has really put France in check this time." As the Altar Eagles sank in their seats, Napoleon's voice rose unexpectedly with determination and anger. "In fact, just before your arrival, Benedetti informed me that the press has issued a report on their meeting; and, quite deviously, Bismarck appears to have edited the Kaiser's response. The reply that the world and, more importantly, my Frenchmen are hearing is that *the Kaiser had nothing further to say to the ambassador.* Hence, the Prussians refuse to negotiate. There have already been uprisings throughout France, all clamoring for war. The Prussians have waved the red flag before the bull, and it is time for France to charge!"

"Not the Prussians, you mean Bismarck," Angelo huffed.

"Yes, Bismarck *is* Prussia," Napoleon acerbically declared. "The Chess Master has shrewdly maneuvered the French king into check, and now it is my duty to fight for all of France and pray that I can avoid checkmate."

Liszt rose to his feet. "What can we do? Just name it?"

Angelo followed. "I'll do whatever it takes."

Sophie eagerly chimed in, "I'm at your disposal, Sire."

Finally, Saint-Saëns stood up, and bellowed proudly, *"Viva la France!"*

Napoleon smiled. "It is noble actions like *that* that make dismal moments like *this* bearable."

Just then, the chamber door swung open, as a guard anxiously stuck his head in. "Excuse me, your Highness. But there are crowds mounting throughout the city. The people are enraged and asking what our response will be."

Irritated by the intrusion, Napoleon waved him away. "They'll have my response soon enough."

As the guard nervously closed the door, Napoleon gazed down at his guests. "I apologize that these pressing matters of state have coincided with your arrival." Looking at Sophie, he said, "Regrettably, my dear, I won't have the honor of hearing you play. Perhaps some other time, under clearer skies." Then turning toward Saint-Saëns, he said, "Keep the faith and transmit that faith to our French brothers." He then looked at Angelo. "Forever hold on to that fiery Italian spirit, that I and my great uncle share, but temper it with forethought." Finally his eyes fell upon Liszt. "And you, my dear friend, what can I say? You have graced me with your sublime God-given talents, as well as those of your flock, and have offered your life and those of your Altar Eagles to aid my endeavor—a cause that, I believe, stands as the last and only bulwark against this belligerent wave of Prussian hegemony."

With a tear welling in his eye, Liszt grasped Napoleon's hand and kissed it. "May God be with you and with all of us in our fight against tyranny."

Napoleon smiled, yet gently pulled his hand away. "The humble reverence of your kiss was unnecessary, but your words are most comforting, especially coming from such a selfless and noble man as you. You are a visionary giant in your field and a shining example among Christian men. I pray we meet again under better circumstances."

"I know in my heart that we *will* meet under clearer skies, your Highness. Until then, we remain your loyal servants," Liszt declared with resolve.

As the foursome bowed their heads, Napoleon gratefully nodded and looked back at Liszt. "I have but one immediate favor to ask of you?"

"Anything, Sire."

Napoleon handed Liszt a document. "Since your ex-son-in-law, Emile Ollivier, is my Prime Minister, I would like *you* to deliver my Declaration of War to him, so that we may officially commence this dirty business."

Liszt nodded as he received the Document of War. "As you wish, Sire. And, please, do not fail to call upon us again. We stand ready to serve you and France at a moment's notice."

Napoleon smiled warmly, yet his eyes shimmered with caution. "Your services will become even more frequent and dangerous once we engage battle, so please take all precautionary measures. I will have someone contact you at the appropriate time. I bid you *adieu,* my precious Altar Eagles. May you fly silently and safely."

Honoring Napoleon's request, Liszt dutifully located the office on the ground floor and delivered the document to Emile. Their brief meeting was bittersweet, bringing back warm memories of better days, when Emile and Liszt's daughter Blandine got married and the many family gatherings, but also the nightmare of Blandine's tragic death after childbirth. The paper now placed in Emile's hand had now only added an even greater weight of sorrow to their load and, more painfully, to all of Europe's.

As the Altar Eagles made their way toward the exit of the Tuileries Royal Palace through the main lobby, Sophie turned and stopped. She pointed down one of the long corridors. "The Louvre is down that way."

Angelo huffed. "I'm really in no mood to view artwork at a time like this, Sophie. Besides, the Louvre is outside, just around the corner."

"No, it isn't," Liszt said. "Well, actually it is, but the two buildings are attached."

Angelo rolled his eyes. "I still don't care to see any—"

"No, not art," Sophie interjected. "My newest recruit said he'd meet me at four-thirty in front of Delacroix's famous painting *Liberty Leading the People*. So, at least that's an appropriate work of art at a time like this. No?"

"No!" Angelo retorted. "Because that Revolution failed. I'd much rather see the marble bust of Marcus Agrippa."

"Marcus Agrippa?" Sophie said, her face radiating bewilderment. "I never heard of him."

Angelo shook his head. "It amazes me how so many women fawn over the pretty works of Boucher or our friend Ingres, but they have no clue about history or the men that truly shaped our world."

Sophie's feline spirit rose up and she verbally clawed back, "Oh, please! Spare me the male-greatness routine. You men have done nothing but make a mess out of everything!"

Angelo laughed. "Ah, yes, the aqueducts that Agrippa engineered caused a real mess, didn't they? What a shame that mankind was afforded the pleasure of bathing, or was supplied with water to drink and to wash clothing, or to flush our toxic waste away. Imagine the real mess we'd be in if men hadn't devised even that one marvel of ingenuity. And what about windmills, to grind our grain; or ships, to sail the seas; or complex architecture, to build our cities; or steam locomotives, to—"

Sophie was truly steamed, as she interrupted, "And who starts all these wars, like the one that was just launched right here today? Obtuse *men,* like Bismarck, Kaiser Wilhelm, Ivan the Terrible, Genghis Kahn, Nero, Alexander the really Great Murderer and a long chain of primitive barbarians."

"Oh, and I suppose *men* like Lucius Brutus, Augustus, Agrippa, Hadrian, Constantine, and Justinian were of no value to civilization? And that's just a short list of some of the great men who not only shaped their world, but largely created our advanced civilization."

Sophie peevishly put her hands on her hips. "I don't even know who half those men are, but—"

"Exactly!" Angelo declared. "That's my point. You, and, in fact, people in general, primarily focus on the evil monsters of history but not the enlightened molders of history. And to settle the score about only men being evil, I'll submit to you that women who attained any position of power throughout history proved to be no different from men. Care to hear a few names?"

Sophie's eyes turned and stared emptily at the opulent lobby wall, as Angelo commenced, "Well, there's Agrippina, wife of Emperor Claudius, who poisoned her husband to put her evil son Nero on the throne; the Hungarian Countess Elizabeth Báthory, branded the *Bloody Countess,* who is said to be one of the most prolific serial killers in history; then we have that lovely Queen *Bloody Mary* of England, who seemed to have a fondness for burning flesh; and there's even a serial killer out there right now, named Mary Ann Cotton, who's killing more people in England than the Steel Blade!"

"Shh!" Liszt hissed. "Tone it down, Angelo. That's enough." Gazing at both spirited youngsters, he continued, "Your points have been made and duly taken. But one thing I will not stand for is a house divided. So this debate is done." Glaring at Angelo, he added, *"Finito! Capisce?"*

"Si," Angelo replied respectfully, knowing that when Liszt spoke Italian it was an irrefutable command, yet graced with fatherly concern.

Liszt then performed the age-old practice of reconciliation by coaxing the two together and requiring them to 'kiss and make up'. With pseudo grins, Angelo and Sophie hesitantly leaned over and quickly pecked each other's cheek, then separated.

Feeling somewhat relieved, Liszt gave a paternal nod, then flipped open his pocket watch. He gazed down at the time, and snapped the lid shut. Pivoting around in the center of the lobby, he waved his hand for them to bring it in, and turned toward Sophie. "So the plan was for you to meet our newest member in front of Delacroix's *Liberty Leading the People*, correct?"

"Yes, at four-thirty."

"Very well, it is only four o'clock, so we have a half-hour to kill. So we might as well spend some time in the Louvre."

"Fine," Angelo said. "But in all honesty, I doubt my interests are the same as all of yours, and I'm not trying to be a royal thorn, but I'd rather explore some artifacts that I truly have an interest in. So I'll rendezvous with you at the Delacroix at four-thirty. Fair enough?"

"That's fine," Liszt replied. He then looked at Sophie and Saint-Saëns. "Are *we* at least in agreement to stick together?"

As the two nodded, Liszt exhaled. "Very well then. Let's examine some artwork."

Strolling down the corridor, they came upon the ground floor entrance to the Louvre. Making their donations, the threesome veered right and headed toward the stairs, while Angelo veered left.

As Angelo strolled down the hall, a troubling thought crossed his mind; namely, a half-hour would never be enough time to view all the artifacts he wished to see. With that, Angelo accelerated toward the Roman Antiquities wing. As he made his way through a motley array of people, he spotted a directional sign in the distance with an arrow pointing to the right. However, he noticed that the closer he got, the fewer people he saw.

Off to his left, Angelo spotted an old museum guard and decided to stop. "Excuse me, sir. Is the Roman Antiquities section closed? It appears there's nobody down there?"

The old guard seemed to have just awoken from his slumber, as he sluggishly looked over. "Oh, no, son, it's open. It's just that most people go to the Painting galleries upstairs."

Angelo's eyes rolled as he thought of Sophie. "So I see. Thank you very much."

Propelling himself down the corridor, he gazed up at the arrow, then made a quick right at the corner. As he did, he slammed into a lanky fellow, knocking him backwards. A metallic sound clattered as the young man quickly turned and picked up the object. Looking back at Angelo, his eyes squinted as he angrily shoved the metal, two-headed eagle into his pocket and then scurried off. Angelo turned and beckoned, *"Excusez-moi!"*

As Angelo swung around, his eyes suddenly beheld a most magnificent and heroic sight. Some twenty-feet away was the bust of Marcus Agrippa. A smile chiseled itself onto Angelo's statuesque face. Reverently, he approached and gaped at the incredible man who had fired his dreams. The workmanship of the ancient relic was stunning. Agrippa looked alive, as if someone merely whitewashed his face and then added faint shades of grays, blues, fuchsias and ochres.

The bust's strong features clearly captured the essence of the man, the loyal pillar who firmly supported Augustus, not only by engineering the great aqueducts that made Rome truly come alive with the all-important lifeline of water, but also by being the greatest general of his day. Agrippa was the unrivalled tactician and warrior who turned seemingly insurmountable odds into the most stupendous and influential victory in ancient times, allowing Augustus to give birth to the mighty Roman Empire.

Angelo stood in awe for an unusually long moment, wholly mesmerized by one of his all-time idols. He had often read the fascinating stories of the man's many struggles and victories, but he now found himself staring at Agrippa face to face—it was as if the elusive man in his dreams, who he hoped would empower him to make the Altar Eagles a success, was now transmitting his strength to Angelo, as though passing the baton and urging him to take the gift and run with it.

Meanwhile, upstairs, Sophie was immersed in her own world, one of blithe refinement. Drawn to François Boucher's idyllic French Rococo style, she happily gazed at the master's gracefully pleasing nudes in *Diana Bathing*.

Liszt and Saint-Saëns, on the other hand, had drifted two galleries away, and were scrutinizing and discussing the works of Jacques-Louis David, particularly his famous and dynamic equestrian portrait, *Bonaparte Crossing the Alps*.

Having examined David's slick and colorful technique, Liszt stepped back to capture the overall composition with its gallantly rearing horse. "It is truly an amazing piece. Yes?"

Saint-Saëns nodded. "Most certainly. And to think, David made five versions of this work. He's very much like you."

"I reckon so," Liszt said with a smile. "Some pieces compel the artist to make small alterations or even completely new versions. But not only is this work powerful, Camille, so too was the subject."

"Yes," Saint-Saëns replied as he scratched his beard. "But too bad that power got to his head."

Liszt's face grew solemn. "Yes, it did, but I must say, I wish our good friend Napoleon III had some of his uncle's military expertise. He'll need it now. However, I do admire his judicious nature, Camille, for making broadminded concessions. After all, he even appointed my liberal ex-son-in-law Émile Ollivier as his Prime Minister."

"Yes," Saint-Saëns replied wearily, "but now France stands alone against the Prussian Empire in this awful war, and as you say, Napoleon III is a good man, but no general."

"Oh, my! Wars for liberty. That reminds me," Liszt said, as he pulled out his pocket watch. "We're late. It is a quarter to five."

The two quickly scuttled to the Delacroix gallery, only to find a crowd of Parisians gathering in front of *Liberty Leading the People.* The news was out about the outbreak of war, and the Parisians were growing restless. Liszt and Saint-Saëns pushed their way through the crowd, looking for Sophie, but all they saw was a sea of strange, agitated faces.

A concerned look washed over Liszt's face as he turned toward Saint-Saëns. "Where on earth could she be? She's not one to ever be late."

"Maybe she met our new member and went someplace less crowded. After all, the Delacroix is kicking up a stir here."

"Indeed, it is," Liszt acknowledged, as he motioned towards an opening. "Let's go to the Boucher section. That's where I saw her last."

Pushing their way through the mounting crowd, the pair soon entered the next gallery. Walking past some of the exuberant works of Fragonard, Saint-Saëns looked up. "We must be getting close."

Liszt pointed. "I last saw her right there, looking at that sensual painting of women."

The two looked around some more, then tried several other galleries. Liszt turned and looked at Saint-Saëns. "This is beginning to worry me. Just what did Sophie say about this new member?"

"Well, I know she's never met him," Saint-Saëns replied anxiously. "But evidently he described himself so Sophie could recognize him. I believe she said he is thin with blonde hair and blue eyes. And his name is Karl." He then corrected himself. "Oh, no. Actually, his name is Kiel. Kiel Leiche."

Liszt squinted as he looked left and then right. "I think we had better go back near the Delacroix."

"But that gallery is becoming a madhouse."

"Yes, but haven't you noticed, we never saw Angelo either."

Saint-Saëns rubbed his bristly mustache. "Well, perhaps Sophie also met up with Angelo, and all three are at the café."

"Splendid idea, but let's pass the Delacroix on our way."

As they approached the gallery, the throng of patriotic Parisians was growing rapidly. Liszt and Saint-Saëns anxiously scanned all the seething and worried faces, but, again, no signs of their two friends. Moving down the corridor, they finally came upon the café. To their utter dismay, still *nothing*. Heading back towards the Delacroix, Liszt's head swiveled like that of an eagle seeking its lost fledglings. "Fine," Liszt said anxiously. "I'll give it fifteen more minutes before reporting this to the police."

Saint-Saëns' face registered his anxiety. Sending messages was one thing, but this deadly espionage game was starting to rattle his passive nerves. "Do you really think it's that serious?"

Liszt's eagle eyes continued scanning the crowd. "Well, it's just that you said this new member's name is Kiel. And after Napoleon said that our missions will become more dangerous in this Prussian war, I am truly hoping this Kiel Leiche is not an operative for the Steel Blade."

Just hearing those two chilling words made Saint-Saëns' frayed nerves all the more ragged. Adding further to his worries, he suddenly spotted a hefty young man barreling toward them with a crazed look on his face.

Saint-Saëns fretfully elbowed Liszt. "Dear God! Could this be the Steel Blade?"

Liszt's keen eyes perceptively noticed the young fellow's white collar underneath his plain clothes. "No, no. Not *steel.* He's a man of the *cloth.*"

Inganni almost collided into Liszt, having all he could do to stop his momentum. As Liszt recoiled, Inganni bellowed frantically, "You must help me stop him!"

"Stop whom?" Liszt asked, perplexed.

"Kiel," Inganni cried. "We must find him, *fast!* The lunatic has really gone mad!"

"Kiel!?" Liszt exclaimed.

"Yes, I can explain later, but your friend Sophie is in grave danger. Kiel must be stopped. Do you have a firearm?"

"No, but where in Heaven's name are they?" Liszt pressed.

"I'm not sure," Inganni moaned. "He only said he would meet her by that Delacroix, and kill her. That was before he assaulted me." Inganni turned his head and pointed to his swollen cheek and red ear, then added, "As I've said, you really should have a weapon. Kiel is dangerous and must be terminated." He moved his head to and fro as his intrusive eyes scanned their garments. "Are you sure neither of you have a firearm?"

Liszt huffed. "I said we're both unarmed. We'll just have to track him down." Quickly, Liszt turned toward the stairs. "He certainly would want to steer Sophie away from this busy crowd. So I suspect he cajoled her down to the ground floor, and may have already exited the building."

Liszt and Saint-Saëns sprinted to the staircase and flew down the steps, as Inganni struggled to keep pace. Reaching the bottom, they were overcome by a wave of emotions as they scanned the area.

Liszt's eyes suddenly lit up. "Let's go to the Roman Antiquities gallery."

Saint-Saëns grinned. "Right. *Angelo.*"

As they ran down the corridor, the same dozing guard looked up and yelled, "Hey! *Slow down!* What's your rush? None of these statues are going anywhere."

Liszt stopped, as the others kept running toward the gallery. He then peered at the crotchety old guard. "Did you happen to see a young Italian-looking fellow, about twenty-one years of age, with a thick mane of black wavy hair?"

"Actually, I did. Twice," he snarled.

"I see, so he went into the Roman gallery and then left?"

"Yes," the guard grumbled. "I remember him well because he asked me if the gallery was open. Then he ran out of here, just like you three rascals. But, I must say, you three look too old to be horsing around like this. You should all be ashamed. Show some respect, for God's sake. After all, you're in a—"

"Thank you!" Liszt said, truncating the conversation. He quickly turned and called out, "Camille, this way!"

As Liszt backtracked to the lobby, Saint-Saëns and Inganni followed in quick succession.

Meanwhile, Angelo was up on the first floor in a dark corner of the building that was sectioned off for renovations. He had burst through the double doors and into what would soon be an exhibition of works by Caspar David Friedrich.

Friedrich's dark and mysterious works hung on the walls, adding a foreboding gloominess to what Angelo now feared—there before his eyes was Sophie, her eyes staring wide and her mouth covered by Kiel's boney hand. Pressing at her throat was a razor-sharp metal pendant of a Prussian two-headed eagle.

Flashing his yellow dagger-like teeth, Kiel hissed like a python, as he constricted his prey. Sophie felt the sting of fear running rampant through her veins, but didn't want to end up a corpse. She thrust her elbow back and tried to wriggle free, but Kiel pulled her head back and slid the steely blade-like edge of the pendant across her neck. As the eagle's talons scratched a shallow gash in her skin, a thin bead of blood formed.

Angelo yelled, "Stop! Why would you want to kill an innocent woman?"

Kiel snarled. "Innocent woman? No. She's a damn traitor, Angelo."

Angelo flinched. "How do you know my name?"

"I know the names of *all* you Altar Eagles. And *none* of you are innocent."

Angelo crept forward. "Well, I'm sure we can work this out, somehow. What exactly do you want?"

Kiel sniggered. "I don't know, perhaps to kill you all."

Angelo squinted. "So did *you* kill our four comrades?"

Kiel hesitated, but then an eerie look of depraved pleasure washed over his sinister face. "Uh, yeah…I sure did. You must admit, the way I slaughtered them was pretty shocking. I sure know how to make headlines." He paused, as his crazed blue eyes rolled downward. "But I'm fed up that no one knows my name. However, that *will* change, today."

Hearing the unstable cretin boast of his wicked deeds, capped by his desire to seek eternal fame, Angelo feared the worst, and took a larger step forward.

Kiel looked up and dragged Sophie back, as he snarled, "You better stop where you are, Angelo, or, I swear, you *will* see how I carve up my victims. And it won't be pretty."

Angelo froze in his tracks. His eyes had already spotted a crowbar on the scaffold just to his right; he only needed another three feet to be within reach. He decided to keep distracting the deranged braggart while he ever so slightly inched sideways. Swallowing hard, Angelo began speaking as he imperceptibly moved. "Very well, but I must tell you, I truly doubt that you killed my fellow Eagles. First of all, look at you. You're a scrawny little weasel." Kiel's lips twisted with rage, as Angelo strategically continued, "Second, you're holding a Prussian pendant. As you must know, three of our friends died by the cross. So I think you're just a little vermin trying to steal someone else's handiwork."

Kiel's spidery neck veins almost burst, as he blasted, "Steal someone else's work!? Are y-you k-kidding?" he stammered angrily, as his mind short-circuited. "I'm sick of that fat fool Wally t-thinking he deserves all the c-credit. And I'm s-sick of him calling me stupid. I had enough, and it's time I get some g-goddamn respect! I'm more of a man than he'll ever be."

Angelo shook his head. "It doesn't take a man to kill someone, it just takes hate—and it certainly isn't manly to kill a woman, so why don't you let her go, and we can settle this man to man? Or is the pathetic little weasel too scared?"

Kiel's sorely maligned ego surged to critical mass, as Sophie adroitly kicked his shin and Angelo grabbed the crowbar. Bringing it around, Angelo hammered Kiel's arm, knocking the deadly pendant out of his hand. Sophie bit down hard on Kiel's other hand as Angelo kicked the metal eagle away and lunged for Kiel's throat. The bulging veins in Kiel's neck, along with his windpipe, were now pinched, as he feverishly gasped and choked for air.

Just then, the double doors of the gallery swung open as Liszt flew in, followed by Saint-Saëns and Inganni.

Liszt yelled, "Angelo, stop!"

But Angelo's ears were blocked with rage, as he tried to block the oxygen from feeding Kiel's evil lungs.

Sophie grabbed Angelo's muscular arms and pulled, but it was useless.

Liszt shouted in Italian, "Angelo, *Basta!*"

The peremptory order deactivated Angelo's homicidal hex, as his hands slowly released their deadly grip. With his enraged mind beginning to clear, Angelo's hands fell to his side as he stepped back.

Saint-Saëns swiftly grabbed Kiel and firmly sat him down. Grasping a piece of rope off the scaffold, he tied Kiel's hands. Meanwhile, Sophie wrapped up her injured neck and then picked up the pendant and crowbar. Thoughts of using them flashed through her mind, but she managed to hand the pendant to Liszt, opting to hold on to the crowbar, just in case.

Liszt shook his head angrily, as he turned toward Inganni. "This is outrageous! I demand some answers."

Inganni smoldered with animus. "Very well, this all began four years ago. And I must confess, Maestro, that I deplore your evil music, as that started this whole evil chain of events."

Liszt squinted. "My evil music? What in God's name are you talking about?"

"I'm talking about your deadly *Dante Symphony, Signore* Liszt. And I mean deadly in more ways than one."

The Altar Eagles all looked at one another, not sure just how much this equally mysterious young man knew.

Liszt entreated him. "Tell me, how so is it deadly?"

Inganni haughtily crossed his arms. "I know your fiendish symphony evokes evil spirits—just because I was unable to decode your little secret doesn't mean something sinister isn't going on. And the blasphemous laughter that your infernal music clearly emits is even marked in your score. I've seen it with my own eyes."

Liszt snickered. "Sometimes I don't know if I should laugh or cry at fanatical critics like you. But it just so happens I know most of my musical critics—who take great joy in smearing my name and music in the tabloids—but you, young man, are no music critic. You are, however, clearly a fellow brother of the Catholic Church. So, just who are you?"

Inganni self-consciously tried to cover his collar, but then proudly unveiled it, as he piously raised his nose. "Actually, I am Monsignor Waldo Inganni, and it is utter blasphemy that you think you're a man of the cloth. I also know, *Signore* Liszt, that you use your *Dante Symphony* as a cipher for Emperor Napoleon. So there is little I do not know about *you* or your Altar Eagles."

Angelo stepped forward. "Yes, Kiel, over there, just told me that they've been following us for years." Then looking at Inganni, he added, "So for you to claim being so righteous, when your friend was killing us off, doesn't make you—," Angelo's train of thought suddenly switched tracks, as his eyes widened. "Wait a minute! Who's to say that *you* didn't commit some of those murders yourself?"

Kiel looked up. "Yeah, he did! I'm not taking all the blame for this. I used a Prussian pendant to kill my enemies because I'm loyal to the Prussian Crown. But the high and mighty monsignor always used crucifixes to do God's work. Look at him!" Kiel blasted with incriminating venom. "The fat zealot killed in the name of the Church. And I'm sick of covering for him and his stupid crusade."

As they all turned and stared at Inganni, he stepped backward, startled. "Now wait a minute! Think for a second. Why in God's good name would I come to alert you that Kiel was going to kill Sophie? Huh? Tell me that?"

Saint-Saëns looked at Liszt as he rubbed his bearded chin. "Yes, he did. This is getting very confusing."

Inganni stepped forward with confidence and waved his hand. "No, no. It's not confusing at all. Allow me to explain. Kiel and I grew up together in Leipzig. Yet as you can see, he is profoundly unstable, and has always been an avid Prussian. And like a true Prussian, he often does cruel things. As such, I felt compelled by the good Lord to act as his big brother to rectify Kiel's perpetual lapses into sin. So, yes, I did ask him to help me shadow you, but that was just to gather evidence; proof that your *Dante Symphony* not only emits dissonant words of the Devil, but also transmits your coded messages for the French Crown. He's the one with an evil political agenda. I never had any intentions of killing anyone. After all, I'm a monsignor. *He's your killer!"*

"You sanctimonious rat!" Kiel blasted. "You're nothing but a religious butcher!" With that, Kiel sprang to his feet and lunged at Inganni. Angelo quickly grabbed Kiel's tied hands and subdued him, while Sophie took delight in gagging his mouth with a dirty rag she had found on the floor.

Liszt shook his head. "Take the rag out of his mouth, Sophie. There are two sides to this crazy story and we must hear his as well, despite his already criminal actions towards you."

Sophie leaned over and grudgingly yanked the rag out, as Kiel cleansed his teeth with his tongue and spit the gritty saliva on the floor. Looking up at Liszt with his youthful, crazed eyes, Kiel pleaded his case. "Fine, I hated school and dropped out. Big deal. So did many kids in my village. Just because Wally's father made him a bigwig in the Vatican doesn't mean he's smart or an innocent man of God. In fact, he's a filthy traitor to my Lutheran heritage and a murderer. And what crime is it to love your country? Aren't all of you fighting for *your* country?"

"That's true, Kiel," Liszt replied. "But we are fighting to *defend* our nation or religion. Meanwhile, Prussia is a belligerent *instigator* of war, and that's an entirely different matter. And although I'll agree with you that many people forgo getting an education, or have deep national sympathies, what I cannot condone is a person who does not question those sympathies when their nation is violently pulverizing others with an iron fist. And it doesn't require any schooling at all to realize the difference. In your case, all one needs is a solid foundation in morals, not a diploma. Now I shall ask you one last time, who killed my three students with bronze crucifixes?"

Without blinking an eye, Kiel squealed, "Monsignor Inganni!"

With that, Inganni spit in Kiel's face and made a break for it, pushing his way out the double doors. Angelo quickly ran out after him and grabbed his collar. With a sense of vindication, he gripped the wily monsignor in a headlock and dragged him back, making sure to use his head as a battering ram to open the doors. Inganni squirmed and squealed, but Angelo held on firmly to his catch.

Liszt shook his head, stunned in disbelief. "Well, I think that's as good of a confession as we'll ever get."

"Oh, I'll gladly confess," Inganni snapped. Unexpectedly, he pulled out a bronze crucifix and lunged at Liszt's neck. Liszt recoiled while Angelo grabbed the weapon and subdued Inganni once again, and spat, "That certainly was a dramatic confession, Monsignor." He slapped him in the head, and added, "But this time just use your words!"

Inganni snarled. "Very well, you heathens! I was chosen by the Lord to serve *Him,* but Kiel is a lunatic who idolizes the Kaiser! Moreover, he's a traitorous Lutheran who had the temerity to assault *me,* the Lord's Praetorian Angel, and threatened to reveal and steal all the glory of my sacred mission. For that, Kiel should be *shot!"* Wiping his heated lips, he pointed at Kiel. "That Jackass Judas had targeted Sophie due to her political leanings, which interest me not. Your Lady Eagle harbored no religious agenda, and *that's* why she was worthy of salvation in my merciful eyes. I should be lauded, not lampooned! Meanwhile, *you,* my deceitful abbé, are a satanic snake, one that spews the worst kind of venom. You're a charlatan. And your vocal chords should be severed, just like those of your disciples'—*by the cross!* Who the hell are you to come out of nowhere to bewitch the Pope with your music, while I struggled through school and the seminary only to be ridiculed and reprimanded by that unPius fool? I am a far holier man than you, Abbé Liszt, and a true servant of the Lord. *I despise you!"*

Angelo twisted Inganni's arm behind his back and gave it a good solid yank. As he groaned, Liszt stepped closer. "Monsignor, I confess that I have not lived a life by the Good Book in every regard, but then again, neither has any other mortal who ever walked this earth, despite what they may say. We have all sinned at one time or another, hence the need for confession and contrition. But to live a life of giving back to one's brothers and sisters has truly been a lifelong practice of mine, a practice that I don't engage in to judge others, but rather to help others. I, too, have worked my fingers to the bone, Monsignor, practicing eight to fourteen hours a day for many years and performing for kings and queens like a show dog in a circus. Believe me, it almost drove me mad with depression, but one must pick oneself up and focus on the true goals that God has planned for us. So, can you truly say that brutally murdering my students was God's plan for you? And are you pleased with your gruesome deeds?"

"Yes!" Inganni blustered. "I am most pleased. Many have read the Bible—including petty abbés *like you*—yet they overlook or choose to ignore critical passages. My father may have been a domineering bastard, but at least he was wise enough to drill these passages in my head, such as Luke 19:27, for even Jesus said, 'Bring me my enemies who will not have me reign over them, *and slay them before me.*' And, *you, Signore* Liszt, and your evil litter, are God's enemies. Do you think I'd allow your disciple Kristian to sing of your praise on the organ in Church? Not a chance! And your two other winged demons I managed to silence in alleys. So, guided by the Lord, I have slain God's enemies. My only regret was not being able to silence *you!*"

Liszt shook his head pityingly. "Monsignor, you have fixated on a verse in the Bible that just so happens to be out of character for Jesus, and took it upon yourself to radically act upon it. I do not believe every word in the Bible to be the utter truth; after all, it was not written by God, but rather by Jesus' mortal, and quite fallible, disciples some forty to seventy years after his death. Hence, misinterpretations or fanatical fabrications must exist within our Good Book. Yet, some people have a tendency to become obsessed with passages that advocate violence, thus giving them a fraudulent free pass to commit crimes or even murder. Evidently your father put you on a most ungodly path." Liszt looked Heavenward.

"Dear Lord, please forgive this lost child, who is consumed with hate, and may he find the true light of your grace."

The double doors swung open as two policemen entered with drawn pistols, followed by the same old museum guard they had encountered earlier. The disgruntled guard waved his finger at Angelo, then at Liszt. "They're the two fellows I saw running, officers! I knew they were up to no good."

One policeman smiled. "Master Liszt! How good to see you."

"Marcel?" Liszt replied. "Is that really you, wearing a police uniform?"

"Yes, I do apologize," Marcel said, somewhat embarrassed, "but after learning how difficult it was to be a concert pianist, I decided to get a normal job."

Liszt smiled. "Well, it won't be normal much longer, once I tell you how *abnormal* this situation is. Let me explain."

Marcel listened to Liszt's deposition, then turned to interrogate the suspects. All were taken aback by Kiel's horrifying confession, including Inganni, who had no idea of the extent of his former friend's political intrigues or homicidal madness. Kiel revealed his covert affiliation with the Steel Blade, but then boasted of his twenty-seven kills; giving gruesome details of how he surgically sliced or brutally chopped up his victims. It was painfully clear; Kiel was insane, yet extremely proud to have beaten the monsignor's record. His feeble mind had been plagued by inadequacy, indecision, hatred, and revenge, but Kiel now seemed to glow in an eerie light of self-exultation.

Meanwhile, Inganni held his swollen cheek as he damned and demeaned his deranged old friend in typical fashion, all while maintaining his self-righteous air of innocence. Afterwards, Marcel stated his plans. Kiel would be handed over to Napoleon's private guard for further interrogation, while Inganni would be extricated and sent to Rome for the triple homicide. Each, he said, would then be a potential candidate for an insane asylum. Marcel and his partner grasped Inganni and Kiel and escorted them out to the *fourgon cellulaire*. With a crack of the whip, the horses bucked, and the prison wagon rode off.

Meanwhile, the pestering old guard, after learning the identity of the celebrities before him, graciously allowed the Altar Eagles to view the Caspar David Friedrich Exhibit, seeing that they would be leaving town soon. He lit the gas lamps and moved the scaffold to the center of the gallery, giving them access to view all four walls of paintings.

Sophie enjoyed gazing at *Chalk Cliffs on Rügen*, but found Friedrich's other works too dark and mysterious. Saint-Saëns wasn't thrilled about viewing the German's artwork, now that France was at war, however Angelo and Liszt found Friedrich's work mesmerizing. Caspar's dark and twisted Romantic landscapes were imbued with symbolism, and it opened their imaginations to exploring metaphysical worlds of time, space, and their own mysterious existence.

As Liszt and Angelo circled the room, they savored Friedrich's haunting *Graveyard under Snow*, and then moved onto his arresting vision, *The Sea of Ice*. At first sight, they were struck by its dramatic and almost abstract quality, yet it immediately became tragic upon seeing the wrecked ship, entangled in the icy shards of ice and snow. Nearing the end of the gallery, both men stopped in their tracks. In awe they gazed at *The Wanderer above the Sea of Fog*. Here they saw a solitary man perched at the top of a rocky mountain, peering out over an immensely vast and cavernous vista laden with fog. At first glance, it appeared as if he stood bravely at the top of the world, yet, with his back to the viewer, perhaps he was fearful of the cavernous drop or even mindful of his own insignificance. Liszt and Camille felt compelled to put themselves in the wanderer's shoes, as the conflicting feelings of exhilaration, fear, and insignificance collided, forcing them to draw their own conclusions. Liszt smiled, elated, as Camille squinted, unsettled.

Breaking their reverie, the guard nervously informed them that their private showing had to be terminated—the curator was on his way with the work crew. As they were exiting the gallery, Liszt spotted Friedrich's last painting, *The Cross in the Mountains*. It was unlike any rendition of the crucifixion he had ever seen. Here, Christ's lone cross stood atop Golgotha in the distance, as a trinity of rays illuminated the sky behind him. Liszt crossed himself, then ran to catch up to his valiant Eagles.

As the curator and renovation crew walked past, the Eagles gazed at each other with mischievous smiles. Liszt, however, was pained when he heard the curator give instructions to dismantle the "potentially riotous German exhibition." Despite the Kaiser and Bismarck's quest for hegemony, Liszt knew very well that not all Germans were monsters, nor were the millions of others from foreign countries who were now at odds with France or the Papacy. He had always prided himself for being a worldly man who embraced all countries and tolerated all religions, but, with the volatile world now spinning out of control, it seemed to offer fewer chances to embrace all these brothers at war.

As they made their way toward the exit, Liszt peered at Angelo. "I meant to ask you, how did you ever find Sophie?"

Angelo grinned. "Well, for once, I decided not to be late for a rendezvous. So I ran upstairs to get there first, hoping to impress all of you. But, to my surprise, no one was there, except that odd-looking specimen that I had earlier bumped into downstairs—namely, Kiel."

Liszt chuckled. "How odd, indeed. But despite Kiel looking a bit strange, how did that make you suspicious?"

"Well, it wasn't so much his peculiar looks. You see, when I bumped into him earlier, that Prussian, two-headed eagle pendant fell from his coat. Not being too trusting of

Prussians these days, I found it odd that he was standing by Delacroix's painting of the French Revolution, especially since he clearly looked like he was waiting for someone. And, lo and behold, Sophie appeared. I decided to stay out of sight and follow them, but then that pesky old guard caught me in the hall again, browbeating me with warnings." As Liszt laughed, Angelo added, "Luckily, I managed to run down the corridor where I had last lost sight of them, and, fortunately, I arrived just in time."

"You can say that again," Sophie interrupted.

As the team looked over, Angelo inquired, "So, how is that neck of yours doing? A little while ago I wanted to ring it, but it now appears that I saved it."

As they all laughed, Sophie smiled. "Yes, indeed, you did. And that reminds me, I haven't thanked you yet."

Sophie walked over, affectionately wrapped her arms around him, and genuinely kissed him on each cheek.

Angelo humbly nodded. "My pleasure, sister Eagle."

As they exited the Louvre, Saint-Saëns turned to bid his good friends *adieu*. He would now leave the Altar Eagles to put on a uniform to fight for his country. Despite his resolve, Camille expressed his fear of war and the greater fear of Prussia's seemingly invincible forces. With a last embrace, they parted, as the Altar Eagles returned to the Gare du Nord and took the next train back to Rome.

Nine days later, on July 28, 1870, Napoleon III left Paris for Metz. Against the better judgment of some of his advisors, the Emperor assumed command of an army that he was told would grow as the French mobilization progressed. Napoleon was given all indications by his military leaders that his forces would be twice the size of his enemy's. It wasn't.

The battle would be exceedingly short, yet excruciatingly disastrous. In one month, Napoleon was ensnared in a losing battle at Sedan, and humiliatingly ushered before Bismarck.

The Prussian Chess Master had indeed cornered the French Emperor and thrust France into checkmate. That Napoleon had opted to personally lead his army into war meant that his Second French Empire fell with him.

The dreadful news of defeat spurred the French to quickly form a makeshift Third French Empire. Even Garibaldi rode to their rescue. Yet, it, too, would fall a mere five months later. The Prussian's siege of Paris ignited total chaos, giving birth to the Paris Commune, a last ditch effort by the proletariat. Yet the bloody writing was on the wall.

During this time, Saint-Saëns managed to be discharged and fled to London, as Karl Marx began writing his pamphlet *The Civil War in France*. Marx praised the Paris Commune for being a working prototype of his earlier devised and strongly advocated Dictatorship by the Proletariat. Neither Marx's idea nor the Commune proved effective and France collapsed, giving Bismarck's Prussian Empire a full-blown victory and a larger chunk of Europe.

The Prussian triumph also caused repercussions in Rome, as Pope Pius IX lost his friend Napoleon's support, thus ending the sovereign status of the Papal States and stripping the papacy of all its temporal powers. The downsized and now politically impotent Vatican would never again be a factor in the political landscape; that domain was now dominated by Bismarck's newly united and enlarged German Empire.

By 1888, Bismarck's longtime friend and Prussia's figurehead, Kaiser Wilhelm I, had died, leading to the rise of his nephew Wilhelm II. Young Wilhelm was not enthralled by Bismarck's unfettered powers or his patronizing manner, and this led to bad blood. Open disagreements finally led to Wilhelm's insistence that Bismarck resign. As such, Kaiser Wilhelm II now assumed full control of the German battleship, thus "dropping the pilot" and boldly sailing into a new and bloody chapter of world history. The new Kaiser would befriend and empower the chemist Fritz Haber after the turn of the century to create a whole new method of warfare, one with blistering consequences.

During these turbulent years, Liszt died in 1886, yet his stalwart Eagle, Angelo Senior, kept pursuing the dream, despite the fact that the Altar Eagles officially disbanded upon the death of their beloved Master. With Liszt's paternal guidance and covert training, bolstered by the spirit of Agrippa surging through his veins, Angelo Senior dedicated his life to his secret mission of sabotaging the German war machine at all costs, a mission that he vowed never to reveal to his son Angelo Jr., born in 1880—his only surviving kin, after Lisa and Angela met untimely deaths. He resolved also never to tell his son of his own impetuous nature or weaknesses, hoping to prevent fate from passing on his flaws. He would groom young Angelo to acquire all the attributes he so admired in Liszt and Agrippa, and would do anything in his power not to jeopardize his precious son's life. But fate is unpredictable.

*S*CENE V: BERLIN, ROME & BASEL [1934]

Angelo Jr. and Mildred returned to Berlin from Basel, Switzerland on January 30, 1934. Their heads were still numb with the shocking news of Fritz Haber's death. After all of Angelo's shadowing and the near-death confrontation in the park, Fritz had died of natural causes, which the doctors labeled 'Heart Failure'. Yet, Angelo wondered—had *he* brought on the heart attack with his altercation down by the Rhine? Worse yet, had Haber's pleas of innocence been truthful, or had Haber lied and deviously killed his father? Now he would never know.

The next morning, Angelo and Mildred arrived for work as usual at the Kaiser Institute. As they walked into the lobby, a large congregation of scientists, administrators, and dignitaries were gathered to commiserate the loss of one of their leading scientists. However, with the new Nazi regime in power, not all mourned the loss of the Jew-turned-Christian-turned-silent-Jew who had died in Switzerland only a few days after touring his homeland in Jerusalem.

Being greeted by a barrage of Hitler salutes, which was now a state obligation, the couple tepidly raised their right hands in return and made a brief round of small talk. Angelo then signaled to Mildred with a shift of his eyes, as the two slipped away down the hall and entered his office.

"My God," Mildred said, unnerved. "What's happening to Germany? I just don't feel at home here anymore."

"Nor do I," Angelo said, "especially with this crazy Hitler salute and all those red banners with swastikas everywhere." He walked over to his desk, yet as he peered down, his eyes froze. "Oh, my God! Someone stole my score of the *Dante Symphony*."

Mildred rushed over and looked down. The bottom drawer of his desk had been pried open—the wood splintered and the lock broken. "Who do you suppose did this?"

Just then, Rudolf Hein walked in. "I did."

Angelo and Mildred turned.

"I figured as much," Angelo smirked. "But where do you come off breaking into my desk? That score is a priceless heirloom."

Hein abruptly kicked the door shut, then stood militantly erect with his hands behind his back. "I suggest you two sit down and pay close attention this time. I made it perfectly clear—even before you left on your little vacation—that there's been a change of command around here."

As Angelo and Mildred unhappily took their seats, Hein continued, "This no longer is a private operation; the Nazi state now calls all the shots. And thank God for that, because I was growing sick and tired of that flimsy liberal Weimar Republic and its pathetically degenerative ways. Hitler has rightly begun the very open process of eliminating the Jews from all positions of authority. No more cover-ups! So get this straight, the Socialist Bolsheviks are being discharged, and the Third Reich is the New World Order!"

"You mean Disorder, don't you?" Angelo snapped sardonically.

Hein cracked a sinister grin. "Very funny, Angelo. Almost as funny as when your father died trying to sabotage the efforts of our beloved Bismarck and both Kaisers."

Angelo sprang to his feet. "Watch yourself, Rudy, I don't care if you *are* the new Bismarck around here, I'll—"

"Shut up!" Hein barked. "Sit down! Or I'll have my guards drag your ass out of here before you can even blink."

Mildred grasped Angelo's arm. "Honey, please sit."

Angrily, Angelo sat, as Hein chuckled. "How sweet. I suspected you two would bond. You both have weak constitutions, and I know that *you,* Mildred, are not even a pedigree. Your rich Aryan blood has been contaminated with Tuscan impurities. So you truly deserve one another."

Angelo's face radiated contempt. "Is this what your little meeting is all about—blowing your pompous Aryan horn."

Hein's haughty grin turned dead serious and direct. "No. Actually, it's a warning and an offer."

"So, let's hear them."

"The warning is this: you better decide which team you're on, *mine* and the Nazis, or *yours* and the Nonentities."

Angelo shook his head. "It doesn't look good for you, Hein. So, what's the offer?"

Hein revealed the *Dante* score he held concealed behind his back. "It's simple: join my team, and I will provide you with privileged information regarding your father's death."

As Hein repeatedly tapped his fingers on the leather bound score, Angelo looked at Mildred.

"Ah, ha!" Hein exclaimed. "The first sign of a castrated male. You must purge that feminine liberal nonsense from your head and crotch, Angelo. I asked *you,* a male scientist, this question, *not* Mildred, a mere, feline secretary. Women are of little use to me."

"Of course women are of little use to you, Rudy. We all know you find men more attractive."

Hein slammed the booklet down on the desk. "You're trying my patience, Angelo! This is the last time I'll ask you. Are you joining me or not?"

Angelo took a deep breath and exhaled. "Fine! Yes."

"That had better be a genuine yes," Hein said as he wiped the hair out of his domineering eye, "because if I find out you're still playing around with this *Dante* score, and going on wild goose hunts, I *will* take firm action, not only against you, but also against your pretty little *Fräulein* here.

Angelo had all he could do to restrain himself, as he retorted, "Fine! I understand. But how did you know I was going on—"

"Know this," Hein interrupted. "I know everything around here, so there's no sense in trying to outsmart me, because it won't happen. I'm much older, wiser, and seasoned. I have scratched my way up to the top and even have the full clout of Ernst Röhm and others backing me. I could have easily taken Max Planck's position here, but like Röhm, Göring, Goebbels, Himmler, Hess and many other new friends of mine, I understand that greater power can be wielded from the sidelines—in the shadows." Hein whipped his head back in his uniquely vain fashion, and placed one hand on his hip. "So, now that we've got that out of the way, allow me to enlighten you about your father's little score."

Angelo and Mildred's eyes followed Hein as he began pacing. "Your father was meddling in affairs that he shouldn't have been. Although his dossier had little *bona fide* information as to what sort of activities he was engaged in, it seemed apparent that he was just a small-time rebel."

As Angelo grew fidgety, Hein intrepidly continued, "Back in those days, I was just an assistant to Fritz Haber, but we developed many unique compounds together—some being completely of my own invention. So I fully intend to go through the records to properly assign which chemicals he produced and which ones I created. However, this brings me to your father and the mystery surrounding his death. Kaiser Wilhelm II would not tolerate any delays in getting our poison gas to the battlefields. So, naturally, when we learned that your father was planning to destroy our production facility, he had to be stopped."

"Hold on!" Angelo interjected. "I'll admit that my father may have been involved in some sort of minor spy ring, but now you're telling me it was high-level military sabotage? I don't buy it."

Hein stopped pacing, as he, once again, brushed the hair out of his eye. "Why else would he be eliminated?"

"Wrong again, Rudy. The newspapers and death certificate said he died of a ruptured appendix."

Hein laughed as he picked up the booklet. "I've seen you and Einstein many times fondling this score, and there's no way two scientists, especially of Einstein's caliber, could miss the poison stains on here."

Angelo's tense and half-risen body softly sank back into his chair. "Fine, so we deciphered the poison. Go on."

Hein smiled. As he resumed pacing, he again tapped the score against his open palm, savoring his ever-winning arguments. "So, the question that I know has been driving you mad for quite some time is this: Who put the poison there?"

"And I suppose you're just going to tell me?"

Hein grinned. "Why not? After all, we *are* intelligent scientists that run on cold logic, not hot emotions, and you *are* on my team, correct?"

Angelo forced a smile and an amicable nod, which even he was proud of.

Buying the gesture, Hein threw the score onto Angelo's lap. "Well, I hate to ruin all your hard work searching for the answer to this painful mystery, but the culprit is now dead. It was our good friend and colleague Fritz Haber."

Angelo's mind was buzzing. He had believed from day one that it was Haber, but now Rudy seemed to throw a wrench in the killing machine. He seemed too cocky. And why did he offer this information now—because he's guilty and Haber is conveniently dead? Or is he telling the truth? After all, Haber had been the kingpin, and many of his colleagues did say Haber was guarded with his early discoveries. Angelo's mind was churning the damning data like a gristmill. *When will this damn wound ever heal?*

Suddenly, Angelo recalled his father's often-repeated motto, to tame the nerves and hone the wit. Taking a deep breath, Angelo regained his calm, as he tactically looked up. "Actually, that's what I suspected, Rudy. Of course I was never able to prove it unequivocally, but Haber *was* the greatest inventor of poison gases."

"Well, I wouldn't go so far as to say *greatest*, but—"

"Oh, yes, I forgot," Angelo smirked. "There was you, too."

Hein grinned. "Well, yes, of course, but there was also our French adversary, Victor Grignard. Yet, his chemicals were no matches for ours, and we Germans proved to be the real *Victors* in that department."

Just then, there was a rapping on the door. Irritably, Hein turned and barked, "Come in!"

As the door swung open, a secretary popped her head in. "Oh, there you are, Herr Direktor. There are some Gestapo officers out here looking for you. Should I say you're busy?"

"No, no! I'll be right there," Hein replied eagerly. Looking over at Angelo, he added, "Well, I hope that puts to rest this whole *Dante* score nonsense, because you *must* be one-hundred percent focused on your work. The Führer demands it." Hein thrust his arm out and barked, "Heil Hitler!" then marched out, slamming the door behind him.

Angelo rolled his eyes and, in utter exasperation, looked down at the score on his lap. "It seems this damned *Dante* mystery will never be put to rest."

Mildred placed her hand on his shoulder. "That's the one thing crazy old Hein said that I agree with. Why don't you just let it rest? After all, it must have been Haber; he even died on the same day as your father. What better twist of fate could there be? And as I told you, Hein is just a slimy leech, a scavenger. He steals people's ideas, credit, and financial rewards. There's no way that he developed the poison."

"Yes, but he could have stolen it from Haber and used it. Or Haber could have ordered him to do it. So, there's no way this is a closed book."

Mildred fell silent as Angelo opened the *Dante* score. As he began skimming through the pages he suddenly stopped.

Mildred recognized the sign. "What is it?"

Angelo's head popped up. "It's just that Liszt was naturally paying homage to Dante, and that reminds me of how much time Liszt and my father spent in Italy—namely, Rome. There must be someone there, or some clue, that can help me solve this mystery."

Mildred rolled her eyes. "Oh, dear! Here we go again. So, I guess I should book two railway tickets to Rome?"

Angelo turned and smiled. "I'm glad you said *two* tickets and not one, because while in Rome, there is something very special I'd like to show you."

Three days later, the pair boarded a train for Rome, which arrived at the Roma Termini late Saturday morning. Although Mildred would have preferred stopping for a cappuccino at a quaint café before getting down to business, she knew better to even suggest it. Angelo was on a mission; and like a treasure hunter with a mental compass, he paced impatiently down the streets of the Eternal City, while Mildred tried her utmost to keep up. Eventually, he spotted in the distance what appeared to be the Monastery of the Santa Francesca Romana.

Crossing the Roman Forum, with its array of ancient ruins from a long line of Caesars, they finally approached the medium-sized building with its attractive façade.

Mildred gazed up. "So this is where Liszt stayed?"

"I believe so. It even feels right for some reason." Angelo stood and spun around to scan the Forum. "It certainly is a great spot. It must be the place. What a splendid view."

"It certainly is," Mildred replied. "Now we just need to see if we can uncover some splendid clues, because we can't stay here long. You know darn well that Hein will get suspicious if we call in sick on Monday."

Angelo waved his hand. "Ah, never mind that glittering old dandy. Let's go see what we can find."

As they ascended the stairs, Mildred shook her head anxiously. "I think Hein is more than a harmless butterfly, Angelo. The evil vultures he's been hanging around with are brutal hacks, and I never did trust him, not one bit."

Reaching the front porch, Angelo waved her comments away, as he looked up at the huge wooden doors and knocked. Within moments, the thick door swung open. A youthful Dominican priest—about five feet tall and even too young for facial hair—looked up and smiled. "May I help you, my son?"

Angelo peered down and grinned. "Well, you look far too young to be calling me *son*, but I sure hope so, Father."

Even the priest chuckled, as Angelo went on, "Actually, I'm curious: This *is* the place where the great Hungarian composer Franz Liszt resided, is it not?"

The fledgling priest squinted. "Liszt? He was an old, famous composer, right? I strongly doubt it. This is a monastery. But there are plenty of other lodgings nearby."

Angelo's hopes began to wither. "Are you sure? I thought for sure Liszt stayed *here*."

Just then, an older priest, having heard their conversation, walked over. "Yes, I believe he did. But the person you really need to speak with is Father Perlino."

The perplexed young priest turned and smiled. "Of course! If Liszt did stay here, Father Perlino would surely know. He's so old, I'll bet he even baptized Liszt."

The priests began chucking, as Angelo prodded impatiently, "Excuse me, but where can I find this Father Perlino?"

The older priest turned. "Oh, yes, of course." He stepped out onto the porch and pointed to the side of the building. "Just proceed around this corner, and you'll see a small side entrance. He should be awake by now."

"It's past noon," Angelo replied. "A late riser?"

"No, he needs his naps. And they seem to be getting longer every day."

Angelo said thanks, grasped Mildred's hand, and quickly ran down the stairs and breezed around the corner. Excitedly, he rapped on the door. A moment later, it opened.

"What's all the racket!? I may be old, but I'm not deaf!" The elfin priest blasted.

Angelo and Mildred recoiled. The bald and wrinkled little priest looked like a gnarly gourd with tiny poppy seeds for eyes. After the initial shock, however, Angelo began to notice a caricature-like charm about the cleric that made him chuckle. He quickly covered his mouth. "Please excuse me, Father."

"There's *no excuse* for being *rude*, my son," the grumpy little priest belched.

"No, no" Angelo said. "I meant no disrespect. I rather find you amusing."

"Nobody around here ever finds *me* amusing," he retorted with an oddly endearing huff.

Angelo stifled a chuckle. "Forgive me, Father. May we please come in?"

Father Perlino's head jerked back. "Come in? Why?"

"Just to chat a bit. Besides, I can sense that underneath that raw, tiny exterior of yours is a tender man with a big heart, one as pure and rich as gold."

Father Perlino was caught off guard in a delightful way. "Oh, why, yes, how *rude* of *me*. I mean, yes, please come in," then glancing at Mildred, he added, "and don't forget to bring your beautiful little lady along with you."

Mildred smiled and thanked the Father, as they entered and closed the door behind them.

Angelo looked around the room. It was barely larger than a bedroom and sparsely furnished. "My, it's awfully cramped in here, and you hardly have any possessions."

Father Perlino turned. "Simplicity! That's the way Jesus lived, my son." He then turned toward Mildred. "Can I offer you a glass of wine or a biscotti, young lady?"

Mildred smiled. "Oh, no, thank you."

Meanwhile, Angelo was doing a 360-degree scan of the room, as his eyes desperately sought some sort of a clue.

"Looking for something, my son?"

"Yes, actually—*my* father."

"Well, I assure you, he is not here."

Angelo chuckled. "No, I don't mean here, right now. You see, my father died a long time ago, back in 1914. But he did come here often to visit his teacher and mentor, Franz Liszt."

"Ah, yes!" Father Perlino exclaimed, as a smile surprisingly added a few pleasant wrinkles to his face. "Franz Liszt. What a good soul. And a fine abbé, I'll have you know."

"So I've heard from my father and many people, but you say you knew him, as in personally?"

"My dear boy," Father Perlino replied. "As you can see, I'm no spring chicken. In fact, I'm ninety-eight years old, I'll have you know."

Angelo smiled. "Wow! You don't look a day over eighty."

The little, old gourd laughed. "Very funny! And *eighty*. My, my, that was a long time ago. I could actually see back then. It's these darn old eyes that now fail me, and that's a most dreadful thing, my son, not to be able to read." He then turned and pointed to his stack of heavily worn books. "Those are the only ones I've been able to keep, as the text is rather large, but I've given hundreds away, hoping they will enlighten others as they have me."

Mildred spotted his telescopic-sized glasses on his small, plain dresser. "May I get you your glasses, Father?"

Pivoting around, he grinned. "Why, thank you, Signora. But I assure you that I don't need glasses to see your stunning beauty. You are indeed a paragon of perfection, just like Beatrice."

Mildred squinted as she passed him his glasses. "Oh, was that your mother or a friend?"

"Oh, no. My mother was indeed a beautiful woman, but I see you, like many your age, don't read much. Beatrice, my dear girl, was Dante's sublime vision of the ultimate purity of women, and she was the woman who guided him through *Paradiso*."

Angelo's head sprang up. "Of course—Dante!" Stepping toward the old priest, he added, "You said you knew Franz Liszt. Did he ever mention his *Dante Symphony* to you?"

Father Perlino adjusted his glasses as he tilted his head backwards to look up at Angelo's face. "Oh my God!" he exclaimed.

"What?" Angelo queried, now excited. "You remember Liszt speaking about it?"

"No, no, my son," the wrinkled cleric replied, as he moved his head left and right, perplexed. "It can't be."

Angelo suddenly felt a bit spooked. "What, Father? What can't be? You're making me feel like you're looking at the Devil."

"No, no, my dear boy—not at all. It's just that you remind me of, of—"

"Of whom!?" Angelo urged excitedly.

"I can't say," he replied, as he turned away and hobbled toward his stack of books.

"Why not?" Angelo said, overcome with curiosity.

Father Perlino spun around. "Well, I suppose there's no harm in telling you. It's just that, with that thick crop of hair and features, well—you remind me of a young student of Liszt's. His name was Angelo Di Purezza."

"Angelo Di Purezza!" Angelo blurted, as Mildred's eyes widened.

"Yes, Angelo Di Purezza," Father Perlino repeated. "Why? Do you know him?"

"Know him? Dear God," Angelo replied happily. "He was my father. I'm his son, Angelo Junior."

Father Perlino staggered. As he wobbled and grasped a chair, Mildred rushed to assist him. He looked up unsteadily. "Dear God, indeed. How? Why? I mean, what are you doing here?"

"To be honest, Father, I'm trying to find evidence that will lead me to the man who murdered my father."

The cleric's shocked face turned guardedly solemn as he turned his head away. "Uh, well…perhaps that is a quest best left undone, my child."

Angelo squinted, his mind churning. "I'm curious, Father. Surely you must know that my father's death was widely publicized as being of natural causes. So, how can you casually tell me to abandon my quest for his *murderer?* Either your memory fails you, or you're hiding something."

Father Perlino squirmed uncomfortably in his chair as he looked over at Mildred. "Can you please pour me a glass of wine, dear? It's right over there in that decanter."

As Mildred acknowledged his request and handed him the glass, Father Perlino took a healthy swig of the dry and potent grape juice.

Angelo stepped in front of him and went down on his knees, his hands now clasped in supplication. "Father, please! Tell me what you know?"

The gnarled old priest pulled a handkerchief out of his black cassock and wiped his damp forehead. He then adjusted his thick glasses and looked dotingly into Angelo's eyes. "My poor, dear child, the pain you were forced to bear is even too unbearable for me."

Angelo glanced down, then up again into the priest's magnified poppy eyes. "Father Perlino, my father died a long time ago, so the pain is long gone. What remains is the pain of not knowing who killed him. Surely you can understand this. I am his son, his flesh and blood."

The wrinkled little gourd reached out and grasped Angelo's shoulders and drew him warmly into his frail chest. He then kissed the top of his head, and slowly pushed him backward. "My dear boy, I remember you as a little *bambino,* and the pain I'm referring to is not the pain of your father's death, but the pain of knowing you have lived your life thinking he is dead."

Angelo recoiled. "Father, has that wine gone straight to your head? That's a cruel thing to say. And…and, what? Did you say you knew me when I was a child?"

Father Perlino nodded lovingly. "Yes, Angelo. You were your father's precious gem. And for that reason, he never wished for you to know about his covert life or about his feigned death."

Angelo's face blanched as a devastating wave of mixed emotions began to wreak havoc internally, while externally turning his olive complexion chalky white. Mildred gasped, not only from the shocking news, but also from the visible pain that now marred poor Angelo's face.

"Feigned death!?" Angelo asked, his voice cracking with distress. "How? Why? And are you saying that he's still alive!?"

Tears began to flow out of Father Perlino's eyes, making their way downward into the crooked crevices that lined his cheeks and onto his round little chin. "I swore to your father that I'd never tell a soul, including you. But, yes, Angelo, it is true. Your father is very much alive."

Angelo staggered as Mildred rushed to support him. Lifting him slightly, she maneuvered him into another chair facing the Father.

"I can't believe it," Angelo uttered, gazing aimlessly at the floor. "I don't understand? I don't know whether to laugh with joy or scream with anger." His head rose, as he looked at Perlino with sad eyes. "Why would he do such a thing? Why would he abandon me like that?"

Father Perlino reached over and, grasping Angelo's knee, firmly shook it. "Angelo, please understand that your father loved you, loved you more than anyone in his hard and turbulent life, especially after your mother and sister passed away. And he did everything possible to nurture you into being a strong and educated young man."

Angelo shook his head, bewildered. "But why did he—"

"He contrived his death to protect *you,* Angelo. His precious lone gem, the jewel that he had to make sure would never be defiled or destroyed by the evil demons in this world—the brutal monsters that he dedicated his life to hunting down and rooting out."

"Hunting down?" Angelo asked, still confused. "So I've been told, but I suspected that he only helped Liszt to transmit messages?"

Father Perlino nodded. "He did at first, but with the inevitability of war looming at the start of this century, and his discovery that Germany was developing horrible toxic gases, he decided to take a more aggressive role. You see, as a teenager, your father often fancied himself as Agrippa; and Liszt, his master, as Augustus. Oddly enough, both great Romans were only teenagers when they bravely confronted the seasoned Marc Antony and the Roman Senate to achieve the grand goals *they* envisioned. As such, that instilled in your father a great deal of courage to continue *his* quest, even after Liszt had died. And I must say; he had quite honorably taken on some of Agrippa's laudable attributes." The priestly old bookworm's mind seemed to wander, as he added absently, "In fact, that was an intriguing chapter in history that I taught him, but, unfortunately, I believe I no longer have that volume." Turning around, he began sifting through his pile of history books.

Angelo smiled sympathetically. "There's no need to find it, Father. I, too, recall my father speaking quite often about Augustus and Agrippa, even mentioning that it was a priest who taught him history—evidently *you*. But, *please*, do you know where he is? I must see him."

Father Perlino looked back and nodded. "Yes, of course. How foolish of me." He grasped his Bible, then placed his hand on the heavily worn cover. "Please, come here, and place your hand upon this Bible. First, I must say a prayer."

Angelo placed his powerful hand next to the Father's wrinkly, chicken claw, as the old priest looked up and incanted, "Oh, my Lord, God, and Savior, may the Trinity look down upon Angelo Senior, Angelo Junior, and myself. Please forgive me for breaking my vow to Angelo Senior and please guide this devoted son back to his loving father. With your divine wisdom and loving grace, please reunite and bless these two separated souls."

Angelo glanced pensively at the floor, as Father Perlino placed the Bible back on the pile. Angelo then looked up. "Excuse me, Father, but you just prayed for *God* to *guide me* to my father. Does that mean you don't know where he is?"

Father Perlino's thin, gray eyebrow furled. "I'm sorry, Angelo, but I only know the city in which he now resides."

Angelo's broad shoulders dropped. "Only the city? That's really not what I was praying for."

"Angelo, you must understand that your father's safety, and that of all of us, has depended upon his total disappearance. The world had to believe he was dead, particularly the Germans, since they had attempted to kill him on several occasions. As such, he feigned his death not only to end their lethal manhunt, but also to protect our lives. He knew that if they kept failing to eliminate him their next step would have been to hunt us down, whereby using us as hostages to draw him out of the shadows. He was also painfully aware that if such a scenario were ever played out, they surely would have killed all three of us. So, basically, your father sacrificed *his* life so that both of us could live *ours*. And that's the sort of man he was and is—totally selfless."

Angelo nodded somberly, yet understandingly. "Well, I guess that makes sense, Father. So, which city is it?"

Father Perlino took the last swig of his wine, and pronounced, "Basel, Switzerland."

Angelo almost choked. "Basel, Switzerland!"

Meanwhile, Mildred sprang to her feet.

Father Perlino looked up at both of them. "My Lord, dear children, what's so shocking about Basel, Switzerland?"

"That's where Fritz Haber recently died. He's the man who developed the poison that I thought had killed my father. And I had suspected that he might have been the one who administered the deadly poison, as well. So it just seems extremely odd that they both were in the same city at the time of Haber's demise."

"Yes, I suppose it is," Father Perlino said, as he rose unsteadily to his feet.

Angelo and Mildred each grasped one of his arms as they all walked toward the door. He looked up at Mildred. "My, you certainly are one beautiful lady." Then turning toward Angelo, he added, "You are a very lucky man, Angelo. Treasure her like your father treasured your dear mother."

As Mildred blushed, Angelo grinned. "Well, Father, Mildred and I are not married."

Father Perlino's wrinkled face emitted a sagacious smile. "My dear boy, I know how men and women lovingly gaze at each other when they're in that sublime zone where souls collide and fuse for eternity. And that also goes for the times when even they themselves don't realize it."

Angelo laughed. "And how would *you* know, being a solitary priest for ninety-eight years?"

Father Perlino laughed. "I know from keen observation, Angelo. And that look you have is the same exact one that your father so proudly wore." Then turning toward Mildred—who was also beaming—he added, "And that goes for your gorgeous stare, too."

Pulling them together, he then clasped their hands in prayer. "May God look over you both and one day unite you in marriage." Looking Heavenward, he added, "And if you would, dear Lord, kindly allow me this addendum: please safely guide *both* these souls to their rightful and most joyous destinations."

Father Perlino warmly embraced the loving couple, then walked them to the door. As the two departed, he gently waved and called out, *"Addio e fortuna!"*

As Mildred and Angelo returned through the Roman Forum, they found themselves standing before the magnificent Coliseum and the Arch of Constantine. While marveling over the grandeur that was ancient Rome, Angelo bent down and respectfully touched the ground, feeling the same paved stones that Augustus and Agrippa walked on so many centuries ago. Upon rising, Angelo spotted the huge dome of Saint Peter's Basilica off in the distance. "Come, I want to show you something."

He grasped Mildred's hand and excitedly began walking at a brisk pace.

"What? Where are we going?" Mildred asked, with a smile and a giggle.

"Don't you remember?" Angelo said. "Before we left, I said I had something very special to show you. And despite the amazing news we just heard, this happens to be extremely important, as well. So, please, just follow me." Veering off the main route, Angelo led Mildred across the Ponte Mazzini. Looking back at the handsome bridge, Angelo relayed how it was named after Giuseppe Mazzini of the *Risorgimento,* and then expounded upon that turbulent time in history, which his father lived through and had taught him.

Walking up along the Tiber River, they finally came upon Bernini's massive circular colonnade. As the pair entered the wide rotunda, they gazed up at the towering façade of Saint Peter's Basilica on the far side. Standing directly before them, however, was the eighty-one-foot tall obelisk, to which he now led Mildred. As they neared the towering needle, startled pigeons flew upward all around them.

Mildred put her hands over her head. "I hope one of these little guys doesn't poop on me."

Angelo laughed as he slowly crouched down and extended his arms toward a white pigeon walking nearby. Unhindered by the noisy tourists, Angelo made odd clucking sounds, and seemed to drift off into another zone, where he communicated directly to the bird. To Mildred's surprise, the pigeon not only crept toward Angelo, but it appeared as if the bird knew him, as it willingly walked right into Angelo's hands.

"Oh my God. Where did you ever learn to do that?"

Angelo gradually stood up and cuddled the bird in an odd and playful way. Peering over at Mildred, he replied, "From Saint Francis of Assisi."

Mildred smirked. "Very funny. Saint Francis lived a thousand years ago."

"Actually, only seven hundred years ago," Angelo corrected, playfully. "But, seriously, it was my father who taught me how to handle pigeons. He loved these little guys, even though so many people think they're dirty, pestering eyesores. But look at this little fella. He's pure white and purely delightful."

Mildred walked closer. "He *is* actually quite beautiful. In fact, he looks like a dove."

"Yes, pigeons and doves are both from the *Columbidae* family. And like humans, some are dirty and loathed, while others are pure and beautiful—like *you!*"

Mildred released a heartwarming smile as Angelo motioned for her to stand in front of him.

As she stepped cautiously closer, Mildred felt a bit nervous. "Are you sure he won't fly away?"

"No, don't be afraid."

Then, quite unexpectedly, Angelo placed the bird in her hands. "There, you see. He likes you. In fact, I think he has something to give you. Look!"

"Oh, dear, I hope it's not a dollop of doo-doo!"

Angelo laughed. "No, no. Look!"

As Mildred lowered her head, her eyes bulged as her heart pounded. "Oh, my God! Is that what I think it is?"

"It sure is." Taking the diamond ring off the white bird's little leg, which he covertly attached a moment earlier, Angelo held it in his hand as he knelt before her.

"Mildred, I love you. After living an unfulfilled life, I never thought it possible to find a woman as beautiful as you. You have brought joy to where sorrow and loneliness dwelt. You have truly turned the desert that once was my heart into a lush Paradise. And it could never remain such without you. I love you with all my heart and soul, as Dante loved Beatrice. You are my paragon of beauty and purity. And so I ask you, Mildred, will you marry me?"

Tears of joy streamed down Mildred's face, as she released the bird and covered her mouth with her trembling hands. Trying to regain her composure, Mildred closed her eyes and took a deep breath, then joyously cried out, "Of course I'll marry you! I couldn't live another day if you ever married someone else."

With that, Angelo rose to his feet and slid the ring on Mildred's finger. As the couple embraced, a swarm of white pigeons flew upward all around them.

Angelo looked into her eyes. "I think it was destiny that led me here to Rome, for not only did Father Perlino somehow know that I intended to propose to you, but he also graced my life with the good news that my father is still alive."

Impulsively, Mildred smiled. "What do you say we go back there *right now* and have Perlino marry us?"

Angelo was gleefully flustered. "Are you serious? No wedding? No celebration?"

"What better blessing could we ever hope to receive? Everything has aligned here. Our love, and new doorways to our future have all been opened to us right here. This place is, and shall always remain, our sacred spot. What better celebration could two people ever ask for?"

The two warmly embraced and shared a loving kiss. Then, with arms entwined, Angelo and Mildred returned to the Monastery of the Santa Francesca, where they excitedly knocked on Father Perlino's chamber door. When the door finally opened, the old priest greeted the pair with a loving grin and a clairvoyant twinkle in his eyes. "What took you so long?" he bellowed, followed by a warm chuckle. "Come in, come in, my children!"

Upon entering, Mildred and Angelo discovered the tiny room had been converted into a charming nuptial altar, with beautiful flowers gleaned from the monastery's gardens and fragrant candles burning. Mildred's eyes watered as her diamond-clad hand rose up to cover her mouth.

Angelo simply stood in awe as he shook his head. "My God, Father! How could you possibly have known we'd return?"

The smiling cleric closed the door, then escorted the couple to his aromatic altar. "Well, it was just a hunch, Angelo. As I told you, I'm a pretty good judge of character. But, if you hadn't returned, well, then I suppose I would have had a most delightful candle-lit dinner tonight among all these beautiful flowers."

Angelo and Mildred smiled as they warmly embraced the dear old priest who had so quickly become a defining factor in both their lives. With a few traditional words from the Good Book, Father Perlino joined the loving couple's hands and souls in marriage.

After bidding the endearing priest another fond farewell, the newlyweds spent that night and the following day in Rome on their honeymoon. Touring the great city, Angelo pointed out the huge Monument to Victor Emanuel II. Designed by Giuseppe Sacconi in 1885 to celebrate the unification of Italy, it was just in the final stages of construction as the loving couple gazed up at the colossal structure. Built of pure white marble, the monument came to be nicknamed the 'wedding cake', which seemed rather fitting to the newlyweds. However, with the thought of food now on his mind, Angelo ran into a nearby *alimentari* and emerged with a bag in his hand. Mildred shook her head, smiling, as the two strolled north, then up the Spanish steps. Sitting at the top, to take in the view, Angelo pulled out two tasty prosciutto and mozzarella sandwiches, some olives, roasted peppers, and two drinks. The two lovingly hugged as they watched the clouds morph and pleasantly change colors until the sun finally took its leave, thus ending the magnificent light show, as it seemed to bow and then disappear behind the dark earthly stage. Wishing to make one last stop, Angelo grasped Mildred's hand and walked her back several blocks to visit the Trevi Fountain. The streaming water seemed to dance in the moonlight as its molecules fell into the huge watery basin, akin to how the couple's hearts seemed to dance as their tossed coins fell into the same watery font. Looking at each other with eyes and hearts ablaze, Angelo and Mildred made their wishes—albeit knowing that the most important one was already granted. It was truly a magical evening.

But, alas, work beckoned, and they hopped on a late train Sunday night. Upon arriving home, however, their hearts dropped; Hein's new Hitler-styled Kaiser Institute was a jarring and harsh follow-up to what had been the best two days of their lives. Yet they soon realized something else; their new sacred bond fortified them, giving them the strength to brave Hein's new cult-like atmosphere, which Angelo privately dissed as "Nazimania."

With poise, Angelo somehow managed to outwardly keep his cool with Hein, but thoughts of his recently resurrected father burned on the inside. With Mildred unable to take a leave of absence, Angelo decided he couldn't wait a moment longer—he would go to Basel alone.

Calling in sick Tuesday morning, Angelo kissed Mildred good-bye and caught an early train. As the noisy locomotive pulled into the Basel Bahnhof, an eerie feeling crept into his bones, becoming more intense as he stepped out onto the platform. It was the same wooden deck where he had stalked Haber only a few months earlier. As he walked down the main street (*Elisabethenstrasse*) under the bright, warm rays of the sun, Angelo could only think of that jarring cold night when he wrestled Haber to the ground in the park. Replaying the altercation in his mind like a looping film, he kept pausing where Haber professed his innocence, then fast-forwarding to the moment when the Gas Man attempted to kill him with his own pistol.

Trying desperately to purge the torment, he recalled what Mildred had rightly said—Haber's poisons had inflicted mass murder, and now that Haber was dead, he was out of Angelo's reach and stood before God. With his mind clear, Angelo spent four grueling hours making inquiries in town, but to no avail. Dejected, Angelo shook his head as he turned left down *Rittergasse* (Knight Lane). Walking in a haze, he suddenly turned, only to find himself standing in the shadow of the massive Münster Cathedral.

Curiosity awakened his senses and drew him toward the main entrance. Gazing up to fixate on the ornate spires of the two large towers, Angelo squinted from the blinding sun. His eyes inevitably gazed down along its Romanesque façade lined with Gothic windows, and past the clock mounted on the right side. But then they did a double-take as they landed upon two large sculptures flanking the main entrance; each was of a knight on horseback.

At that precise moment, a voice boomed. "That's Saint Martin of Tours."

Startled, Angelo turned to see a jolly-looking old priest with a bulbous nose and a beer-barrel chest. "I figure many from your generation don't know who or what these statues represent, so please excuse my intrusion."

"Not at all," Angelo replied politely. "In fact, I love learning about our past. Thank you, Father—?"

"Jakob, Father Jakob. And your name is?"

"Angelo. So, tell me, who is the knight on the left side? Is it Saint George?"

Father Jakob turned and looked up. "Yes, good guess, Angelo," he acknowledged with a grin.

"Well, he's wielding a lance and slaying a dragon, so I suppose it had to be either Saint George or Saint Michael."

Father Jakob nodded. "A fine deduction."

"It's funny," Angelo thought out loud, "every time I see a lance, I think of how my father told me that Franz Liszt 'hurled his lance into the future.'"

Father Jakob suddenly turned and rubbed his chin as he looked up at Angelo's face. "Hmm, that's really rather queer."

"Queer? What's so odd about that?"

"Well, I've discussed this statue with many curious passersby, and that's just not something that ever arises in conversation, except for one time, just several months ago."

Angelo's curiosity was piqued. "What happened?"

Father Jakob scrutinized Angelo's face, as he replied, "Well, one elderly fellow and I had a conversation that, by God, I must say was very queerly like the one we just had. And the more I look at you, by golly, you even sort of look a little like him."

Angelo's heart began to race. "Please, tell me what else you remember about him?"

The priest's head tilted downward as his eyes oscillated to search his memory. He then gazed up. "That's it! His name was Hans Geist. I may be old, but I can remember people, places, and sometimes even trifling details."

Angelo's left brow furled. "*Hans Geist.* Are you sure?"

"Absolutely. Especially since *geist* means ghost, and that's not the sort of name one's likely to forget. I was standing right about here when I heard a voice ask me about that Saint George statue. I turned, but saw no one. I was actually a bit spooked. You see, at the time, there was some construction going on, and Hans was standing, hiding really, on the other side of some scaffolding. As he spoke, I finally located his face, and only his face, mind you. He was peering out between piles of wooden planks and bricks on the scaffold. After our discussion—in which he, too, mentioned Liszt's lance—he vanished and I never saw him again. It was most queer, as if he were a ghost." Father Jakob grinned. "That's a little trick I use to remember people's names. I associate the person with something interesting about them that relates to their name. It can be something as simple as what they were doing at the time I met them, like with Hans, or maybe what they were wearing—you know, little things like that. For example, four years ago I met an old lady who was wearing a pretty rose print dress; and wouldn't you know it, her name was Rose. So I always remembered her name. Or like the time this man—"

"Excuse me, Father." Angelo tried to be polite, but he wanted to know more about the mysterious ghost that he now suspected was his father, not the old priest's proprietary memorization system. "Please, is there anything else you remember about Hans Geist? I believe he might be a long lost relative of mine. Did he say where he lives?"

"Oh, oh, I see," Jakob stuttered. "Let me think...I know he lived right here in Basel, yet, by golly, where? Um, give me a minute, son." His eyes, once again, did their data-seeking dance.

Angelo's hands were clenched in anticipation. "Take your time, Father," he said, barely able to contain himself.

Jakob's rolling eyes briefly looked at Angelo and winked, then resumed their scanning. Finally, he looked up. "Oh, yes!"

"Well?"

"He never actually told me where he lived, but I did deduce the general location."

Angelo was skeptical, fearing that the priest's deduction might lead him on a wild goose chase all over Basel. "How did you manage to figure that out, may I ask?"

Father Jakob's plump cheeks swelled. "Quite simple, my son. You see, Hans had mentioned that he enjoyed doing his own farming. Naturally that rules out the city here, so that would have to mean just across the Rhine."

Angelo's low expectations fell lower. "But there are miles and miles of farmland out there. He could be almost anywhere."

"Oh, no. Not exactly," the chubby old priest said reassuringly. "You see, he also mentioned that the one thing that bothered his peaceful farm life was the loud noise of trains traveling over the nearby trestles. And there are only three or four to be found."

Angelo's face beamed with excitement. "Please, tell me how to get to these trestles?"

Father Jakob shrugged his hefty shoulders. "Why sure. Just cross the *Wettsteinbrucke* over the Rhine, then take *Freiburgerstrasse* just a few miles, and you'll come across three railway trestles on your left. On the other side of that narrow canal, you'll see plenty of farmland. He must live somewhere near there. But, tell me—what long-lost relative of yours is this Hans Geist?"

Before the priest even finished the last sentence, Angelo had already thanked him and vanished. Left standing alone,

Father Jakob scratched his head: *Hmm, I guess I'll have to remember that lad as Angelo "Liszt's Lance" Geist II.*

Angelo had crossed over to the other side of the Rhine and scurried down *Freiburgerstrasse.* Just as Father Jakob had said, he came upon three railway trestles to his left. Just then, a train rumbled over the first trestle. Angelo waited for it to pass, then ran across the graveled bed alongside the tracks to the far side. There before him, fields of rolling farmland stretched as far as his excited eyes could see. He knew his father's farm had to be somewhere close, and he opted for the dirt road that ran parallel to the tracks, rather than the one that led up into the mountains.

As Angelo progressed, the row of trees lining the uneven trail grew denser. It was then that he almost past a small dirt path to his left. It was heavily overgrown, and it probably would have never been noticed if not for the small shred of newspaper clinging to a branch. Angelo stepped back and picked the torn piece of paper off the prickly twigs. At the edge of the torn fragment, he saw the date: May 19, 1934. Today's date!

Angelo eagerly pushed his way through the thick brush. The further he advanced, the wider the path became. Finally, he was able to see a small field of crops up ahead. To one side was a quaint little green house with white shutters and a fairly large red shed standing beside it. The colors felt right. *Could they represent the colors of the Italian flag?* he thought. He started to walk faster, when, suddenly, a stern voice bellowed, "Stop where you are, or I'll shoot!"

Angelo froze in his tracks. Nervously, he turned his head toward the voice. There, through a sparse mesh of trees, he saw an old man with an ample crop of gray hair pointing a Carcano M91TS bolt-action rifle at his head. Before he could say a word, he heard the bolt cock, as the man blustered, "Don't move, mister. You're trespassing! Who are you and what do you want?"

Angelo's face went pale, not so much from the deadly rifle, but more so from the old man's dead-on striking resemblance to himself. There was no mistaking it. In a voice broken with emotion, Angelo cried, "Papa! It's me, Angelo."

The old man took his trigger finger off the rifle and used that hand to shield his eyes from the glaring sun. As he took several steps forward, he suddenly felt lightheaded—the rifle fell and he clung to a large branch to support himself. Angelo pushed his way through the small trees and grasped his father's arm to steady him. They gazed into each other's eyes, not truly believing what they were seeing. Angelo Senior saw himself some thirty years younger, while Angelo Junior saw the exact opposite. The resemblance was as spooky as Angelo Senior's pseudonym, *Geist*.

"How in God's name did you ever find out, or find me?" Angelo Senior asked, his voice breaking with emotion.

With tears welling in his eyes, Angelo replied, "Well, it certainly took a long time. Twenty years to be exact."

After a profoundly emotional embrace, Angelo was disconcerted to see his father's shaky health, accentuated by a terrible, hacking cough.

"Pop, you really need to sit down. Let me help you back to the house."

Angelo Senior looked firmly into his eyes. "Angelo, I've been living on my own for twenty years, and despite a considerable down-turn in health over the past few years, I've managed just fine."

"I understand that, but now that I'm here, I want to help you in any way I can."

Angelo Senior smiled. "You have no idea how glad I am to hear you say that. I imagined that, if ever this day came, you'd never understand my decision and would hate me."

Angelo nodded solemnly. "If I were younger, perhaps I would. But I'm fifty-four years old now, Pop, and, hopefully, a bit wiser and certainly more understanding. A man has to do what he truly believes in, and dedicating your life to pursuing villains and protecting your loved ones from repercussions is very admirable. Yet, in another regard, I find your solitary life a bit lonely and sad. No disrespect intended."

"Angelo, as you know, some of us have to make tough sacrifices in this world. As a Catholic priest chooses a life of celibacy to commit himself fully to his *holy* task, I have committed myself *wholly* to a solitary and covert life with the task of eradicating evil."

As the two walked slowly back toward the house, the elder Angelo pointed to his small farm, explaining how he had just enough crops and animals to sustain himself—a perfect system with no waste. As Angelo looked at all his father's heavily worn farming tools, he smiled. "How do you manage to do all this? You're eighty-five years old, for Christ's sake."

His father smiled. "That's exactly why I'm still able to do it. Because I do it. Just as they say 'an idle mind is the Devil's workshop', I believe an idle body is the Devil's disease lab. One must keep moving. But no matter how much one moves, no one can out-run time, Angelo. And that's why, when I saw my health begin to decline, I took my covert operation to another level two years ago."

"What new level would that be?"

Grasping a shovel, his father began scooping up cow dung and tossing it onto a compost pile. "Well, initially I just stuck to relaying intelligence. But, with the advent of the Kaiser's toxic war, I moved up to sabotaging military production facilities. Then, once I realized how Hitler and his band of thugs were skillful organizers with their Nazi Party—as well as cunning underminers of both the Weimar Republic's passive socialists and Hindenburg's unorganized Prussian Old Guard—I just had to take the radically aggressive next step."

"Radically aggressive? How radical?" Angelo asked, yet suddenly the 1932 date flashed in his mind. "Wait! Don't tell me. Two years ago!? Were you in Berlin in 1932?"

His father stopped shoveling and looked up. "You're a smart boy. I'm glad I directed you towards math and music, as I believe they heighten the abilities of deduction and creative thinking. But, to answer your question, yes, I was."

Angelo shook his head. "Oh my God! That was *you?* I was with Albert Einstein when I heard the news of Hitler's assassination attempt. I was only five miles away at the Kaiser Institute. I can't believe it!"

His father nodded with a pained expression. "Yes, it was not an easy decision to make. You know—taking another man's life. But I truly believed that I was trying to kill a destructive virus, not a man. Hitler *is* the malignant root of that virus, and his ugly branches include thorny pricks like Hermann Göring, who made power plays in Hindenburg's weakening regime, and Joseph Goebbels, who began to physically act out the Party's hatred of Jews as early as 1927—ordering his thugs to smash Jewish shops in Berlin and beat up anyone who even looked Jewish. Yet, as I said, the repulsive ringleader of this Nazi virus is Adolf Hitler. Unfortunately, I failed to eliminate him in 1932. And, as you know, the lethal germ was appointed Reich Chancellor only months later, just as I had feared. Worse yet, his despotic regime continues to assume control over every facet of government and business." Resuming his shoveling, he continued, "Hitler and his Nazi disease are like this manure, Angelo. If someone doesn't take action to shovel it away, it will continue to pile up and overtake the entire yard, turning it into a toxic waste dump that spreads disease and defiles the air with its horrid stench."

Angelo stood almost in a trance, gazing pensively at the ground. "I still can't believe you were responsible for the assassination attempt." Unexpectedly, he grinned and looked up. "Actually, I'm proud of you, Pop. I share your mindset. But, speaking of assassinations, you must tell me: What happened back in 1914 when we all thought that you were killed? Was it Fritz Haber or Rudolf Hein?"

Angelo Senior suddenly flinched, as he held his chest and barked out a mean cough. He turned his head, then spit out a bloody glob of phlegm on the ground.

Angelo quickly grasped his father's arm. "Hey, Pop, that's not good! This is more serious than you might think. I should call a doctor."

His father looked at him with knowing eyes as he broke out into a cold sweat. "It's too late for that, my son. I have tuberculosis. My days are numbered, but I have very few regrets—one being, not spending the time with you that we could have enjoyed together."

Angelo slowly walked his father to a nearby lawn chair, then sat on a tree stump beside him. Angelo's face withered with anxiety as his father pulled out a handkerchief and wiped his bloody lips. Shoving the soiled cloth back into his pocket, he then turned toward his distressed son. "Please, Angelo, wipe that sad look off your face. First, by sheer will I have managed to rise above the pain and achieved *almost* everything I wanted to in this life. And second, you know darn well—we don't live forever. So I have no need for sympathetic frowns or useless laments." Before Angelo could even respond, his father forged onward, "So, as for your question, 'was it Haber or Hein', I guess I should backtrack to 1913." As Angelo beamed with pride, his tough old man continued, "That was when I learned of Fritz Haber's experiments with poison gas. He was by far the leading expert in his day, and the Kaiser took a keen interest in his poisons for possible use in warfare. As a result, Haber was given his own unit. He was the brains of the operation, while Rudolf Hein, on the other hand, was nothing more than his laboratory lackey. But there was one military man assigned to Haber's unit, named Karl Kramer. And after Haber learned that I tried to sabotage his lab, I always suspected Karl of being his hit man."

"Hmm, I never heard of that name while at the Kaiser Institute."

"I doubt you would have. Like I said, he was part of the military branch, and he died during the Great War. So I lost interest in hunting down Haber or his team, and my thoughts began to focus elsewhere, like sabotaging Richard Fiedler's development of the flamethrower. But, for the past five years, I've been trying to destabilize Schirach's disturbing brainwashing program—the Hitler Youth. It's a serious problem. But, when I caught wind that you joined the team at the Kaiser Institute, well, that rekindled my interest in that murderous old prick, Fritz the Fumigator." Angelo chuckled as his father added, "So, several months ago, when I discovered that Haber was taking his vacation right here in Basel, I just had to pay him a visit."

Angelo's eyes bulged. "*You* visited Fritz the night he died?! Oh my God, so did I."

Angelo's father grinned. "How odd, indeed. Judging by your earlier question, it's apparent that you never learned who the hit man was."

"No, did you?"

His father smiled and noncommittally raised his hand. "Hold on. Let me finish. Anyhow, I had snuck into the Basel Hotel, where I knew he was lodged, and I waited in the maid's cleaning room. It was very late when I finally saw Haber strolling down the hall. He looked like hell and was holding his chest."

Angelo nodded. "Yes, that's because he and I had a near-fatal scuffle in the park that night. The dirty bastard even managed to grab my revolver and took a shot at me. Luckily he missed."

Angelo Senior shook his head, distressed. "I really never wanted you to get involved in all of this nonsense, but it seems we can't always control our children's lives the way we plan. Anyhow, as soon as Haber entered his hotel room, I walked over and knocked on the door. When the door opened, it truly looked as if Haber had seen a ghost. I now wonder what went through his head, after being assaulted by you in the park, and then seeing me—your father, a dead man back from the grave, calling upon him for revenge. It's almost comical."

Angelo chuckled. "Yes, it is. That really must have been one heart-stopping moment for poor Fritz."

"Indeed it was. As soon as Fritz saw me, he gasped and clenched his heart. In immense shock and pain, he eagerly offered up his friend Hein as his (shockingly incompetent) assassin, and then fell dead on the floor. Christ! I knew I had looks that could kill, but that takes the cake."

The two looked at each other and instantaneously burst out laughing. In between laughs, his father spurted, "It appears…Old Fritzy boy…was looking to absolve some of his sins before Judgment Day."

As Angelo caught his breath, he queried, "But hold on. So, Rudolf Hein is the one that physically tried to kill you?"

"Evidently. But you don't have to worry about him anymore, Angelo. In fact, I think when you return to Berlin, you may be getting a promotion."

Angelo's head recoiled. "What do you mean?"

Angelo Senior put his hand on his son's knee. "First of all, my son, I just want to say that I'm extremely proud of you. Making it into the Kaiser Institute is a great achievement." As a tear of joy welled in Angelo's eye, his father continued, "I know your mother would have been very proud, as well. But, as for Hein, let me tell you. I just returned this morning from Berlin. You see, I paid Hein a visit, too. And he had that same, shocked '*geist*' look on his face that our buddy Haber had. But his heart was too strong to make him just keel over, so I helped him along with a dose of his own toxic medicine."

"Dear Lord! You poisoned him?" Angelo exclaimed, with a mixture of shock and relief.

"Yes, son. That mystery has finally been put to rest. In fact, I bought the newspaper this morning, and it's already in the news. Look there." His father pointed to the newspaper on the ground, which, coincidently, had a small corner torn off.

Angelo smiled. "Yes, indeed, how peculiar," he said, recalling Father Perlino's 'guiding prayer', which led him to Father Jakob, and then to the shred of newspaper. His mind, however, rapidly jumped back to his father's deadly story. "But how did you avoid getting killed by the poison that I found on the *Dante* score? That booklet was found in your hands the day you supposedly died. And speaking of your death, how on earth did you manage that stunt?"

Angelo Senior coughed with a chuckle. "Yes, that was a clever stunt alright. As I said, the Germans had caught onto me, and like those Hollywood gangsters often say, I knew they'd be sending a hit man to bump me off. Except Haber's team wouldn't plug me full of lead, they'd try to poison me with some strain of sulfur mustard. You see, I had learned of the deadly poison's garlic and mustard odor, so when I came home late that night from a concert, I smelled it as soon as I entered my undercover apartment in Lichtenrade."

Angelo gazed at his father with an analytical stare. "Let me guess; I'll bet the concert you went to featured Liszt's *Dante Symphony,* with a few special cryptic notes added. Right?"

"Yes, the *Dante Symphony* is rather special," his father replied with a grin. "So you picked up on that, too?"

Angelo nodded. "Yes, I know you were using it as a cipher, but neither I nor Albert Einstein could figure out Liszt's code. So that's pretty darn impressive."

His father laughed. "Well, that, too, was part of my plan." Angelo's head tilted with curiosity as his father continued, "You see, when I came home that evening, I smelled the poison. And, as sure as the Hell in the score itself, I noticed the deadly scent of Haber's Hellish poison on the booklet. My cover was blown. It was then that I saw the ideal chance to create the perfect subterfuge. I would feign my death to get them off my tail forever while also protecting you."

"Go on," Angelo prodded, intrigued.

His father coughed. "Well, I called my good friend Marcel. I had met him through Franz Liszt one night at the Louvre museum in Paris. He was a former piano student of the Maestro that turned Parisian cop. But after the Franco-Prussian War, he decided to make the best of the new German world order and moved to Berlin. Anyway, thanks to Marcel, he fed my story to the press; basically, the headlines read that I died of a ruptured appendix, and the photo showed me with the *Dante* score in my hand to dupe the Germans that their poison worked. They, or rather Rudy Hein, had laced my wine glass and my personal copy of Liszt's score. So it was easy enough to wash the wine glass, but the score posed a problem. Even though we were able to dilute and deactivate the poison, we couldn't get rid of the stains or that unique scent. However, the scent had faded substantially."

"Fine, so I understand how Marcel managed to fake the report of your death, but what about the matter of your dead body?"

"Marcel was a captain and had pull. He made sure it looked like my body was properly handled and promptly cremated according to my will."

Angelo scratched his head. "But the far greater mystery is that bewitching and elusive *Dante* score. Like I said, even Einstein couldn't figure out Liszt's code. I always recall you telling me as a little boy how brilliant Franz Liszt was, but to outsmart Einstein—now that's pure genius."

His father choked with a laugh. "Well, it was, indeed, a brilliant code that Liszt devised, but you can stop wracking your brain over how elusive and undecipherable it is."

"How's that?"

"Well, Angelo, when I saw that they poisoned my personal copy of the score, I was actually relieved. Because that copy does *not* contain any coded messages."

Angelo almost fell off the stump. "You must be kidding!? I've spent years scrutinizing that score, along with a solid month of Einstein's help, all for nothing, simply because it was the wrong score?"

His father laughed. "Yes. As they say, sometimes the best solutions are simple ones. That score, with its nice leather binding, was a gift from Liszt, and it would never be circulated. Most importantly, it didn't contain the code. I had made it a practice to tell all the conductors who played our coded scores that they could only perform the symphony if they agreed to destroy the scores afterwards. You must remember, Angelo, before the advent of radio or the phonograph, people could only listen to live performances, and only musicians purchased sheet music. So it was an ideal vessel to transmit messages. But, once these new-fangled inventions came about, people began to learn these pieces very well, some knowing every note by heart. So I decided not to use the *Dante Symphony* score any longer." His father hacked and spit, and then continued, "However, I always attend performances of the work, because it became such an important part of my life. I love the amazing work of art it truly is, as well as what it allowed Liszt and myself to accomplish—namely, to root out the Hellish evil in this world that Liszt so ingeniously portrayed in his symphony."

Angelo rubbed his chin. "Yes, Einstein and I scoured the *Inferno* movement of Liszt's symphony in great detail."

His father chuckled. "Well, that was another clever move on Liszt's part. He knew most critics and any possible spies would focus on that infernal movement, so he only put his code in the final *Magnificat*."

Angelo shook his head as he chuckled. "So even if Einstein and I had a coded score, we'd still probably be scratching our heads, all because we were examining the wrong movement."

"Well, I don't know about that, perhaps only more time would have been required, but how we managed to pull it off was twofold. First, like I said, without radios or recordings, the majority of spectators and even most musicians couldn't remember the full details of a symphony. Adding to the unfamiliarity was the fact that Liszt was known for making revisions to his works, always fine-tuning a phrase here or a note there. And this particular symphony even featured an alternate coda. The *Dante Symphony* normally ends on a soft ethereal note that fades away, yet Liszt had also written a brief alternate ending where the orchestra swells up to a triumphant conclusion. And it was within this alternate ending that we would modify the notes to form a code, which we then supplied to undercover agents. As you know, a musical scale consists of eight notes, from A to H, if you include the bass note in the next octave, hence giving us ample letters to devise a code. Liszt also utilized Morse code to add to the complexity, while using Dante's poem as our key."

Angelo nodded. "Ah, yes. Just like Liszt did with his *Fantasy and Fugue on B-A-C-H,* when he paid tribute to J.S. Bach. And adding Morse code into the mix, along with needing the poem as the key to piece it all together, was very clever. And the other reason?"

His father grinned. "Well, the additional beauty of Liszt's idea was that music is the universal language. He knew that, no matter how turbulent political tides were, or how closed state borders became, music would always find a way to sail across these nasty waters to all nations. Therefore, Liszt was able to send messages to Russia, Hungary, Austria, France, Britain, Spain, Italy, Denmark—you name it. It truly was an ingenious operation in all regards. The man was brilliant. More importantly, Franz Liszt was also like a father to me."

Angelo squinted. "I guess I was about six years old when Liszt died, so how come I never met him?"

His father coughed, then wiped his mouth. "Actually, you did, it's just that you were a little boy at the time. You see, after witnessing the humiliating defeat of his good friend Napoleon III, Liszt's attention shifted elsewhere. He was getting older, and he devoted his life to writing mostly religious compositions or even some lugubrious little piano pieces, some quite bewitching, actually. But basically, our paths separated. I was bitten by the political spy bug and never looked back."

"So you never told me—what happened that day when you tried to assassinate Hitler?"

A smile, laced with regret, washed over his father's face. "These really aren't the type of stories I thought I'd ever be relaying to my son, but here it goes. I knew Hitler would be at the Berlin Opera, and I realized, quite unexpectedly, that the *Dante Symphony* was on the program. As I said earlier, we had stopped using it for coded messages long before, so I really felt as though it was an act of God that it would be playing the day I intended to eliminate Satan's anointed madman." Angelo grinned, as his father coughed and continued, "But I was equally surprised when I heard the *Magnificat* played with the alternate ending, which Liszt had officially rejected. As I listened, I was taken aback that the score being used *did* contain a coded message. Yet, it was one that I had written some forty years earlier. Evidently, some conductor didn't dispose of the coded score as directed. So I knew that, after I killed Hitler, I'd have to get my hands on that score to destroy it. Not that it really matters at this point in time, but I don't like leaving loose ends. I guess that just became a standard protocol for me, doing what I do."

Angelo's head dropped, and then he looked up again. "Well, then, I'm sure that loose end of failing to kill Hitler must really eat at you?"

Angelo Senior bent over and coughed again, as he said, "It sure as Hell does, just like this damn disease eating at me." He looked up into his son's eyes. "It's amazing, Liszt really did hurl his lance into the future in more ways than one. I have a sketch by the famous illustrator Gustave Doré inside. He drew it as Liszt described a burning vision he had of an evil monster that would plague the world. You must see—" he suddenly keeled over and violently barked out a bloody mass of phlegm. This time it was far more serious.

"Pop!" Angelo cried in fear. "That's really *not* looking good. I better call a doctor, and quick!"

He wrapped his arms around his father's shoulders and slowly lifted him to his unsteady feet. As he guided him toward the house, chaotic sounds of unrest emanated from the shed. His father turned and looked up. "Please, take me there instead."

"But, Pop, this is no time to do any work, or anything foolish."

"Never mind that. Please, Angelo, just take me there. There's something I'd like to show you."

As Angelo helped his father to the large red shed, the rumbling noise had grown almost ecstatic. Reaching the double doors, his father raised his hand, signaling caution. "Wait! Let me open the door. They need to see me first."

As he opened the large wooden door, Angelo's eyes widened. "Oh my God. You never gave up your love of pigeons."

His father smiled as he walked into the middle of a flock of fluttering white birds. Like Saint Francis, the birds all lovingly flew toward him and onto his arms as he stood in the shape of a cross. As his father spun around to face him, Angelo was overcome by a truly miraculous vision. A halo of bright white light radiated behind his father from the rear window—illuminating a spiritually moving specter, one of heavenly transcendence, yet also one of inevitable gloom.

As he stood mesmerized, his father was obviously in a state of utter peace and otherworldly love as the pure white pigeons seemed to carry him away from all his earthly pain. Yet, in an instant, Angelo was thrust into a dark world of earthly pain when his father suddenly collapsed.

Angelo immediately rushed over, and lifted his head. "Papa! Speak to me? Pop! Please! Don't leave me."

His father's eyes barely opened as he muttered, "I'm so sorry, Angelo, that we didn't have more time together. But, I'm glad you found a beautiful woman to love. During my reconnaissance I learned about Mildred. Love her as I loved your mother...but, I'm sorry...it's time, time for me to go... fulfill your destiny...I love you, my son."

Angelo's heart dropped as he felt the last warm current of his father's blood cease to flow—the electrical spark of life had turned irrevocably off. His own world went black.

The next morning Angelo had somewhat recovered from his emotional blackout by the time he woke to Mildred's warm smile and loving embrace. Trapped within his gloom, Angelo could only mumble the bad news.

Mildred's head dropped. "I'm so sorry, Angelo. But try to focus on the gift you both shared of being reunited. It was truly a miracle."

Angelo just lay in bed as tears began to stream down his cheeks and into his ears. He had arrived home late in the middle of the night, as if in a trance, and gone straight to bed. He had carried out his father's wish to be buried near his shed, having found his will that was tacked to a corkboard in the kitchen. All that remained was to sell off the property, but the emotional reunion had been much too short for Angelo, with its dramatic yet dreadful ending. Still, the haunting last words of his father kept tolling in his tear-filled ears: "fulfill your destiny."

Angelo turned his head and pointed to the dresser. "Can you please hand me that envelope?"

Mildred stood up, grasped the manila envelope, and brought it back. "What is it? Your father's will?"

"Not exactly, but then again, maybe it is what he willed for me."

Mildred looked confused. "What do you mean?"

Angelo opened the flap and slid out a large piece of paper. Filled with curiosity, Mildred leaned over. Although unable to get a full view, she didn't expect to see what she saw. "Oh my! What in God's name is that?"

Angelo just lay there semi-dazed, staring, until finally he said, "It's a drawing by Gustave Doré of a vision that Franz Liszt had."

Mildred shivered. "It's creepy."

"Yes, it is. Especially since Liszt envisioned this some sixty-eight years before it came to fruition."

"What came to fruition? That demonic image looks like Armageddon."

Angelo looked at Mildred. "I'm afraid that's where we're heading. Look closer, look at the central figure."

Mildred grasped the illustration. As she spun it around in full view, she froze with shock. "Oh my God! That looks like Adolf Hitler! How can that be?"

Angelo grabbed the sketch. "Because in more ways than one, Liszt hurled his lance into the future, foreseeing the evil that would plague us, and he passed the baton to my father, who in turn has passed it on to me."

"What are you saying?" Mildred prodded with anxiety. "What baton? And just what has your father willed for you?"

But Angelo had drifted back into his vexing trance, his eyes just staring at the ominous illustration.

G. Doré 1866

FINALE: BERLIN, RASTENBURG & BASEL

[1935-45]

A year had passed since Angelo awoke from his trance, a deep catatonic hex that was only broken when Mildred uttered two powerful words: *I'm pregnant.*

On that morning, Angelo's dark menacing visions miraculously seemed to vanish upon hearing the news, like the sun evaporating dark stormy clouds to warmly reinvigorate the earth. With the birth of Angelo III, Angelo paused to re-gear his thinking; he now had a family to commit to, while also still devising a plan to accomplish all that he felt compelled to do.

Having been selected to fill the vacancy of Director left by the unexpected death of Rudolf Hein—which the papers declared had been a tragic accident due to his neglect of safety protocols—Angelo decided to stay on for the financial security as well as for the insider tips for his undercover operation. Given his dangerous covert activities at the Institute, coupled with the Nazis' accelerated toxic behavior, Angelo opted to hold onto his father's farm and moved Mildred and young Angelo to Basel, Switzerland. Fortunately, his new position of power allowed him to draft his own schedule, thus he was able to go home on weekends and for a full week every six weeks. He had expected this arrangement to be temporary—it wasn't.

After the births of three more children, Angelo decided to stay on longer in Berlin than anticipated; and with the outbreak of World War II in 1939, his covert operations had to be ramped up to support the German, French, and Italian resistance movements. Having stayed in contact with his old friend Einstein, Angelo relayed a bit of intelligence that he knew Albert would gasp over; namely, that the Nazis had actively engaged in atomic research. Angelo's startling reports presaged what the physicist Leo Szilard so zealously impressed upon Einstein weeks later, basically that it was imperative for the United States to actively begin serious research to develop an atomic bomb. It was no longer a matter of *if* such a bomb could be built, but rather *when*—and failure to take on the Nazis and win this race would be catastrophic. This intelligence prompted Einstein to write a cautionary letter to President Franklin D. Roosevelt, leading to the development of the Manhattan Project.

Oddly enough, Angelo had also made contact with a former math student of his from his tenure at the Scuola Normale Superiore in Pisa—his name was Enrico Fermi. Angelo's star pupil had gone on to win the Nobel Prize for Physics in 1938 and, like Einstein, he, too, had fled to the United States. The war years rolled by, and Fermi's brilliant research at the University of Chicago led to the development of the atomic pile in 1942; and what had once been but a mere possibility of a nuclear chain-reaction had become a hard reality. Fermi would eventually take on the role of leading consultant at Los Alamos. During all this time, Enrico received constant updates by way of Angelo regarding the Nazis' progress.

Angelo had long hoped that he could simplify his life to spend more time with Mildred and his four children, yet the frightful events that kept spiraling out of control across the globe kept chaining him to the war effort. Despite these pressing times, however, Angelo had commendably delegated many tasks to his eager compatriots, thereby maintaining his regular schedule to visit his farm. Mildred clearly understood the immense load that Angelo had been forced to bear and was often too busy herself to dwell upon their lot, knowing very well that millions of others fared far worse. This was mainly predicated upon the harrowing news that Angelo relayed to her.

Amid his surveillance, Angelo had discovered that Haber's laboratory developed a new lethal gas, called Zyklon-B. Angelo had followed the paper trail of the lab's sales receipts, which led to a well-concealed factory in the outskirts of Berlin. While there, he had witnessed the manufacturing and delivery of small, round canisters to a concentration camp in Auschwitz. Itching with curiosity, he had watched as an endless procession of trains arrived like clockwork; each packed with Jewish prisoners, as if cattle. Meanwhile, huge mysterious plumes of black smoke billowed from smokestacks in the distance. The nauseating odor had choked Angelo's lungs, but it was only upon further investigation that the horror truly set in—the putrid stench had been from burning human flesh! As if thrust into the darkest circle of Dante's Hell, Angelo trembled as he watched Nazi butchers shoveling emaciated dead bodies of men, women, and children into furnaces, as if contaminated animal meat. Meanwhile, others had been systematically led into gas chambers, awaiting their turn to be processed in Hitler's diabolical slaughterhouse of mass murder.

Angelo was profoundly shaken by the paradoxical nature of Haber's posthumous contribution. The Gas Man's legacy would now include his killing of Jews en masse—Haber's own kin. Moved by these disturbing events, Angelo setup underground networks to traffic Jews across Germany's tight borders to safe havens. Even overriding Angelo's concerns for his family's safety, Mildred had used their own farm (with its huge cellar and food supplies) for sheltering and feeding Jewish refugees on their desperate journeys to freedom.

Yet, despite all the noble efforts, Angelo still had trouble sleeping nights, as his father's dying words often tolled in his mind like an ominous gong: *fulfill your destiny.*

His father had deeply regretted not killing Hitler and now the wicked 'loose end' was raping and scorching the earth—foretelling the very end of civilization.

On July 12, 1944, Angelo managed to arrange a meeting in Berlin at the *Bendlerblock*, some four miles away from the Institute, with Colonel Claus von Stauffenberg.

Walking alongside the *Landwehrkanal* (Militia Canal), Angelo could see the huge *Bendlerblock* building with its vibrant orange roof and stately beige façade. It had become the headquarters of the German Resistance and Angelo could now see Colonel von Stauffenberg and General Friedrich Olbricht standing on the sidewalk near the building's entrance.

As Angelo approached, Stauffenberg turned—his striking, black eye patch unmistakably identifying the wounded colonel. "I take it you are Director Angelo Di Purezza with that blackish-gray crop of wavy hair?"

Angelo nodded. "Yes, I see my description was clear enough for you to identify me."

Stauffenberg smiled. "And I know my black eye patch was even easier for you."

"Indeed, it was," Angelo said. "There's certainly no mistaking *you*, Colonel."

Angelo extended his hand, yet as he gazed down at Stauffenberg's right arm, he suddenly recoiled—his whole right hand was missing!

"I apologize for not shaking your hand, Director," the Colonel said, "but, as you can see, I no longer have one to offer you."

A slight chill ran down Angelo's back. "I'm so sorry, Colonel von Stauffenberg. You didn't mention that over the phone."

General Olbricht, with his receding hairline and glasses, extended his hand. "Greetings, Angelo. As you can see, I do have a hand to offer you." As they shook hands, he added,

"And don't worry, Claus has very thick skin, so such minor setbacks cause him little concern and no mental hardships."

Stauffenberg grinned. "Yes, in fact, I don't wish to give you the creeps any further, Director, but I also have only three fingers remaining on my left hand."

Swinging his left arm up to display his disfigured claw, Angelo's lips twisted uncontrollably. "Again, I apologize, Colonel. It's just that I can't get used to seeing all these tragic consequences of war. I recall my father telling me how Franz Liszt used to visit the wounded and play rousing tunes for them to lift their spirits. Now I understand why."

Stauffenberg nodded. "Yes, I find music to be very therapeutic, and I guess that explains why some of Liszt's other works were emotionally charged with pathos."

"I believe so," Angelo replied. "And evidently some of that music was too dark and gloomy for some people to understand." Angelo looked back down at the Colonel's missing hand and squinted. "So how did it happen, if I may ask?"

Stauffenberg hooked Angelo's arm with his handless stump and began to walk along the canal, as General Olbricht flanked Angelo on the other side. "Sure," the Colonel said, "It all happened in Tunisia, just about a year ago. I was driving my vehicle, when a formation of British fighter-bombers swooped down and opened fire. My vehicle and others were strafed; and actually, some of those *Kübelwagens* sustained a hell of a lot more damage than I did. They had to be junked; meanwhile, I only lost my left eye, right hand, and two fingers on my left hand."

Angelo shook his head. "You're one hell of a guy, Colonel. I don't know what *I* would do in such a situation."

"Listen," Stauffenberg said jovially, "to be honest, I never really knew what to do with all those fingers anyhow."

"Do you see what I mean?" General Olbricht interjected. "The man is like a rock."

"So I see," Angelo replied. "Now then, how can I help you?"

General Olbricht peered around as they walked. "Well, Director, the Colonel tells me that you have been cleared, so I'll take his word for it. I hear you have done many covert operations, all successfully, and that you are committed to the German Resistance—*Ja?*"

"With my life, Herr General."

"Very well," the General said. "Have you been apprised of Operation Valkyrie?"

Angelo hadn't been, but he found the operation's name too inviting not to jest. "No, Herr General. But I assume it must have something to do with Wagner's *Ride of the Valkyries*. Are we escorting slain heroes to Valhalla?"

Stauffenberg chuckled. "I like a man with a sense of humor *and* good taste in music."

Meanwhile, General Olbricht remained unamused. "No, this has nothing to do with Richard Wagner, but rather Adolf Hitler."

Angelo's smile vanished. "Excuse my levity, Herr General, but anything to do with Hitler has my full attention."

"I certainly hope so," the General replied, having become somewhat skeptical of Stauffenberg's recommendation.

"I'll have you know," Stauffenberg interjected defensively, "that Director Di Purezza's father was responsible for the assassination attempt on Hitler back in 1932. So, don't disparage our new comrade."

General Olbricht looked across Angelo's face at Stauffenberg. "Very well, Colonel. But do watch your tone, you're speaking to a general. And remember, I, as well as Henning von Tresckow, devised this operation."

Stauffenberg looked at the General with his one glaring eye. "With all due respect, General, you and your friends in the *Wehrmacht* have all been dragging your feet on this mission for two and a half years. Let's not forget yesterday; I had Hitler and Göring sitting at the Berghof with my bomb planted right next to them. Yet when I phoned you to confirm and execute our plan, *you* called it off."

Angelo—uncomfortably caught in the middle—just observed, as General Olbricht fired back, "That's because I want to get Himmler, too! We must get all three if we're to make the rest of the operation a success."

"At this point," Stauffenberg countered, "to hell with seeking perfection. It rarely, if ever, comes in battle. So we must take what is given us—seize the moment! And to do that, one needs guts, General, not excuses."

Olbricht shook his head. "Oh, yes, the half-blown-up war hero wishes to recklessly execute a dangerous mission without planning and precision. That's why you look the way you do, Claus. I've known many men with blaring bravado, just like you, and almost all now lie six feet under the ground."

Stauffenberg had heard enough of the personal digs, and he uncharacteristically lost his temper. "Call me anything you like, General, but I'm fed up with all your delays. Apparently, you have no balls!"

Olbricht's face twisted. "I'd rather have no balls and a brain, than the reverse, Colonel! And watch your—"

"Excuse me," Angelo interjected—losing his patience, and unclasping his arm. "I didn't come here to listen to your internal problems. The real problem is *Hitler*. And if you men can't see to it to act in unison, then I'd rather go my own way, just like my father did. After all, I'm doing pretty well so far."

General Olbricht smirked and peevishly looked outward at the trees lining the canal, while Stauffenberg aimed his single orb at Angelo. "Listen, Director, the General is a good man and we're both committed, it's just that we're all under a great deal of stress. Moreover, I know you want to do more than just help supply resistance fighters with intelligence and weapons, or help refugees, so, please, hear us out. Yes, I've lost a great deal of patience, but I'm fervently committed to serving that end goal that all three of us seek—killing Hitler!"

Spotting a bench facing the canal, Angelo took a seat to collect his thoughts. The Colonel and General followed, again, flanking Angelo on opposite sides.

General Olbricht exhaled. "Getting back to Operation Valkyrie, Director, it is actually not my plan, *per se*, but rather a contingency plan that has been approved by Hitler. You see, the Führer is very concerned that the unrelenting bombings by Allied forces will cause civil revolt in our cities, not to mention uprisings by all the foreign subjects that are now forced laborers under the Third Reich. His policies had originally allowed these foreigners a minuscule amount of autonomy, yet with signs of Germany possibly losing this war, they're starting to get more vocal and demanding—and Hitler is not one to hear demands, especially by non-Aryan laborers. As such, Hitler's reprisals have become harsh and swift. Some three and a half million Soviet prisoners have been executed or died of starvation. With resentment and vengeance brewing in their guts, the probability of revolt in these territories is a major concern for Hitler. Therefore, Operation Valkyrie is a military backup plan that would utilize a Reserve Army to maintain civil order and control so Hitler can continue his dirty business as usual."

Angelo sneered, "Well, the madman is right to think that the people are eager to revolt. So what is *your* plan?"

The General adjusted his glasses and looked at Angelo. "My plan is to convert Hitler's Operation Valkyrie into Operation Coup d'état." As Angelo's eyes widened, Olbricht continued, "I intend this military unit to take control of our cities and then rapidly neutralize Himmler's SS."

Angelo nodded. "I certainly approve, but two things concern me: First, do you have enough German soldiers willing to challenge the Nazis? And second, how do you propose to kill Hitler?"

Upon hearing Angelo's remark about Germans, the General turned indignant, as he looked at a passing boat, and replied irritably, "Yes, we have plenty of loyal Germans willing to oppose Hitler and his malicious Nazi regime, Director *Di Purezza,*" his voice emphasizing his Italian name.

"Well, no offence, Herr General," Angelo countered, "but it certainly took long enough."

The General turned and gazed at Angelo—seething. "You, of all people, should talk. Your Italian brothers are spineless worms that wriggled listlessly under Mussolini's thumb. Then when Allied forces landed on Sicily, they fell like dominos all the way up to Switzerland. Useless. All of them!"

Angelo grit his teeth and nodded. "Yes, Italian soldiers get a great deal of tongue-lashing here in Germany, but they have wisely chosen not to fight for a lunatic like Mussolini. That's why Toscanini refused to play his Fascist anthem, thus was put under house arrest. But the people rallied for the great conductor until the goons set him free. Arturo, like others and myself, fled Italy. Those that remained may have put on a uniform, but they didn't mindlessly buy into the madman like the majority of your fellow Germans did with Hitler. And that's why *Il Duce* was deposed a year ago. Yet, if a man like Garibaldi were at the helm, it would be quite a different story, one that would have had Italy siding with the Allies, rather than the Axis." As Angelo continued, his anger began to build into a crescendo. "Furthermore, Hitler claimed this war started because of the harsh reprimands by the Treaty of Versailles that included taking away some of your land. But those territories in Poland or Czechoslovakia, for example, have people living there for many generations that *do not* want to be Germans. How would you Germans like it if we Italians wished to reclaim all the territories that our Roman ancestors held for thousands of years? That would mean *all* of Europe, Northern Africa, parts of the Middle East and much of the Balkans. The Italian people, however, are content with what they have and know that these other territories all have their own cultures now, and everything can and should be just swell. But, no! Hitler, on the other hand, wanted his little parcels of land back, and a hell of a lot more. And now, the world must suffer through his Hell just to survive." Angelo aggressively stood up and peered down at the General. "And I'm sick and tired of hearing how dedicated German soldiers are. All I see are young Nazi cadets being sworn in as they make their *Reichswehreid*. Your Realms Military Oath mindlessly brainwashes your youth to swear to God a holy oath of unconditional obedience to Hitler. How profane and insane is that?"

General Olbricht sprung to his feet, his face red, and only inches from Angelo's. "That oath is exactly why I dedicated my life well over two years ago to take down this evil madman and his insane regime. And that is also why Hitler *must* be killed, because only his death will defuse his fanatical warriors."

Angelo's body remained firm, as he retorted, "That's all well and good, but I'm afraid I agree with Colonel von Stauffenberg—what the hell is taking you so long!?"

Stauffenberg rose to his feet and patted Angelo on the back. "I knew I liked you."

General Olbricht exhaled in disgust. "You two have no idea how much planning is required to pull off a plot like this, none whatsoever! This is not some little deer hunt; we're talking about trying to get close enough to kill the most powerful man on earth, a man surrounded by a pack of sick angry wolves, no less!"

"Well, Herr General," Stauffenberg retorted, now exasperated, "I think I'm done sitting around and waiting for *your* plans. After General Helmuth Stieff screwed up our plans three days ago, by backing out on his assassination plot in Salzburg, and then you, in terminating my attempt yesterday, I'm taking this operation into my own hands."

General Olbricht laughed. "You mean *hand*—and a screwed up hand at that!"

Stauffenberg wrapped his stump around Angelo's shoulder. "Come on, Herr Director, let's go back to the *Bendlerblock.* We can discuss *my* plan there, a stratagem of *action,* not words."

As the two were about to turn, General Olbricht uttered, "Listen, Colonel, you know you can count on me."

Stauffenberg peered back, neither rattled nor ruffled. "I know, Herr General. Like I said, we're all just under a great deal of pressure, so losing our heads is to be expected. Please excuse my earlier outbursts, but I will no longer wait or miss opportunities that present themselves. I will contact you later to keep you apprised of what my plans are. As you know, we all must act together to make this work, especially the important second phase of this operation once the time comes, as I don't trust General Fromm."

General Olbricht nodded. "Nor do I. His being in charge of the Reserve Army is a critical role, and I just can't figure the man out. He seems to be on the fence, and that can be most dangerous. So, in the interim, I will continue to cajole him to our way of thinking and assure him that we *will* be successful."

Stauffenberg nodded. "Yes, that's why I *must* kill Hitler, Herr General. All these failed attempts understandably make all of our coconspirators very uneasy, or should I say extremely fearful. So I can't blame them."

With that, General Olbricht patted Stauffenberg on the back, as the two exchanged warm glances. The Colonel looked back at Angelo. "Let's go."

Returning to the *Bendlerblock,* Stauffenberg escorted Angelo up to the third floor and entered an office where he introduced him to his adjunct, Werner von Haeften. As Angelo and Werner made their introductions, Stauffenberg gazed out the window at the picturesque city of Berlin. He may have been determined and eager, yet Stauffenberg harbored reservations. With the successful landing of Allied forces on the beaches of Normandy only a month earlier, he believed that to assassinate Hitler now seemed almost futile. However, when he turned and expressed these concerns to his two compatriots, they insisted that it was important for the German Resistance to show not only their fellow countrymen but also the world that not all Germans condoned Hitler's brutal regime. Apparently, Stauffenberg just needed to hear again what he already knew, before relaying his plot.

It would take place on July 20, 1944, at *Wolfsschanze* (Wolf's Lair). The secret complex of bunkers, situated in the middle of a dense forest, was located in East Prussia (formerly Poland) and had been built for Hitler's Operation Barbarossa when the Führer was making his exhausting assault on Russia. Recently, however, Hitler and some of his top command had scheduled a meeting there, and Stauffenberg was among those invited. The Colonel's plan went thus: Werner would carry two bombs in a briefcase to the site and meet up with Stauffenberg at a predetermined spot. There, they would activate the bombs and the Colonel would then enter the meeting, put the briefcase down, and leave.

Angelo agreed; simplicity was often the best solution, and he wanted to be a part of the operation. Stauffenberg assured Angelo that being a prominent scientist at the Institute would pose no problems, since Hitler's suspicions centered on ambitious warriors in uniforms. The days leading up to the fateful meeting were spent in careful preparation, with all three men faithfully rehearsing their roles. Angelo's task was that of distracting any officers at the meeting from fouling up the process. With the heightened state of tension in Hitler's inner circle—due to the Allied advances that were pummeling their way inland—Stauffenberg was happy to have another set of hands on the job, especially since he himself was somewhat lacking. However, despite his lack of a hand and some fingers, Stauffenberg was a hands-on sort of guy with three assassination attempts already under his belt. So when July 20th came, he and his two accomplices were primed and ready.

Catching their flight, the team sat mindfully quiet for three hours—landing on an airfield in Rastenburg, some half hour away from *Wolfsschanze*. Driving through the dense forest, they passed through three checkpoints, each crawling with SS guards examining their papers. To their relief, the two brown briefcases were not inspected. After enduring those nerve-wracking moments, the team finally arrived at the Führer's secret bunker complex. Almost immediately, Angelo and Werner were disconcerted to hear that their plans were already beginning to unravel; the meeting had been pushed up a half hour earlier to accommodate an unexpected visit by Mussolini later that afternoon. Therefore, the briefing would begin in just thirty minutes!

Stauffenberg, the seasoned veteran, remained calm and determined, as he strolled casually over to General Fellgiebel. He needed to confirm that Fellgiebel was ready to do his part, which was to inform their fellow conspirators back in Berlin to initiate the militant takeover once Hitler was dead, then cut all communication lines at *Wolfsschanze*.

Within moments, another unraveling layer of bad news came; their meeting, originally scheduled to be in a subterranean bunker—where Stauffenberg's explosives would be contained and cause more damage—was relocated to an aboveground wooden barrack. Worse still, Stauffenberg was having his own troubles in another barrack, hiding in the bedroom of a fellow conspirator. Using the excuse that he needed to freshen up, Stauffenberg was having a difficult time using the special pliers with his disfigured left hand to insert the fuse that would activate the bomb. An unexpected rapping on the door startled him as a sergeant urged him to hurry—the meeting was about to commence! Able to activate only one bomb, Stauffenberg placed it in one of the briefcases and started walking towards the barrack.

Meanwhile, Angelo was inside the conference room making small talk with Colonel Heinz Brandt. Angelo's undershirt was now soaked with perspiration, more so from nerves than the sweltering mid-day July sun. The Nazi high command had already filed into the small briefing room, yet there were no signs of Stauffenberg or Hitler. Angelo's eyes darted from face to face, then back toward the doorway. Suddenly, Adolf Hitler walked into the room. Angelo's heart beat faster as the throng of militant, cult worshippers all shot their right hands up and chanted, "Heil Hitler!"

Making his way across the room, Hitler's beady eyes locked in on Angelo's face—there was something oddly familiar about it, but he couldn't draw a connection. Instinctively, his eyes darted over to Colonel Brandt, who gave the Führer a nod of confirmation. Without further ado, Hitler sat at the center of the hefty, oak map table, with his back to the door, as his deadly disciples all converged and took their places around the table's perimeter.

Angelo stood against the wall with Colonel Brandt and two SS guards, wondering what happened to Claus. *Was his cover blown?* he wondered, as a number of calamitous scenarios flashed through his mind. Angelo was about to step out to investigate when Stauffenberg suddenly appeared.

Slipping into the room, Stauffenberg gazed at Angelo, offering a slight nod that all systems were go, then calmly approached the table. He placed the brown briefcase containing the activated bomb under the conference table and pushed it with his foot closer to Hitler—being only six feet away. It would detonate in five minutes!

The Führer only briefly glanced up at the colonel, being far more interested in the war maps, as his eyes feverishly scrutinized the positions of the Red Army and his faltering troops. Meanwhile, everyone was stunned into silence as General Heusinger solemnly relayed the depressing news—the mighty *Wehrmacht* was being humiliatingly slaughtered. The eastern front was a disaster.

With a signal from Stauffenberg, Angelo knew they only had two minutes left to escape the deadly blast. Yet, with Heusinger being the only one speaking and commanding the rapt attention of all, it would be far too obvious, not to mention precariously rude, to leave at such a time. As a bead of sweat began to trickle down from Angelo's moist hairline, the Führer finally opened up the floor to his henchmen. As they began pointing at the maps on the conference table and offering strategies for counterattacks, Stauffenberg turned quietly and walked past Angelo, then straight out the door.

Angelo leaned over toward Colonel Brandt. "Excuse me, I need to go to the lavatory. Do you know where it is?"

Brandt looked at Angelo quizzically. "Sure, it's just outside, several feet to the right. But where did your colonel friend go?"

"I imagine the same place." Angelo said.

With a heightened sense of suspicion, Colonel Brandt suddenly noticed how profusely saturated Angelo was; his hair was drenched and his face streaming with sweat. "Nervous, Herr Director?"

Angelo cracked an edgy smile. "Well, perhaps a little. You know—being in the presence of a great man like Hitler can do that, and this *is* my first time."

Colonel Brandt's cold analytical stare swiftly warmed. "Ah, yes, I recall my first time, too. It's kind of like sex—the first time is a killer, isn't it?"

"Yes, a *killer* indeed," Angelo replied wittily and somewhat relieved. However, knowing what he knew, his mind could almost hear the ticking of the clock growing louder and louder, as each second brought him closer and closer to certain death. "Well, I really must go, you know—nature is calling."

"Oh, of course, go right ahead," Brandt said.

As Angelo made his way to the door, he peered back. His heart began to race even faster—Brandt was now reaching down for Stauffenberg's brown briefcase. Having been unable to lean over the map table to get a clear view, Brandt was now unsuspectingly moving the deadly briefcase from being near Hitler's feet to the other side of the table, behind its massive oak leg. As the few seconds remaining would soon tell, this insignificant action would save Hitler's life and alter the course of history. Meanwhile, Angelo turned anxiously and walked quickly out the door. Making his way down the corridor and out of the wooden barrack, he spotted Stauffenberg and Werner just up ahead. As he ran through the tree-lined path to catch up with them, an earsplitting blast rocked the ground and rattled their nerves. Turning around, they saw the small barrack blown apart. Smoke was billowing wildly as fire feverishly twisted its way out of gaping holes and shattered windows.

The three saboteurs looked at one another, smiled, and ran headlong to their vehicle. Making their rendezvous at the airfield, they boarded the plane and took off for Berlin.

As they disembarked upon landing, the three shook hands and parted—Angelo making his way back to the Kaiser Institute, while Stauffenberg and Werner activated the second phase of their operation. However, Stauffenberg was soon enraged when he heard that General Olbricht's command to mobilize the coup had hit a brick wall, namely General Fromm. Refusing to believe that Hitler was dead, Fromm kept the confused Reserve Army in limbo, hence rendering the *putsch* useless. Within hours, their bold power play turned horrifically ugly as General Fromm—having received word that the Führer had indeed survived—ordered a wave of retaliatory strikes that trampled the coup. Shortly after midnight, Fromm had all the main conspirators rounded up, including Stauffenberg, Werner von Haeften, and General Olbricht, and all were summarily shot dead. Although Fromm had been ordered to only capture the conspirators, the wavering turncoat didn't wish to be implicated, and so all ties to the Valkyrie *putsch* had to be eliminated. Meanwhile, General Olbricht's coconspirator, Henning von Tresckow, would commit suicide hours later.

As daybreak came, Angelo picked up a newspaper and read the astounding headline: HITLER SURVIVES ASSASSINATION BLAST, CONSPIRATORS SHOT DEAD.

Angelo's head fell.

Distraught at the loss of his brave compatriots and for failing to prevent Brandt from moving the briefcase, even if impossible, Angelo suffered weeks of melancholy. But in time, he slowly regained his vigor and resumed his covert operations. Although he took comfort in the mounting Allied victories, Angelo continued to be plagued by his father's unfinished business—*his* unfinished business. It was now April 30, 1945, and he could hear the bombings and gunfire of the advancing Soviet troops. The Red Army was consuming Berlin, and it was now only a matter of hours or days before the Nazis' Third Reich would collapse.

Sitting in his office, Angelo's mind reeled as he contemplated his next move. Should he simply let the Allies capture Hitler and hold him accountable for war crimes? But what if he was only given a life sentence? Could Angelo tolerate knowing that Hitler was alive in a jail cell? He knew he could not—yet another, far more troubling thought entered his mind: what if Hitler escaped Berlin and disappeared? This thought truly rattled Angelo to the core.

Angelo felt certain that Hitler would never surrender. In fact, he knew the deranged leader had already commanded his brainwashed troops to fight until the death and had already ordered his scorched earth policy, that of spitefully destroying German industrial complexes to deprive the enemy of acquisition or glory.

Angelo sat pensive, with his elbows on the desk and his chin resting on his clasped hands, as his right knee bounced feverishly. He couldn't get over how Hitler's burning self-destruction of Germany so chillingly mirrored Richard Wagner's Immolation Scene from *Twilight of the Gods.* He thought of how ironic it was that Franz Liszt was often criticized for his venomous *Dante Symphony,* which some feared would corrupt innocent minds, yet it truly offered a positive Heavenly message *if* listened to in total. Meanwhile, Wagner's proudly touted Aryan works had a profoundly dark influence on Hitler, who used the *Rienzi Overture* for his Nazi Party's anthem and was now incinerating all of Germany in an Immolation Scene just like the one that ended Wagner's tragic *Ring Cycle.* Hitler's twisted worship of these works had evidently become a warped blueprint for the evil madman, and Angelo found this whole situation not only ironic, but infuriating.

Springing to his feet, Angelo knew that every minute now counted. Angelo had carefully contemplated several assassination plots over the past year, so he felt a surge of confidence. Reaching into his desk drawer, he pulled out his revolver and then slipped it into his jacket pocket. He grasped a briefcase and ran down to his laboratory, where he stuffed the case with two bags of chemical compounds—both essentially inert. Spotting his Liszt pendant, which was pinned to the inside of the lid, he smiled and closed the briefcase. Knowing that Hitler was stationed in the Reich Chancellery, Angelo stormed out the door of the Institute.

Running through the war-torn streets of Berlin, Angelo gazed up at the burnt-out and demolished buildings. Smoke and fire streamed out of empty windows, as the acrid smell of sulfur and ash choked his lungs. The once beautiful city now looked like a Hellish nightmare. In frustration, he gazed down at all the demoralized and fear-stricken Berliners as they pathetically scurried about. Dead bodies of thousands littered the streets; some being casualties of Soviet artillery fire, while others were victims of their own fanatical suicide—having mindlessly sworn an oath to their maniacal Führer to never surrender. The wailing of survivors could be heard all around, as Angelo's eyes spotted an odd and jarring sight; a young woman was caressing her dead charred baby, her mouth wide open, yet her cries silent—her voice giving way to the excruciating stress and torment. Angelo grit his teeth; Berlin, and the world, had chillingly become like Dante's *Inferno.* A vision of Doré's horrific sketch flashed before his mind's eye, recalling Liszt's prophetic omen. Angelo now saw the Armageddon before his eyes as the end result of a Prussian-German nation steeped in aggression, racism, and hatred, which now finally reached fruition all because of one obstinate, and initially unchecked, madman—Adolf Hitler!

Slowing down to a quick pace, Angelo discreetly removed the revolver from his pocket and slid it down his pants by his crotch. He then turned down Voss Street, finally arriving at his destination. Looking up at the once magnificent Reich Chancellery building, Angelo shook his head—sorrowful, frustrated, and angry. The political epicenter of Germany was literally blasted away, as chunks of its stately façade now littered the sidewalks. All around him buildings had been reduced to rubble—Hitler's rubble!

As Angelo approached the main entrance, two young guards drew their rifles. "Halt!" they barked.

Unaffected, Angelo sized the two up, then stared deep into the more aggressive guard's eyes. "I must see the Führer. I'm Director Di Purezza from the Kaiser Institute, and I have crucial information."

The stern-faced guard stepped forward, and grunted, "Your papers?"

Angelo reached into his jacket pocket, pulled out his wallet and flipped it open. "There, you see! Now let me in."

The smug guard looked at Angelo severely. "Just because you're a director from the Institute doesn't mean you're permitted access to the Führer."

Angelo's hand squeezed his briefcase harder in an effort to relieve his frustration, as he countered, "Just tell Traudl Junge that Mildred's husband Angelo is here—waiting impatiently!" Then with dagger eyes, he added, "I think you'll find yourself regretting this imposition, soldier."

The guard's cocky demeanor mellowed, knowing very well that Frau Junge was Hitler's personal secretary. As such, it was highly probable that the Director's intimate terms with Traudl meant that he was also close to the Führer.

Angelo felt a rush of confidence; he was at the top of his game and running on all cylinders. He recalled how Mildred had helped Traudl with her secretarial skills and resume several years ago. Mildred had even taken a liking to the young Austrian who had dreams of becoming a ballerina, yet ended up dancing alongside the most heinous psychopath to ever stomp across the earth.

The guard looked at Angelo's unflinching face and called back to his partner, "Keep your rifle cocked and ready." He laid his rifle against the Chancellery building, and said, somewhat apologetically, "Do excuse me, Director, but I'm ordered to frisk everyone that enters."

Angelo put the briefcase down and lifted his arms outward. "Go ahead, make it quick."

As the guard's hands cascaded over Angelo's waist and then down his legs, Angelo quickly sought to divert his attention when his hands neared his dual set of pistols. "Listen, as I said, I have extremely important information in that briefcase to deliver. So hurry up!"

The gullible guard stepped back. "Ah, yes! I also must see what's in that case of yours, Director."

"Be my guest," Angelo said, relieved. He picked up the briefcase and unlocked it. As he swung open the lid, the brash young guard leaned over and peered inside, his eyes squinting. "What in blazes is this stuff?"

"You're looking at the salvation of the Third Reich," Angelo said, dead serious.

The other young guard lowered his rifle. "Hey, Karl. What is it?" he asked curiously, as he walked over. As they both gazed at the two bags of powder, Karl looked at his partner, then back at Angelo. "I don't get it. What can these little bags of dust possibly do?"

Angelo's voice became dark and sinister. "If these two chemical compounds were to unite, you would witness the largest explosion the world has ever seen. It would lay waste to all of Berlin, leaving just a crater."

Karl's eyebrows pinched with disbelief. "Impossible!"

The other guard stepped back. "Actually, I believe him, Karl. My father had suffered some awful backlashes with the Institute's mustard gas during the Great War, so I can just imagine what these guys have been up to thirty years later."

Angelo smiled. "You're a wise boy, what's your name?"

"Helmuth, Herr Director."

Angelo gently closed the lid. His smile turned cold as he looked at Karl. "You've wasted enough of my time, Karl, and if you're wise, you'll let Helmuth here take me to see the Führer."

Karl grabbed his rifle. "I don't think so. I still think I should call this in."

As explosions and gunfire echoed throughout the air and the rumbling of Soviet tanks could be heard in the distance, Helmuth shook his head and threw his rifle around his shoulder. "Oh, give it a rest, Karl! We have nothing to lose. I'm taking him in, he just might be our only hope."

As the rat-a-tat-tat of dueling machineguns underscored Helmuth's words, Karl stepped back. "Fine, but I just hope those silly bags of tricks save our hides."

Angelo followed Helmuth into the main entrance and through the Marble Gallery until they emerged out the rear portal into the garden. The huge square was handsomely lined with trees and a row of greenhouses on the far side, yet portions of the yard were blown apart, scarred with huge pockmarks and divots from cannon fire.

As they followed the narrow paths, Angelo was scoping out every detail, every exit. "I was expecting a large office, not a garden."

Helmuth spun his head around as he continued to walk in front of Angelo. "Well, the Führer is not up here, he's down below, in the *Führerbunker*."

"Ah, I see. Of course," Angelo said, as he adjusted the revolver over his crotch, "he sure knows how to keep himself safe, doesn't he?"

"Yes, he sure does," Helmuth replied. "And, get this, the bunker's walls are over seven feet thick."

Just then, Helmuth stopped, pulled out his key chain and unlocked a steel door. As he swung the thick metal slab open, its hefty steel hinges squeaked. With an innocent, youthful smile, Helmuth waved Angelo to step in. Sliding through the threshold, Angelo was momentarily unsettled when he gazed down the long flight of cement steps. The concrete stairwell was morbidly dreary, looking like a dark vault leading to a crypt. The musty smell didn't help.

Helmuth closed the door and locked it. Pivoting about, he began descending the eerie stairwell. "Follow me."

With every step Angelo took, his revolver dug deeper into his thighs, forcing him to stop and adjust himself.

Helmuth looked back. "Is everything ok?"

Angelo smiled. "Yes, it's just these damn underwear. My wife uses too much starch."

Helmuth chuckled as he turned and resumed his descent.

Angelo's face grew damp with perspiration, his mind just now coming to grips with the harsh reality of his mission. The stifling forced-air from the ventilation system didn't help matters, as they finally entered a small cement-blocked cubicle used as a waiting room. It was sparsely furnished and painfully drab. The lack of windows, damp air, and dim lighting made the cell only appear smaller, as an uneasy touch of claustrophobia rattled Angelo's senses.

Just then, a guard rapidly approached Helmuth. "Who is this? We have no record of any visitors at this hour," he demanded, as he now turned his gaze at Angelo.

Helmuth pivoted buoyantly and looked back at Angelo, as he said, "This is Director Di Purezza from the Kaiser Institute. He has an amazing new explosive that can destroy whole cities. This man can save the Third Reich!"

The guard's lip twisted. "Is this some sort of a joke?"

Angelo wiped his sweaty brow. "No, what the boy says is absolutely true."

"It had better be," the guard said, "because the Führer has been under immense stress these past few weeks. Even his marriage to Eva yesterday did little to lift his heavy mood."

"Well, I assure you," Angelo said, "this will end his worries forever."

Just then, Joseph Goebbels limped into the cubicle—his weasel-like face pale and visibly marred by intense fear and hopelessness. He had already made plans with his wife to end not only their own lives, but also those of their six young children if all appeared to be lost. And with one glimmer of hope shot down after another, the future of Nazi Germany and the Goebbels dynasty was looking painfully bleak. Closing his eyes, the Propaganda Minister took a long drag from his cigarette, as if it were a kind of medication, then looked over at Angelo with his cold, cadaver-like eyes. "I believe I know you, but I can't recall how or where."

Helmuth—whose youthful optimism was in stark contrast to Goebbels weathered depression—interjected excitedly, "He's a director from the Kaiser Institute."

"Ah, yes," Goebbels said, almost dazed, as he rubbed his greasy black hair. "I've seen your photograph. I know Max Planck. Poor old Max moved out of Berlin two years ago, I think. The bombing was too much for him. I'll never forget how the old fellow tried to uphold Fritz Haber's employment some ten years or so ago, but Hitler refused. As you must know, Haber was a damn Jew, so he had to go. At least I'm glad we were able to put Haber's Zyklon-B to good use."

"Sure, right," Angelo said, trying awfully hard to play along. Yet, unexpectedly, his conscience surged to the fore, as he sharply needled the deranged disciple. "But I'm curious; Max had told me back then that you had spoken very highly of Hitler. I believe it was something like 'I thank providence for having given us this man.' So what exactly is your feeling about Hitler now?"

Goebbels looked at Angelo intently, not sure just how that question was posed, or if he should reveal his innermost feelings. His weary delusion overcame him, as he passively replied, "Well, the Führer told me just days ago that the pendulum of history was about to swing back in favor of Germany. Therefore, I shall not lose hope," he said most unconvincingly.

Angelo smiled. "Well, I don't know about that, but it certainly looks like you've lost sleep."

Goebbels' glazed eyes peered down at the drab cement floor as he took another long drag of his numbing cigarette. His boney hand shook, as he kept the nicotine in his dark evil lungs as long as he could. Blowing out the smoke, like a wounded dragon whose fire was all spent, he gazed back up at Angelo. "Yes, I've been smoking an awful lot lately and taking tons of sleeping pills."

Angelo nodded. "Good for you, that's probably the best thing you can do at this point. But, you'll have to excuse me, I'm here to see the Führer. So if you don't mind, I'd really like to get—"

"Oh, yes, by all means," Goebbels said, sluggishly, "I have to meet up with Martin Bormann anyhow. But, feel free to join us once you're finished."

"Sure, why not," Angelo said, as he counted in his head how many bullets he might have to spare. Meanwhile, Goebbels unsteadily turned and slowly limped away with his deformed clubfoot.

As fate would have it, in 48 hours Goebbels would find himself administering sweet water, laced with poison, to his six children, while he and his wife, Magda, would bite down on their cyanide capsules as if Eucharistic hosts—unwittingly offering their souls to Lucifer for induction into his Hellish Hall of Shame.

Meanwhile, Traudl walked over to Angelo. "Hello, Herr Director. Nice to meet you. Helmuth just told me who you are. How is Mildred?"

Angelo smiled anxiously. "Oh, fine, just fine. In fact, we have four children now."

"That's terrific," Traudl said, as she motioned with her head. "Follow me, I'll take you in."

As Angelo walked alongside her, Traudl looked up at him. "I see Mildred knows how to pick men."

"Why, thank you, Traudl. She's always told me how sweet you were, and I can see that your looks match her description."

Traudl smiled with a gracious nod. "Well, Director, I don't wish to know your business with the Führer, but I must say, please go easy on him." Her face turned sullen. "I just typed up his will. He knows the end is near."

"Indeed it is," Angelo mumbled to himself, as he adjusted the pistol in his pants.

Traudl then entered a much smaller vestibule-like cubicle, as she turned and put up her hand. "Please wait here, I'll inform the Führer of your presence."

Angelo nodded, as she entered Hitler's cell and closed the door.

After his brief encounter with Traudl, Angelo couldn't help but think how innocent people got caught up in Hitler's charismatic charade, even someone so close to this madman as Traudl. As he looked around the cramped tomb-like cell—with its depressing cement walls and dank, stale air—creepy chills rippled over his torso and down his legs. To Angelo, this rotten, dingy rat hole seemed most fitting for the repulsive rodent that was incinerating the world.

Taking a seat on a flimsy wooden chair, Angelo's legs bounced in nervous anticipation, as adrenaline surged through his system like electricity. With each passing minute, another bead of sweat dripped down the side of his face. Angelo had learned to better harness his nerves while actively engaged in a perilous operation, but waiting was sheer murder. Ten minutes passed, when finally the door swung open and Traudl walked out. "The Führer will see you now, Herr Director."

As Angelo stood up, the pistol slid down his pant leg, the barrel slightly emerging as it sat on the top of his shoe.

Traudl's eyes widened as Angelo bent over and picked up the pistol. "It's just for protection," Angelo said calmly, "those damned Soviets are shooting up all of Berlin."

Traudl's anxiety faded. "Of course, what was I thinking? You're a scientist and married to Mildred, you can't be an assassin—now can you?"

Angelo smiled confidently. "Of course not, assassins kill humans. The only things we scientists kill are rats."

Traudl giggled. "Very true. I actually feel sorry for all those poor lab rats."

"You're too kind, Traudl—seriously. You see, rats need to die so we humans can live. It's just a harsh reality of life."

As Traudl's face still registered her gullible compassion, Angelo looked at her with endearing eyes. "Listen, Traudl, you're obviously a nice gal, but please do me a favor and make sure the Führer and I are not disturbed. It shouldn't take long, but I do have a new chemical weapon in this briefcase."

Traudl recoiled. "You mean—a bomb!?"

Angelo smiled. "No, not exactly. It's a harmless miniature testing-module that I use just to demonstrate its volatile nature. So, you see, there might be a little rumble or a loud noise, but don't worry, I've tested this many times at the laboratory, so just make sure no one else gets alarmed."

Traudl nodded. "Certainly, Herr Director, no problem," she said with a smile, "I'm so glad you came. I knew you'd be delivering just what Hitler always needed."

Angelo smiled. "Indeed, he should have received this a long time ago."

As Traudl passed by him, she added, "Just be careful, because like your explosive, the Führer is in a *volatile* mood." She then exited the crude, cinderblock waiting room.

Angelo slipped the pistol in his jacket pocket, keeping his finger on the trigger. Taking a deep breath, he entered Hitler's chamber. There, sitting behind his small drab desk, Hitler hopelessly gazed down at a map, while his left hand shook uncontrollably with a Parkinson-like affliction. The Führer's nerves were fried, yet the scheming psychopath's mind was still burning the midnight oil—obstinately seeking a miracle. Hitler looked up, his tired, beady eyes analyzing Angelo's face. "I've seen you before—*ja?*"

Angelo closed the door behind him, locked it, and took several steps closer. "Yes, at *Wolfsschanze*."

Seeing Angelo lock the door, and now bringing back bad memories of his near assassination, Hitler sprang to his feet—self-consciously thrusting his crippled hand behind his back. "Ah, yes, I never forget a face. So is this another attempt to assassinate me?"

"Well, I must say, you're one tough son-of-a-bitch to kill. Not only did Stauffenberg fail several times, but so did my father many years ago, back in 1932."

"Yes, of course, at the Berlin Opera House," Hitler said with disgust. "I'll never forget that old man's face, either. And now I see the resemblance." Hitler cautiously sat back down—his hands out of Angelo's sight. "But, all of you are incompetent fools, just like all those around me," Hitler said, his face now contorting. "Two days ago, *Reichsführer-SS* Himmler had the audacity to sneak behind my back, sheepishly trying to secure a peace treaty. Can you believe that?" Hitler vented, his voice rising with anger. Angelo just stared, emotionless, as Hitler stridently continued, "Then *Waffen SS* General Felix Steiner was ordered to make a rousing offensive, but the traitorous coward refused to mobilize. The *dummkopf* should be shot!" Hitler blasted, as his tirade escalated, "then General Walther Wenck tells me his Twelfth Army will turn this Battle of Berlin around, and he, too, proves useless. I'm surrounded by *dummkopfs!*" Smashing the top of his desk with his fist, Hitler's demonic eyes glowed with rage as he exploded, "And, then, to top it off, that fat SOB Hermann Göring has the gall to telegram us from Bavaria that *he* should assume command. Ha! Can any of these blundering idiots truly believe that they can make decisions that only *I* am capable of making?"

Angelo slipped the revolver out of his pocket. "Yes, I see where *your decisions* got you and Germany. The Allies are crawling all over our heads right now, destroying Berlin, all because of *your decisions.* You're now trapped like a rat in this tomb, because of *your decisions.* Millions have died and millions of Jews have been incinerated, all because of *your decisions.* The world, my furious and demented Führer, does not need *your decisions!*" With that, Angelo cocked the revolver.

Meanwhile, unbeknownst to Angelo, Hitler had his hand on his Walther PPK 7.65 mm pistol inside his desk drawer. Within the next four seconds, Angelo took aim and squeezed the trigger, yet his eyes suddenly froze with shock—the gun jammed! Simultaneously, Hitler swung up his Walther and squeezed off a shot. As the bullet tore through Angelo's shoulder, he quickly whipped his briefcase around, knocking the Walther out of Hitler's hand. Hitler bent over to reclaim it, but Angelo swung the briefcase up and cracked it down hard on Hitler's head. As the Führer fell flat on his face, Angelo grabbed the Walther. Hitler quickly flipped over on his back and grabbed the base of the coat rack. Swinging the long metal pole down, the spiked head smashed Angelo's arm, discharging the firearm—the bullet boring a huge hole in Hitler's skull.

Angelo dropped the Walther on Hitler's chest, not realizing that it was the same pistol that Hitler's half-niece,

Geli Raubal, used to commit suicide thirteen years earlier. It was an odd but fitting end.

Angelo then looked at the bullet hole in his shoulder and sighed—it appeared to be a clean shot. He used his undershirt to stuff the hole, then took his Liszt pendant out of the briefcase to cover the hole on his jacket. His gaze turned back to the dead Führer on the floor, as a wave of relief and fulfillment washed over him—his father had passed him the baton eleven years earlier, and he had now finally achieved success. Angelo looked up and winked.

As his head swung down, he spotted two phony passports and tickets to Argentina on Hitler's desk. They had been sent to him by Dr. Josef Mengele—the deranged madman who used Jewish prisoners for sadistic scientific experiments. The accompanying letter stated that he was currently hiding in Bavaria, but would rendezvous with Hitler and Eva in the near future. Angelo smiled, all the more happy to have thwarted Hitler's planned escape.

Picking up his briefcase, Angelo stuffed his revolver in his jacket pocket and slipped out the door. As he quickly paced toward the bunker's stairs, he passed Traudl.

"Oh, so how did your demonstration go?"

Angelo didn't even stop or look. "As planned, thank you."

Angelo flew up the bunker stairs, through the garden, and out the front entrance of the Reich Chancellery. As he did, he saw Helmuth standing several yards away. He was looking down at his dead comrade Karl—a mortar had just blown his legs several feet away. Helmuth looked up and spotted Angelo, tears streaming down his face. "You better get out of here, Director. The Russians are storming through the streets and they're heading this way!"

"You better run, too!" Angelo said, as he put his hand over the pendant to apply pressure to the wound. He turned and started to run back toward the Institute. The streets were clouded with smoke and Berliners all scurrying to take shelter, as others ran to greet their liberators. Making it back to his office, Angelo telephoned his doctor who discreetly tended his wound. With the prognosis of a full recovery—requiring some physical therapy—Angelo patted the doctor on the back and thanked him. With the pressing need for his services elsewhere, the doctor nodded and swiftly departed.

Angelo gathered the essentials from his office and packed his suitcase. Taking a deep breath, he sat down at his desk. As he gazed down, he saw the poorly mended bottom drawer that Hein had broken into years earlier. Reaching down, he opened it, and pulled out his *Dante Symphony* score. Memories of all the events that had transpired due to Liszt's enigmatic score filled his mind: Liszt's elusive code, Einstein's friendly assistance to decode it, the hunt for Haber, the run-ins with Hein, his father's feigned death, as well as that final, sad yet transfiguring moment. And then, as if submerged in a warm and soothing mineral bath, all the beautiful memories of Mildred saturated his senses; the faithful woman of his dreams who stuck by his side through good times and bad, the loving woman who gave birth to their four beautiful children, the gorgeous woman who now deserved his full love and attention.

Overcome with emotion, Angelo rubbed the cover of the *Dante Symphony* score as a tear of joy and relief fell from his eye—squarely hitting the light-colored, poison stain and turning it darker, or rather appearing to make the deadly stain blend with the cover, or disappear, at least temporarily. Angelo chuckled at the apt symbolism, as he now wisely understood how the world often gets reprieved by conquering evil, yet unfortunately evil can never be fully eradicated—always finding a way to reappear. However, it was imperative for the righteous to stand up and confront evil, for passivity can be just as deadly as the worst evildoers.

Angelo put the score down and happily gazed out his sunny office window at all the tulips and lilacs that colorfully lined the walkway. With a smile he picked up the telephone and called Mildred—he would be returning home to Basel for good. With his missions accomplished and the dark clouds now all behind him, Angelo and the free world seemed to be given another chance to begin anew. Spring was here in more ways than one and it was time to start building a better life and a better world. Civilization had been saved from ruin and it was up to him and all like-minded souls to preserve it. This was a task not for those who naively say never shall we engage in war again or those simply content to reap the benefits of freedom, rather, it was for all those valiant men and women who were willing to put their lives on the line to defend liberty when duty calls.

As these thoughts filled Angelo's mind, a lump of pride welled in his throat, for he now knew there is nothing more noble and glorious than to be a part of such a breed as his co-defenders of freedom. Leading that pack were those who were perceptive and brave enough to stand up to evil when it first rears its ugly head. With his heart pounding proudly to the righteous rhythm of justice, Angelo's mind and soul buoyantly rejoiced: *God bless Liszt's Altar Eagles, my compatriots, and all future Eagles, and may they all find eternal peace perched on the high altar of Paradise!*

End

HISTORICAL CHARACTERS

Composers & Pianists

FRANZ LISZT: (1811 – 1886)

Liszt composed the *Dante Symphony* between 1855-56 and dedicated it to Richard Wagner, who had suggested that no human was capable of depicting Paradise. Nevertheless, Liszt managed to compose an ethereal *Magnificat* that many, including this author, believe beautifully accomplishes the spiritual requirement and effectively completes the symphony. Additionally, Liszt did write an alternate ending, which he later instructed was not to be used.

Sergei Rachmaninoff is one of many who admired the *Dante Symphony*. Liszt's powerful tour de force gives voice to some of the most advanced harmonies of his day, some anticipating the impressionistic works of Claude Debussy a half century later. In many ways, Liszt did hurl his lance into the future—a metaphor that did become a recurring and appropriate epitaph for this prophetic genius.

As for secret codes, although Liszt did write his *Fantasy and Fugue on B-A-C-H*, which uses a thematic progression of notes that spell out the name BACH to honor Johann Sebastian Bach, he never devised any musical ciphers for covert political or religious agendas. Or at least none that were ever found or decoded.

Franz Liszt was a pioneer of the first order, and an experimenter, much like Leonardo da Vinci, who was more concerned with innovation and progress than personal glory or financial rewards. His noble and selfless dedication to teaching students free of charge—thereby allowing his ideas to flourish and take flight upon the wings of his pupils as they became famous and influential in their own right—remains a highly laudable act that often times gets lost behind the frivolous rumors and catty gossip that the tabloids, then and now, fixate on. As revealed in this novel, Liszt did have a weak spot for women and was continually barraged by them. However, he truly was the conquered soul in most cases. He gravitated towards women who were empowering, yet not always conventionally attractive, as in the case of Princess Carolyne von Sayn-Wittgenstein, to whom he was engaged for a time. As a minute detail, Carolyne, in fact, did give Liszt the pocket watch with the engraving of Pope Pius IX mentioned in Scene IV.

Liszt was a prolific composer and a leading figure of the Romantic period, not to mention the true founder of Impressionism and Atonal music that flourished after his death. I invite all my readers to investigate Liszt's rich harmonic worlds, as they are sure to fire the imagination and lift the soul. And perhaps even scare the Hell out of you in certain pieces. Feel free to visit my Franz Liszt Site at:

www.dvbooks.net/music/franzliszt.htm

CAMILLE SAINT-SAËNS: (1835 – 1921)

Saint-Saëns was a French composer who was heavily influenced by Franz Liszt and the two were indeed friends. However, Camille did not engage in any covert operations, and as the novel indicated, he was discharged from the French army during the Franco-Prussian War and fled to London after Napoleon III's demise, when the future of France looked most bleak. He was a virtuoso on the piano and produced a large oeuvre of masterful works, including five splendid *Piano Concertos, Danse Macabre, Havanaise, Organ Symphony,* and the opera *Samson and Delilah,* among others.

RICHARD WAGNER: (1813 – 1883)

Wagner and Liszt had a close yet turbulent relationship. Having seduced and stolen Liszt's daughter Cosima from Hans von Bülow, Wagner (being only two years younger than Liszt) caused a scandal that ruptured their relationship for several years. Yet the two titanic composers did manage to rekindle a somewhat cordial relationship thereafter.

As indicated in the novel, Wagner's penchant for stealing also carried over to his pilfering Liszt's advanced chromatic harmonies. Wagner wrote a scathing letter to Hans von Bülow admonishing their friend Richard Pohl for blurting out to the whole world that Liszt had in fact pioneered Wagner's new harmonic language, which premiered in his famous *Tristan* prelude. That the chromatic sequence that made the *Tristan* chord so famous was taken almost note for note from Liszt's earlier works confirms Wagner's plagiarism. And, despite Liszt's generosity in praising Wagner, which the German master most certainly deserved, being a genius himself, one cannot escape the fact that the timeline of history places the lion's share of truly pioneering works into Liszt's earlier pockets, which did profoundly influence Wagner's music. Basically, there never could have been a mature Wagner without Liszt. And that Wagner's name dwarfed Liszt's during the Prussian and Nazi years is unfortunate, and demands rectification. In that regard, it is apropos to conclude with Wagner's own words about Liszt, which, unfortunately, he seldom ever voiced:

> "Do you know a musician who is more musical than Liszt? Who holds within his breast the powers of music in richer, deeper store than he? Who has felt more sensitively and more tenderly, who knows more and can do more, who is more gifted by Nature and who, by educating himself, has developed his potential more forcefully than he?"
>
> — *Richard Wagner*

GIOACHINO ROSSINI: (1792 – 1868)

Rossini retired from the stage at age 38, having written 39 operas. He was the most famous opera composer of his day, yet Giuseppe Verdi was fast on his heels, and the world of opera (with the advent of Wagner's music dramas) was changing. It proved to be a very dense and serious style of music that was against Rossini's jovial grain. Scintillating overtures and comic operas were where Rossini's genius shined most, as his *Barber of Seville* is a masterpiece of the genre, yet his skillful hand also penned serious operas, such as *Semiramide* and *Otello*. Abandoning the world of opera, Rossini did become one of the best hosts in Paris, where he entertained eminent guests at his lavish matinées and soirées. He and Liszt were indeed good friends, and Liszt did transcribe many of his operatic works for piano.

SOPHIE MENTER: (1846 – 1918)

Sophie was a star pupil of Liszt's, whom he described as his "piano daughter." Her electrifying performances even prompted the sarcastic and opinionated George Bernard Shaw to claim that her magnificence even exceeded that of the wildly famous Ignacy Paderewski. Sophie did perform Liszt's *Piano Concerto #1*, as indicated in the novel, yet naturally all her dialogue and covert actions herein are purely fictional.

AGNES STREET-KLINDWORTH (1825 – 1906)

Agnes was an attractive student of Liszt's, and lover for a time. Her father Georg Klindworth was a master spy for Prince Metternich and had contact with Austria's Franz Joseph and Russia's Nicholas I, among others. Agnes entered Liszt's school at the Altenburg in 1853, and their discreet relationship remained a secret for fifty years, until private correspondence of the two lovers surfaced. That Agnes was an emissary for her father has led some to suspect that Liszt may have engaged in their spy ring, yet no evidence to support that claim has arisen, at least not yet!

Scientists

ALBERT EINSTEIN: (1879 – 1955)

As indicated in the novel, Albert Einstein was at one time a good friend of Fritz Haber, yet he severed the relationship once he realized that Haber's patriotic zeal for the Kaiser entailed his developing poison chemicals for warfare. Einstein was a staunch pacifist and it is noteworthy that he did partially author the *Manifesto to Europe*. The *Manifesto* rebutted his German colleagues, who condoned World War I as being necessary for the survival of German culture. Einstein's critical declaration occurred just as he was given the Directorship of Physics at the Kaiser Institute, and such anti-war/anti-German sentiments were viewed as treasonous.

Nevertheless, Einstein boldly commented: *"Never before has any war so completely disrupted cultural cooperation."* Even though Germany lost the First World War, Einstein was dismayed to see how fast Hitler's Third Reich grew like a toxic weed, threatening to wreak even greater havoc and destruction upon Europe and the world. At that juncture, Einstein fled Germany and the pacifist became a realist, stating that the only way to remove Hitler was by force.

FRITZ HABER: (1868 – 1934)

It's key to point out that all the dialogue and murderous actions by Haber in this novel in regards to the two Di Purezza characters were fictitious. However, although not an assassin or direct murderer himself, Fritz Haber was the Kaiser's mastermind who developed poison chlorine gas used in World War I, although not mustard gas. He did lead a unit that also developed gas masks, which were distributed to German soldiers at the front. As noted, his wife Clara did commit suicide by shooting herself with his pistol due to his chemical weapons activities. Haber was decorated by the Kaiser and he won the Nobel Prize for Chemistry in 1918. He was born a Jew and did convert to Christianity. Nevertheless, Hitler's pogrom forced Haber to resign. His lab did produce Zyklon-B, and Haber did die of a heart attack in the Basel Hotel on January 29, 1934.

Political & Religious Leaders

EMPEROR NAPOLEON III: (1808 – 1873)

Napoleon III was the nephew of Napoleon Bonaparte, and ruler of France as indicated in the novel. He was a friend of Franz Liszt, yet the entire Altar Eagles covert operation was fictitious. He did support Pope Pius IX, and the events that led to war with Prussia over Spain were true. So, too, was the fatal demise of France when he led his troops into battle, thus being captured and thrown before Bismarck. He would spend the rest of his days (amounting to only two years) living in London in exile with his wife and son.

OTTO VON BISMARCK: (1815 – 1898)

Bismarck's political actions highlighted in the novel, including the excerpt (as spoken by Liszt) of his famous speech that earned him the nickname 'Iron Chancellor' are factual. And although Kaiser Wilhelm I was the figurehead of Prussia, Otto was indeed the Puppeteer and Chess Master. Yet, as indicated in the novel, once Kaiser Wilhelm II rose to power, Bismarck was viewed as a rival; thus came the famous dismissal or the "Dropping of the Pilot," which was a popular refrain at the time, having appeared in the London magazine *Punch*, as a political cartoon.

KAISER WILHELM II: (1859 – 1941)

Wilhelm II inherited the throne when his father Frederick III died after having served only three months. Frederick, in turn, had inherited his brief throne from his brother, Kaiser Wilhelm I, who, as indicated in the novel, was Bismarck's monarchical master. Yet, in reality, Wilhelm I was a figurehead, while Bismarck pulled the strings. Once young Wilhelm II rose to power, however, Bismarck was relieved of duty. In time, Wilhelm II found himself ensnared in a volatile situation when the Sarajevo crisis erupted over the assassination of the Archduke of Austria. As nations clamored for war, Wilhelm II actually looked to avert a full-scale European battle. Oddly enough, his cousin Nicholas ruled Russia, while his other cousin George ruled England, all three with ties to the deceased Queen Victoria. However, war could not be averted, and Wilhelm actually decried the fact that, if Queen Victoria were still alive, she never would have allowed their family feud to explode into outright war—a massive and ugly war that claimed the lives of over nine million people.

POPE PIUS IX: (1792 – 1878)

Pope Pius IX served the Holy See longer than any other pope, amounting to almost thirty-two years. He oversaw the Vatican during a most turbulent time, when its temporal powers were eliminated and the Vatican States were severely reduced to the present single Vatican State. Pius and Liszt were friends, and as indicated in the novel, they did spend quality time together, with Liszt at the piano and the Pope singing arias from Bellini's operas.

Artists

GUSTAVE DORÉ: (1832 – 1883)

Gustave Doré was a French illustrator, artist, and sculptor who illustrated Dante's *Divine Comedy*. Completed into two phases, Gustave illustrated the *Inferno* canto first, in 1857, and then *Purgatory* and *Paradise* ten years later, in 1867. His other illustrated works included Shakespeare's *Tempest*, John Milton's *Paradise Lost*, Edgar Allan Poe's *The Raven*, and many other literary works, as well as scenes from the Bible. Naturally, although a friend of Liszt's, he was not involved in any covert actions. However, he did begin documenting the Franco-Prussian War with a series of bleak illustrations that portrayed the destruction and breakdown of his beloved France under the trampling boots of Bismarck's Prussian soldiers.

The alleged DORÉ ILLUSTRATION OF LISZT'S VISION OF HITLER is a composite image that this author/artist created utilizing various Doré sketches and a portrait of Hitler from the George Grantham Bain Collection. I further manipulated the Hitler sketch to lend a more sinister air to the Nazi leader's diabolical eyes.

CASPER DAVID FRIEDRICH: (1774 – 1840)

Friedrich was a German Romantic landscape artist who produced many visionary works that delved into the mysterious realm of metaphysics. His works often portray nature as a sublime creation littered with the various ruins of mankind, celebrating the divine longevity of nature as compared to mankind's fleeting attempts at permanency and eternal glory. One is always forced to think and contemplate the mysteries of life when viewing a piece by Caspar David Friedrich, and he, too, has inspired this artist/author countless times. There was no Caspar David Exhibition at the Louvre, as indicated in the novel, yet included herein are black and white images of the master's intriguing artwork, which hopefully will incite further investigation.

OTHER CHARACTERS IN THE NOVEL

Here's a list of other historical figures featured in the novel: Hector Berlioz, Countess Virginia di Castiglione, Victor Hugo, Alexandre Dumas, Jean Ingres, Jacques-Louis David, Eugène Delacroix, Jean-Honoré Fragonard, Giovanni Sgambati, Giuseppe Garibaldi, Count Benedetti, Felice Orsini, Ede Reményi, Carl Bechstein, Émile Ollivier, Giuseppe Mazzini, Victor Emmanuel II, Elsa Schiaparelli, Helmuth von Moltke, Max Planck, Leo Szilard, Paul von Hindenburg, Benito Mussolini, Ernst Röhm, Hermann Göring, Heinrich Himmler, Joseph Goebbels, Rudolf Hess, Claus von Stauffenberg, General Friedrich Olbricht, Henning von Tresckow, Colonel Heinz Brandt, General Helmuth Stieff, General Fellgiebel, Baldur von Schirach, Werner von Haeften, Traudl Junge and others.

Napoleon III

Kaiser Wilhelm II

Otto von Bismarck

Giuseppe Garibaldi

Camille Saint-Saëns

Gustave Doré

Sophie Menter

Hector Berlioz

Gioachino Rossini

Hans von Bülow

Cosima Liszt, von Bülow, Wagner

Richard Wagner

Albert Einstein & Elsa

Pope Pius IX

Victor Emmanuel II

Fritz Haber

Joseph Goebbels
Bundesarchiv,
Bild 146-1968-101-20A
Heinrich Hoffmann / CC-BY-SA

General Fromm
Bundesarchiv,
Bild 146-1969-168-07
CC-BY-SA

Claus von Stauffenberg

General Olbricht
Bundesarchiv,
Bild 146-1981-072-61
CC-BY-SA

Wolfsschanze barrack after the bomb

Hitler & Eva at the Berghof

Bonaparte Crossing the Alps
by Jacques-Louis David

Diana Bathing by François Boucher

MARCUS AGRIPPA 63 BC – 12 BC

Works by CASPAR DAVID FRIEDRICH

Graveyard under Snow

The Cross in the Mountains

Wanderer above the Sea of Fog

The Sea Of Ice

Acknowledgements

I would like to thank my wife Eileen, for putting up with my compulsion to engage creative endeavors that pull me away from her and my family. That thanks includes my four children and extended family that many times suffers, or celebrates, in my absence, while I'm busy typing.

Of terrific assistance was my editor James Long, whose knowledge was impressive and invaluable. I must also recognize my assistant editor, Z Hufnagel, for her steadfast support, sage advice, and her patience with this maverick.

And of course I thank the amazing composer/pianist Franz Liszt who has been such a tremendous influence on my life in countless ways. I only wish I could have lived during his time, for a few moments, to have met him. His brilliance at the piano and at writing some of the most pioneering works in his day was compounded by his love of literature, hence giving birth to the *Dante Symphony, Faust Symphony* and many other magnificent works of art. That he was world famous and met most of the great politicians, religious leaders, artists, musicians and authors of his day truly added to his own creative powers and influence.

In regards to the *Dante Symphony,* it is interesting to note that the famous American poet Henry Wadsworth Longfellow visited Liszt at the Monastery Santa Francesca Romana in 1868. The two artists no doubt discussed Dante's *Divine Comedy,* as Longfellow, a year earlier, became the first to translate Dante's masterpiece into English for an American audience. Additionally, Liszt had originally envisioned his symphony being performed with illustrations by Bonaventura Genelli (who had also interpreted Dante's *Divine Comedy*) being flashed across the stage—a multimedia concept that was as far-reaching as his Hellish and Divine symphony. Hence, Dante Alighieri's spark of brilliance was passed along, like a baton, to Liszt, Genelli, Doré, and Longfellow who all aided in making Dante's work more accessible to a larger audience.

And in a very small way, it was my intention to add to that awareness by pointedly focusing on Liszt's amazing sonic masterpiece, which was based upon Dante's literary masterpiece. What Liszt achieved in sound was truly groundbreaking in many ways, and I only hope that this modest novel will make people pick up a recording or attend a live performance of Liszt's *Dante Symphony*, or any one of his many masterpieces. And perhaps even pick up Dante's dense allegory to peruse his pages that have influenced and motivated many others to write about his work or interpret his work; in music, like Liszt, or even visually, like Gustave Doré with his amazing illustrations.

I have always been enamored how creativity spawns influence, which inspires others to create, thus perpetuating a cascade of creativity. May this work be another spark in Dante's centuries-long chain reaction to spur others on to continue the creative charge forward.

THE AUTHOR

Rich DiSilvio is an award-winning author of thrillers, mysteries, historical fiction, Sci-Fi/fantasy, history and children's books. He has also written articles and commentaries for magazines and online resources. His passion for art, music, history and architecture has yielded contributions in each discipline in his professional careers, however, in *Liszt's Dante Symphony*, DiSilvio combines all these elements in a historical thriller that features a stellar cast of great characters from the nineteenth and twentieth centuries.

DiSilvio's work in the music and entertainment industries includes commentaries on the great composers (such as the top-rated Franz Liszt Site), and the Pantheon of Composers porcelain collection, which he conceived and created for the Metropolitan Opera. The collection retailed throughout the USA and Europe.

His artwork and new media projects have graced the album covers and animated advertisements for numerous super-groups and celebrities, including, John Lennon, Elton John, Engelbert Humperdinck, Pink Floyd, Yes, The Moody Blues, Cher, Madonna, Willie Nelson, Johnny Cash, Miles Davis, Jay-Z, Black Sabbath, Alice Cooper, The Rolling Stones, Jethro Tull and many more.

He has also worked on projects for historical documentaries, including *Killing Hitler, The War Zone* series, James Cameron's *The Lost Tomb of Jesus, Return to Kirkuk, Operation Valkyrie* and many others.

As a software developer, DiSilvio pioneered the first interactive courseware for autism in 1999 with the Autism Academy CD-ROM.

Rich lives in New York with his wife and has four children.

www.ingramcontent.com/pod-product-compliance
Lightning Source LLC
Chambersburg PA
CBHW032106090426
42743CB00007B/254
* 9 7 8 0 9 8 1 7 6 2 5 3 1 *